Women and Social Change in Latin America

Women and Social Change in Latin America

Edited by Elizabeth Jelin

Translated by J. Ann Zammit and Marilyn Thomson

UNRISD
United Nations Research Institute for Social Development

Zed Books Ltd
London and New Jersey

Women and Social Change in Latin America was first published
by Zed Books Ltd, 57 Caledonian Road, London N1 9BU, UK, and
171 First Avenue, Atlantic Highlands, New Jersey 07716, USA, in
association with UNRISD, Palais de Nations, 1211 Geneva 10, Switzerland,
in 1990.

Cover designed by Sophie Buchet.
Cover photograph by Jenny Matthews/Format.
Typeset by EMS Photosetters, Rochford, Essex.
Printed and bound in the United Kingdom
by Biddles Ltd, Guildford and King's Lynn.

British Library Cataloguing in Publication Data

Women and social change in Latin America.
  1. Latin America. Women. Social conditions
  1. Jelin, Elizabeth
  305.42098

  ISBN 0-86232-870-5
  ISBN 0-86232-871-3 pbk

US CIP is available from the Library of Congress

Contents

Tables

Contributors*

Lourdes Arizpe, a Mexican anthropologist with a doctorate from London University, is Director of the Museo Nacional de Cultura Populares de México. A lecturer for many years at the Colegio de México, Lourdes Arizpe is also a founding member of the feminist movement in Mexico.

Cecilia Blondet is a Peruvian historian, having graduated from the Catholic Pontifical University in Peru. She had worked in popular education in both Lima and the interior of Peru. Cecilia Blondet is currently a researcher at the Instituto de Estudios Peruanos, and is engaged in an analysis of popular culture and women.

Teresa Pires de Rio Caldeira, a Brazilian anthropologist, is a researcher at the Centro Brasileiro de Analise e Planejamento in Sâo Paulo. She has done research on daily life in the outlying shantytowns, which is published in her book **A Politica dos Outros**.

Maria del Carmen Feijoo graduated as a sociologist from the University of Buenos Aires. She is a researcher at the Centro de Estudios de Estado y Sociedad (CEDES) and a scientific research member of the Consejo Nacional de Investigaciones Científicas (CONICET). At the present time, Maria del Carmen Feijoo coordinates the Consejo Latinoamericano de Ciencias Sociales (CLACSO) Working Group on the Situation of Women.

Telma Galvez is an economics graduate of the University of Chile and a researcher at the Centro de Estudios de la Mujer in Santiago, Chile. Telma Galvez has researched and published on the subject of paid domestic work and acted as advisor to the Sindicato de Trabajadoras de Casa Particular. She is currently doing research on women's work in manufacturing industry.

Mónica Gogna is an Argentine sociologist who graduated from the University of Salvador. She holds a scholarship from the Consejo Nacional de

---

* This information relates to 1987 when the book was first published in Spanish. It is possible that some of the information is now out of date. (Translators)

Investigaciones Científicas y Técnicas (CONICET) and is a member of the Centro de Estudios de Estado y Sociedad (CEDES).

Elizabeth Jelin, an Argentine sociologist, has a doctorate from the University of Texas. She has researched and taught on the themes of urban popular sectors, trade unions, the family, women and social movements in a number of countries. At the moment, Elizabeth Jelin is a member of the Centro do Estudios de Estado y Sociedad (CEDES) and a scientific research member of the Consejo Nacional de Investigaciones Científicas y Técnica (CONICET).

Rosario Leon is a Bolivian Anthropologist. She is a researcher at the Centro de Estudios de la Realidad Económica y Social (CERES) in La Paz and Cochabamba, Bolivia.

Taller de Historia Oral – (the Oral History Workshop), which is under the aegis of the University of Bolivia in La Paz, is coordinated by Silvia Rivera, a Bolivian historian. (See page 208.)

Rosalba Todaro graduated in economics from the University of Buenos Aires and the University of Pennsylvania. She is a researcher and director of the Centro de Estudios de la Mujer in Santiago, Chile. Rosalba Todaro has carried out research on paid domestic work and advised the Sindicato de Trabajadoras de Casa Particular. Her current research is on women's manual work in Chilean industry.

Preface

This volume presents the results of a number of studies on the role of women in social movements and organizations, which were carried out within the context of a research project on Popular Participation in Latin America.

In the Participation Project, the research focused on an examination of the organized efforts made by 'excluded' social groups — peasants, workers, ethnic groups, poor urban dwellers — to increase their control over resources, decision-making processes and the regulative institutions of society at large. It also analysed, in historical perspective, the encounter between such social movements and those social forces, structures and ideologies that maintain an inequitable distribution of power and wealth, examining, in particular, the role of the state in these processes. While the emphasis on the study of social movements reflected a rejection of a technocratic approach to the issues involved, the broader aim of the project was to help clarify the idea of people's participation in order to make it operationally more useful. The project included research, action-research and discussion activities which were linked together through a more general debate on the theory and practice of participation.[1]

Initially the Project was directed by Andrew Pearse and, following his death, responsibility for the project was assumed by Matthias Stiefel.

Many of the case studies provided valuable ideas about the role of women in social movements. At the same time, they served to indicate the specificity of ways of conceptualizing the problems women face as a new collective social actor, which is often innovatory with respect to the ways it intervenes in the public sphere.

Over the period 1985–86, two complementary pieces of research were carried out, one in Latin America, the other in Asia. They examined information obtained from case studies, widening the studies when it was considered necessary. They aimed to find answers to the following questions: what was the nature and extent of the role of women in the social movements and participatory organizations being studied? To what extent did participation by women in such activities influence the results? And, finally, how did women's participation affect their own role in society, both at the local and the national level.

This book, which has been compiled by Elizabeth Jelin, comprises six case studies: on Argentina, Bolivia (2), Brazil, Chile and Peru, and a final concluding chapter. While the six studies present very different aspects of the women's movements selected for study and employ different methodologies, they nevertheless all contribute to the aims of the general study presented here. The present volume offers an overview of the variety of means and methods by which Latin American women organize their actions in defence of their vital family interests and in the struggle for their dignity and their rights.

There is a conceptual difficulty in trying to encompass women's groups and movements and women's actions within the categories traditionally used in relation to stratification and social conflict. This led the authors to think more deeply about the nature and characteristics of new social movements in general, on the basis of the material available. This book, therefore, makes an important contribution to the theory and conceptualization of social movements and is a significant addition to the other studies published within UNRISD's overall Project on Popular Participation.

The writers, as well as Elizabeth Jelin who compiled this volume, are all from a new generation of Latin American social scientists who combine a thorough training in methodology and theory with an effective social and political commitment. This has permitted them to innovate in the field of study of social change.

1. A complete list of the publications resulting from these studies is to be found at the end of this book.

Acknowledgements

Like the theme with which it is concerned, this book is a collective project which forms part of the search for identity and citizenship. To everyone who contributed to its making, many thanks.

In particular, I would like to thank Matthias Stiefel, Mónica Gogna, Fernando Calderón, Mary Feijoo and Leonor Plate for their support and help.

Elizabeth Jelin

Glossary

Achachila and *awilita*:	lit. grandfather and (Castilianized) grandmother. *Achachilas* are also the hills and other sacred places related to the cult of ancestors. (Aymara)
Akullikar:	From the Aymara, *ak'ullina* or from the Quechua, *akulliy*: chew coca leaves
Awayo:	Square woven cloth, usually multicoloured, used by women for carrying their baby on their backs. Also used by women and men to carry loads on their backs.
Ayllu:	Kindred community or territory covering various strata of Andean social organization, from the smallest (homestead or chapter house) to the large or maximum strata (Platt, 1976, cited in Bibliography to chapter 6) covering extensive multi-ecological territories and grouping confederations of *ayllus* organized into two halves (*Aransaya/Urinsaya; Alasaya/Masaya*). (Aymara and Quechua)
Aysiri:	A high ranking *yatiri*, capable of bringing back those people who have gone away. (Aymara)
Chullpa:	Pre-Inca tomb. See also note 17, chapter 6. (Aymara and Quechua)
Ch'ullu:	Male, hand-knitted balaclava-type hat with flaps to cover the ears. (Aymara)
Imilla:	Young Indian woman. Can be used as an insult.
Jaqi:	People. A person recognized as a unit with rights and duties in the community. (Aymara)
Jilaqata:	lit. the supreme chief. Traditional communal authority. This authority was maintained on the estates but in a context of total submission to the landowner and authoritarianism toward the tenants. (Aymara)
Liwk'ana:	Andean work tool. (Aymara)
Lliqllas:	A square woven cloth or blanket. Another name for *awayo*.

Mallku:	lit. condor; it also refers to important or guardian hills. Maximum authority of the *ayllu*. In pre-hispanic times, each Ándean town had two *mallkus*, one for each half. (Aymara)
Marka:	Dual confederations of *ayllus*. Also town or city. (Aymara)
Ojot'a:	Leather sandals used by the Indians. (Quechua)
Ponguito:	Diminutive of *pongo*, meaning unpaid labourer or servant. Can be used as a pejorative term.
Postillonaje:	Obligatory state service by indigenous people since colonial times. It involved carrying post for the Republic's literate people over vast distances and attending to the overnight quarters or staging posts along the roads.
Q'ara:	lit. bald, naked. It refers to the Spaniards, *Criollos* or white-*Mestizos* who, to the Indian, secularly represent colonial abuse and oppression. (Aymara)
Q'owa:	Aromatic Andean plant, with various medicinal and ritual uses. (Aymara and Quechua)
Salt'a:	A portion of textile, which has a more elaborate design and figures in contrasting colours. (Aymara and Quechua)
Tari:	Small rectangular piece of cloth used for holding coca. It is also essential for 'seeing in coca'. (Aymara)
Tarilla:	Diminutive of *tari*.
Tata:	Man, father. (Aymara and Quechua)
Tinku:	lit. meeting. Ritual fights between *ayllus* of different ranks, which are still practised in communities north of Potosi. (Quechua)
Wara:	Staff or baton of command. (Quechua)
Warayoq:	The one who carries the *wara*. Person invested with authority. (Quechua)
Yatiri:	From the Aymara, *yatina*: to know. One who knows. Andean ritualists who combine religious and psychotherapeutic practices with knowledge of traditional and herbal medicine.

Foreword:
Democracy for a Small Two-Gender Planet

Lourdes Arizpe

The current worldwide eagerness for democracy goes beyond traditional political structures and institutions. Indeed, it finds multiple expressions: greater equity is demanded in relations at the international level and, within nations, new as well as old demands for equality are put forward. Women's movements, movements bringing together urban dwellers, and ethnic and ecological movements are among those that currently draw attention. These movements are quite heterogeneous. Yet, the fact that they occur at this moment in history — towards the end of the twentieth century — can hardly be considered a coincidence. It is highly probable that they pave the way to a different future, one whose outline we cannot yet discern.

These and similar movements approximate to the general notion of popular participation. It is one way of taking up again what has come to be known as the anthropological perspective. Even in societies where no political institutions are apparent, politics still exists, albeit expressed in another language and through different actions. The emergence of women's participation is remoulding established models of political mobilization.

The women's cause is an old dream whose periodic surge has always been submerged beneath the major tides in politics. Nevertheless, from time to time, it has the capacity to make itself visible. Even in the more silent periods, women are always part of the script of the works that shape history. It is the actresses, the female chorus, women messengers, rearguard and wage-earners who restrain or urge men to fight. They are, in fact, the warm swell which rises in fury only in times of extremity. But, in general, women are to be found in the interstices which are too personal to be known publicly. That they have always been there should not be forgotten.

It is evident that women's domain has been that of private life. But human life has undergone tremendous changes in our life-time. Today, biotechnology enables us to manipulate life — both its conception and its genetics. Furthermore, technical and economic means now exist to eradicate the majority of human ills. Nevertheless, this planet's inhabitants have never been so close to total extinction. Surely, it is against this flagrant folly that the widespread pressure for democracy is directed, a pressure that women also help to exert.

Twentieth-century women: Characters in search of an author

At the present time it can be said that women are more visible in social movements and that they themselves are creating their own movements. It is worth pausing to consider what gives rise to this phenomenon. Is it due to the spread of feminist ideology, a generous though final cultural death-rattle of the West, or a new imperialist conspiracy? Or, is it women's sincere desire to overcome their situation which is rooted in tradition? Doubtless, all these factors play a part, it takes many streams to form one river.

Possibly two important historical facts have been decisive. On the one hand, the prolongation of human life has breached a demographic dyke. At the same time, the spread of contraception has ruptured the previously existing physiological fatalism. The effect has been explosive with respect to women: women's biological reproductive role has lost its pre-eminence and in many societies it is declining. Consequently, if previously women had to struggle against the maxim 'biology is destiny', nowadays they have to begin the search for an additional purpose in life.

On the other hand, the spread of industrialization in almost all regions of the world (with its ambiguous contributions to the organization of social life) is in the process of overturning the traditional role of women in all societies. To the extent that nowadays the capitalist market and/or the state penetrate daily life, this is no longer the domain reserved mainly for women, but rather for the impersonal institutions that usurp their functions. Women are beginning to find themselves empty handed: few children, small families, fewer social ceremonies and religious rites, highly formalized urban customs, and programmed social practices. In the majority of countries this process is obviously incomplete, especially in Latin America and the Third World, but the evolving features that characterize this process certainly point in this direction.

Because it is incomplete, but above all because it is unequal and riddled with contradictions, the process of distorted development has an important impact on the situation of women. It expropriates or destroys existing modes of production in agrarian societies and propels the inhabitants into industrial economies that are incapable of providing them with work or sustenance. The low levels of working-class income make it essential for women to take on some form of income generating activity.

Technological change also exerts an influence. How nice it is that high-level technology reduces the physical exertion required by male and female manual workers! But it has made their manual skills obsolete. And what a good thing it is that women no longer have to wear themselves out physically in heavy work! But many of their abilities have become outdated. It's also a good thing that high-level agricultural technology offers high returns. Nevertheless, it eliminates male and female peasants from the stock of human resources.

The result is that these workers, peasants and women from many different social groups are no longer valued and therefore lose their power. It is important to be aware of the fact that public institutions and the market for goods and services have captured this power by stealth. And who, in turn, controls them? The problem is that such organisms — which are uncontrolled by the public — tend to centralize this power, although in a diffuse sort of way. These organisms are the multinational corporations, which own the high-level technology and the means of communication, and states, too many of which lack political legitimacy. Under such circumstances, it is difficult not to look for signs that subterranean forces are on the move, emanating from the popular base of society.

We are only engaging in politics

Everywhere, women are mobilizing themselves. This phenomenon, which though not new is only just becoming visible, is the subject that the contributors to this book are beginning to study. It is, therefore, a pioneering work. As Elizabeth Jelin shows so well, the writers have embarked on the search for analytical guidelines in order to form a view on 'how and why women are emerging from the private domain.' This quest is very opportune but it lags behind the enormous changes in the ways in which women's presence is manifested in present-day societies. Participation has already begun and we social scientists have hardly begun to explore the concepts and theoretical tools needed to try to capture it.

The use of the category 'women' as an analytical concept in studies concerning popular participation is intended to create a new conceptual field. But its theoretical laws are still being formulated. One particular concern of the authors of this book — to examine the soundness of this process — is also one of their merits.

The writers seriously question what there is in common between Bolivian peasant women from the Bartolina Sisa Women's Federation, Chilean women trade unionists, mothers from the Plaza de Mayo group in Argentina, Aymara peasant women in Bolivia and the women leaders of the poor neighbourhoods and shanty towns in São Paulo, Lima and other Latin American cities. An initial theoretical proposition is that they are all involved in actions which, through protesting, defending and demanding, make them the active subjects of social change.

Nevertheless, the wide range found in their forms of organization, immediate demands and strategies and tactics raises the question as to whether there are reasons for considering this problematic as a specific field for theorizing. This can be justified in a simple straightforward way by resorting to the notion of feminism — a political philosophy premise — which asserts that there is a specific form of subordination affecting women. But this theoretical field is also justified for use in the social science analysis of behaviour and practice in present day society in general and in Latin American society in particular. In this connection, it can be stated that the differences in the empirical forms of popular participation by women are not an obstacle to theoretical generalization. On the contrary, precisely because these are reflections of women's primary concerns, they constitute genuine social demands. The problem arises when, a) they are not considered to be genuine, which raises an ideological or theoretical problem; or b) when it is impossible to discern common features that unite these heterogeneous forms.

With respect to the first point, it is a fact that the processes that organize political life in formal democracies also restrict the modes and themes of discourse, in order to make them conform to the main lines of political debate. Otherwise, the infinite variety of thousands of genuine demands from all sorts of groups and people would be unmanageable. The various ideological currents and political parties assume the task of amalgamating them, their function being precisely that of negotiating group demands in order to present a common electoral platform.

It is worth asking whether the many diverse forms found in the women's movement are not, in fact, the result of the effective exclusion of women from traditional political space. In other words, it may be due to the fact that traditional political organizations either continue to resist incorporating women's multidimensional problems into their ideological schema or do not know how to do so. It is, therefore, a political problem, which is reflected in a scientific–technical problem.

This can be explained in another way. For reasons which would be too long to go into here, in the hegemonic political philosophies found in Latin America and other regions one finds that the demands relating to the private sphere are almost by definition excluded from general political demands. Women's implicit demand that the personal should become political is, in this sense, revolutionary. Women are insisting that their demands enter the arena of debate and political negotiation. Why? It could be attributed to feminism's insistence on women claiming their rights. But as the studies in this book show, in the case of Latin American women, social and political reality reveals another cause: the repressive state apparatus and the market encroach increasingly on private life, undermining traditional social organization.

If governments kidnap and kill their sons and daughters, women demand a public forum to denounce the situation and cry out for an end to such abuse. If the market causes the level of their husbands' incomes to plummet, obliging women to seek employment and to carry out additional work in the home to stave off hardship, while still being expected to fulfil their valued role as mothers, then women will demand better social services, better urban infrastructure, better wages and more child-care facilities. If their husbands — peasants or miners — find themselves imprisoned both literally and metaphorically by repressive structures, then women will demand the right to speak out on their behalf.

In particular, it is worth mentioning the case of indigenous communities. As shown in a later chapter by the Andean Workshop, the private space in the indigenous sphere is also clearly one of ethnic defence. This is the space where indigenous language, identity and vision of the universe is protected. The destruction of this private space is greater subordination for women and also increased ethnic subordination.

What is important in all this is that, if the market and governments create conditions increasingly intolerable for the private sphere, which is the domain of women, the latter have every reason to move into the public sphere to put their grievances and make demands, *using the same language as used in the private sphere*. But why are they criticized and ridiculed, when they employ domestic language? The answer is clear: neither political parties nor trade unions understand how the private and public spheres are interlinked. And, if they do not begin to understand this soon, they run the risk of becoming relegated to a small corner of politics.

That is why, in Latin America, people speak of 'a new form of politics'. Indeed, one must go further: it is not just a new way of engaging in politics but, as Elizabeth Jelin says, a new form of social relations and organization and, I would add, a new conception of what is political.

We are fighting for people's interests

If we consider people's current central concern, it is clear that the field of politics has widened irreversibly. We can think of many examples: the fact that today the population issue is a central concern in politics as it is in the struggle for hegemony between countries; the high level of unemployment in women's economic activities; women's activities as a crucial element in the survival of the majority of the population; the increasingly clear relationship between political authoritarianism and male chauvinism and the patriarchal family; the major transformations in the family in most societies and the concern for ecological conservation and the quality of life which are now on the agenda. And as politics widens, women are groping with tremendous courage towards the creation of new channels for expressing themselves and putting forward their demands in trade unions, political parties, the Plaza de Mayo, in the streets and in the countryside.

We should not forget that, in this process, women are trying to win something because they have lost something. Under the old order in Latin America, women's realm was the private sphere, which comprised religion, the family, relations with kinfolk and social dynamics. It is the loss of this power which increases the feeling among women that they are being more and more excluded and marginalized.

If we understand everything that has just been said, it seems premature to ask whether these women's movements are merely asserting women's rights and claims or whether they represent an alternative involving profound social transformation. If the question is posed within the precepts of traditional political ideology, the answer will be that they do not constitute such an alternative. This is because these women do not struggle only to vote, be voted for and climb the steps to power.

But, if the question is asked from the perspective of the historical changes currently underway in capitalist societies, the answer is that they may well be an alternative. What is more, changes in the definition of what is the private and public domain (in terms of the role of the state, social reproduction, marital relations and political participation by women, which reflect women's demands) surpass by a long way the programmes for social transformation currently presented by most political parties.

Part of the problem consists in thinking that women's movements have a populist and not a class content. This is true. But, as already indicated, many other movements stand outside the category of class movements, including for example the struggles waged by peasants, ethnic groups, anti-industry groups, ecologists, those against large-scale modern technology, poor urban groups and those against consumerism. This is the case to such an extent that, at least in Latin America, what can be analysed using a political/social class perspective is in fact a very small part of the formal economy. The problem is, then, that it has not been possible to develop a wider analysis which comprises all these movements within the context of a class strategy.

The ebb and flow of domination

This book's most important conclusion can be considered to be its demonstration that the basic question in all these women's movements is the struggle *against all forms of domination*. In all the cases described, in addition to the problems that women face in unions and political parties and in the streets and government offices, the women who give evidence describe their daily battle to persuade their husbands to allow them to participate in public activities. Here, without doubt, is a silent struggle shrouded in guilt, which is specific to women and provides an additional reason for studying the ways in which women participate. It is worth emphasizing that the counterpart of women's double day (economic and domestic) is their double militancy (in politics and in the marriage). In one the woman struggles as worker and mother at the same time; in the other, as citizen and wife.

In this sense, the schizophrenia of the public/private divide in capitalist society imposes on women a double militancy; and this is why feminism has been born as the ideology of the private domain. Going a bit further, we could even say that women are the only majority to have a minority ideology. This is because feminism, especially at its narrowest watershed, apears to be no more than a theory on, by and for women, when it should be a theory of society from the perspective of women.

This directly affects the forms that popular participation takes. As the contributors to this book state, to be able to move from rebellion to revolution it is necessary to have an ideology that universalizes. But perhaps it is historically unjust to ask that women should develop a priori a master plan for an alternative society. We should remember that capitalism, parliamentary and republican democracies and present day socialism have never had such a plan, but have developed through actual practice.

To conclude, what the chapters of this book show is that the governing mechanism of domination is exclusion. It is also shown that the principal and original exclusion of women is being unable to participate in the decisions that define the concepts and procedures by means of which public life is organized. It follows, naturally, that women have to adapt their demands and their struggles to an already existing structure. Let us go further: the exclusion begins with language itself. What this book demonstrates for indigenous women can be applied to all women: if in order to express themselves they have to use the language of the oppressor, 'is not firm silence a form of resistance?'.

The demands made by women's movements are not as yet very far-reaching. We should remember that 'participation' is the weakest of the links in the chain of equality, in contrast with the 'taking of decisions'. To demand participation and not decision-making powers is already a rather modest way of engaging in politics.

Hardly 15 years ago there was little or no awareness concerning the social participation of women. Today, such a consciousness is developing slowly and in an unpretentious way. This itself is already a great step forward.

Lourdes Arizpe
June 1986

Introduction

Elizabeth Jelin

The purpose of this book is to discuss the subject of women's participation in collective actions associated with the struggle for their rights and their identity. The subject matter is located in two fields of analysis: 1) the analysis of social movements; and, 2) that of the institutionalization of legitimized channels of participation. In both cases this is a special exercise, in that the analysis revolves around women, but within the context of a wider socio-political reality in which collective actions acquire meaning.

To some extent this is a new theme, in that interest in it arises from two directions: first, the discovery that, even when culturally they are assigned a place in the private world of the domestic domain, women have always had a presence in collective struggles; second, the impact of a new situation in which there are many more women who have a growing sense of identity based on gender.

Furthermore, this book is based on the collective actions of women from the popular sectors of society.[1] In other words, the theme of gender is articulated — in various ways which we shall try to identify — with that of subordinate classes in their struggle to extend their rights and question the existing forms of social organization and domination.

The wide variety of concrete situations manifested by women's collective actions poses considerable difficulties with respect to comparability and generalization. Each concrete historical situation is specific and it is therefore difficult to compare different situations or to generalize on the basis of just a few of the many varying experiences lived by women. Thus, our discussions and analyses have to combine two dimensions: they must respect the specificity of each case while trying to draw some lessons and make generalizations or, in other words, develop some analytical guidelines which are useful for examining cases that are not similar.

Latin America: a cultural region. A definition of women?

The works comprising this book relate to different Latin American situations. Although it does not cover the whole region, the study of forms of women's participation must take into consideration certain basic cultural features, which have a decisive influence on the situation of women and on the range of alternatives for action open to them.

The Latin American cultural tradition is well-known for the way it defines the role of each sex. While the variations between countries and zones within the region may seem very considerable, when compared with other areas of the world, the situation of women in Latin America appears to be highly uniform with respect to their typical aspirations and to the cultural meanings given to concrete practices.

In the Latin American cultural tradition, the subordination of women is anchored to the strongly cohesive family group that constitutes the base of the whole system of social relations. The patriarchal family is seen as the natural unit around which daily life revolves. The household is the basic unit of reproduction. Within it, the relations between the genders and generations are hierarchical, involving a clear division of labour and areas of activity. Women are in charge of the domestic tasks associated with the private sphere of reproduction and maintenance of the family; men are responsible for tasks relating to the public sphere of social and political life.

The cohesion of the family group has had very different implications for men and for women. For women, subordination is the result; for men, the outcome is a pattern of personal relations based on kinship solidarity, which is transferred to the public sphere of politics and productive activities. This is the basis of the patron–client relationships and paternalism that weigh so heavily on traditional public life in Latin America.

At the macro-social level, Latin American societies are clearly class societies and have been so since early in their history. Capitalist development has superimposed itself over other forms of organization that were evolving to include the class dimension. (Stavenhagen, 1969) Furthermore, the development of class society was linked to the emergence of nation states, with large and complex bureaucracies which exercised influence over the daily life of the population. Consequently, in order to analyse the social position of each sector of the population — and even more so a group so invisible and hidden in history as women — it is necessary to take explicit account of class distinctions and the state.

Social movements, politics and society

Social movements as a theme in social science already has a tradition in Latin America. Or rather, one can state that, on the basis of a certain earlier preoccupation, the last decade has seen a considerable flow of work on popular social movements.

In effect, its strength is related to a social crisis, and one which is implicit in all 'finalist' paradigms, including that of the 1970s concerning the 'relative autonomy of the state and politics'. In face of the confusion caused by the fact that the future did not turn out as expected and, more specifically, by the rise of dictatorships and the closing of channels of popular participation, a search began for manifestations of non-conventional, non-institutionalized forms of participation, (albeit sometimes small, very hidden, and discovered more as a possibility than an actual reality) which are not to be found in the existing models of relations between society and the state. This, in my view, explains the energy with which the study of social movements has developed.

In a recent work T. Evers (1984) put forward some important ideas. According to this author, the social sciences in Latin America, concerned as always with power and the will for political change, were looking at the situation concerning social movements in these countries and concentrating their attention exclusively on questions of power. From the point of view of political transformation, the uninstitutionalized collective expressions of the popular sectors have been interpreted as pre-political protests or as embryonic forms of popular participation which were to be channelled through a vanguard party. The realization that these forms of collective action cannot easily be incorporated into a revolutionary party meant that their political significance had to be reinterpreted. Some social scientists embarked on work which revealed the limited, reactionary or reformist nature of these collective actions. Others, who were more puzzled, began to recognize the urgent need for a more profound internal investigation of these movements, without holding any preconceptions, in order to discover their potential and their limitations within the historical context. Within this new tendency, social movements begin to be identified with 'new ways of engaging in politics'. Nevertheless, power continues to be the theme around which interpretative thought is organized. Perhaps it is now time to return to look at social movements from another perspective. It is not only a question of new ways of engaging in politics, but also one of new forms of social relations and social organization, such that it would be a new society which was in transformation or being engendered, more than a new politics.[2]

The meaning of social movements and their interest from an analytical point of view lies in seeking within them evidence of profound change in social logic. What is in question is a new form of politics and a new form of civil society or sociability.[3] But, at a deeper level, what is being detected is a new way of relating what is political and what is social, the public world and private life, in which daily social practices are linked and interact directly with the ideological and the political–institutional. The immediate question that arises, and which cannot be answered with certainty, is whether it is a question of a 'new reality' or whether social life was always like that, but, with our vision limited by the then predominant paradigms we were unable to see this.

What is important now in the development of our knowledge is to recognize that the field is open and (why not?) reflect on the social conditions in which these reinterpretations of social life and politics emerge. There is no doubt that, at least in the Southern Cone countries, the ideological and repressive offensive of authoritarian regimes has had an important impact on redefinitions of the relation between the public and the private spheres, as also on the interpretative approaches of the social sciences. To quote Lechner:

What has occurred is a transfer from the public to the social. The public is reinterpreted as a consumer public . . . The constitution of the subject no longer refers to the citizen but to the consumer . . . The private sphere is no longer a protection for individuality and is incorporated into the sales publicity of the market. (Lechner, 1982:21–3)

Furthermore, when the conditions of life and action of the researchers themselves change, they, along with the rest of the population and with greater critical awareness, incorporate daily life into their own thinking:

The displacement of the public sphere and the triviality of official political discourse direct attention towards daily life . . . To the extent that routines become problematical — which is normal and natural — the complexity of daily living increases . . . The loss of certainty and the increase in forced decisions combine, generating a painful experience. (Lechner, 1982:24)

Of course, these developments are not exclusive to intellectual work under authoritarian regimes. Many of the factors, which only recently have begun to orient research and become the axes for analysis of politics and collective practices, must be considered important developments for the body of social science at an international level. (Such aspects include the consideration of daily matters as an area for reflection and research, in which the structures and mechanisms of public and social functioning are condensed and revealed in a complex fashion; consideration of the subjectivity of the actors and the researchers; and the analysis of the significance and meaning of actions and practices.) Changes in our knowledge are another influence that, since feminism, means that we should recognize the political dimension of the personal and the rereading of the family as a social–political–public sphere. (Jelin, 1984)

This is the intellectual space in which consideration of social movements is located — in the process of formation, manifesting spontaneity and many different dimensions, lack of institutionalization, ambiguity in their demands and on contradictory paths. Nevertheless, they are based on collective action and practice more than ideological propositions and institutional apparatuses. It is the researcher who proposes reading these practices as social movements, on the basis of an analysis that begins with the interpretation of their insertion in the socio-political context and of their development over time. In other words, the task of the researcher is to seek out the meaning of a collective practice, a meaning that obviously is anchored in the conceptualization of these very subjects, but which goes beyond this conceptualization.[4]

To summarize, we begin our research of the theme with some general pointers to the direction to be taken, as opposed to a theory made to fit. We start with the idea of social movements as objects constructed by the observer, which do not coincide with the observed form of collective action. (Melucci, 1982) To the outside, they may present varying degrees of unity, but internally they are always heterogeneous, with very diverse meanings, forms of action and organization. We interpret social movements as signs of the existence of social conflicts between collective actors in which, explicitly or otherwise, the system of social relations is put in question:

> The movements are not the residual of development or manifestations of discontent on the part of marginal categories. They are not only the product of the crisis, the last expressions of a society which is dying. On the contrary, they are signs of what is being born. (Melucci, 1982:7)

Social movements and popular participation

These two expressions seemingly refer to a single phenomenon: the mobilization of a sector of the population — a social sector — in order to make felt its presence, interests and demands in the public forum of power and in socio-cultural relations. Thus, in one sense, one is dealing with the theme of *presence*. Nevertheless, there arises an immediate need to distinguish between the forms and modalities of presence of subordinate social sectors on the public scene. To go and vote in an election is not the same as participating in a strike. Setting up a co-operative is not the same as joining in a street demonstration, not to mention actions that involve violence.

The history of Latin American societies can be read as a gradual process of incorporating new social sectors or older marginalized groups into the social body. (Germani: 1964) It seems feasible, therefore, to take indicators of this process of incorporation — for example, the history of the extension of the vote, the history of illiteracy or of waged work — and regard them as the social process of extending rights and social modernization. But these processes are neither gradual nor linear. Their history is never complete, nor is it simple or peaceful. Rather, it is a history of social struggles for inclusion, based on the demands of subordinate groups to be given their rights.

The social and political conquests made by subordinate social groups are the result of the confrontation and struggles waged by these groups, rather than from political actions 'from the top down' on the part of dominant classes and social sectors. Therefore, the process of social transformation is one of struggle from below, in which subordinate social sectors redefine their identities and their rights, in an attempt to widen their space for action and extend the boundaries of their social and political citizenship. In this struggle the socio-political space into which the subordinate sectors are incorporated is itself redefined. History, then, is the history of transformation of the stage at the same time as an account of the entry of the actors on to that stage.

Conceptually, the notion of participation supposes a structure or institution within which participation can take place, that is, it indicates incorporation into already existing institutions. But recognizing the existence of social movements highlights collective propositions that question the existing order. Nevertheless, the difference is not so clear cut in the flux of concrete history. There are numerous historical examples of substantive changes in social organization which began with initial propositions that seemed to demand no more than wider participation but which ended up as subversive of the existing order. It is within this framework of gradual but also profoundly transformative processes that the theme of women's participation must be seen.

Women's participation in Latin America: a guide for research

It is perhaps worth beginning by asking why we should want to analyse the issue of women's participation. Why think about the theme of women? In what way is this legitimate within the problematic of popular participation and social movements? Or, in other words, is there a specific problematic relating to women that justifies considering them separately? We know that women do not in themselves constitute a social group; rather, they are a category that cuts across social class, ethnic groupings, communities and nations. But, in order to further justify our proposition, we would also argue that we are witnessing a historical process of the constitution of a new collective subject, with its own identity. Consequently, the problem cannot be reduced to one of exhorting researchers to include the theme of women, to the extent that it is relevant to the purposes of the study. Nor is it only a question of indicating that in the study of popular movements it is important to research the absence as well as the presence of women.

In this respect, a review of recent research and debates reveals that little or nothing has been done in this field, due in part to the lack of women's participation and also to the lack of perception on the part of researchers. In effect, until a few years ago women constituted a forgotten social category, invisible in analyses and diagnoses of popular movements and in the elaboration of strategies for them. This oversight and absence was rooted in the sexual division of labour and in the ideology that justified it. To see men as responsible for tasks tied to the public sphere of social and political life was *natural*. Likewise, it was *natural* for women to be responsible for jobs in the private domain, for reproduction and maintaining the family. The consequence of such reasoning was that changes in the presence or absence of women in popular movements had to wait until the sexual division of labour was modified, as a result of a very wide range of social processes.

All this can be read as an argument favouring the view that there is nothing specific about women's participation that justifies designating it as a case for analysis and discussion. But the situation is more complex and requires efforts to conceptualize and also to penetrate more deeply the outward appearances of social life. In effect, it is necessary to recover the presence of woman by looking for her where she is not seen. She is not seen when she stays at home, tied to domesticity and the sphere of private life. Nor is she seen socially when she leaves the house to take part in collective actions of a public nature, and this is what has to be rescued from oblivion. In fact, the theme of social movements, even *new* social movements, hardly identifies the gender of the participants or asks how gender influences the nature of participation, collective practice or the meaning of action. Our intention is, therefore, to make visible what is hidden, so as to be able to identify its importance and its consequences.

To do this, it is necessary to rethink the relevant dimensions that could serve as points around which to organize the discussion about women's participation. Which are these themes, these relevant dimensions that would allow us to examine the specificity of women's collective action? We propose the following.

The public world and the private sphere
A first aspect to take into account starts from the material and symbolic reality of the sexual division of labour, a division of labour that separates the public and private spheres, the domestic and the political, and which tends to make woman specialize in domestic tasks. This requires us to analyse these domestic activities. What happens within the tasks of reproduction and consumption within the domestic domain? At first sight, women's specialization in domestic tasks seems to constitute an obstacle to any sort of participation in popular movements. In the context of the ideology of the dominant patriarchal society, the two spheres are seen as opposed: in order to participate outside the household the woman must neglect her domestic taks, abandoning her family role. A deeper analysis of what happens in the domestic sphere reveals that, arising from the specific role of woman–housekeeper or wife–mother, women have a potential for organizing, participating and transforming that needs to be discovered and analysed.

Daily life and reproduction
In connection with the previous point, the analysis of women's movements helps us to discover new aspects of social reality that were previously invisible. Beginning with an analysis of women's situations, the social sciences have discovered the existence of domestic work. The 'economistic' emphasis in our thinking, centred as it is on production, causes us to forget that there is another area of analysis which is tied to distribution, consumption and reproduction. In a number of different theoretical strands there have been important debates on the political economy of domestic work, on the reconsideration of the population issue on the basis of an analysis of domestic organization, and also on the link between domestic work and the labour market and so on. Explicit consideration on the theme of reproduction and the organization of daily life is now legitimate and necessary.

Establishing an identity and the development of social actors
There are two aspects to this theme. At the micro-social level, there is the issue relating to the role of women in establishing identities and in the transmission of ideologies. Traditionally, this aspect is included in the analysis of processes of socialization. Retracing the social position of women also involves retracing the mechanisms by which socialization is achieved and identities are created or established. Starting from a perspective in which women are seen as mere

transmission belts of dominant ideologies, we can begin to formulate a hypothesis that sees women as mediator–producers of social identities, with a capacity for social creation and transformation. At the macro-social level, the social process of formation of a new collective protagonist — the women's movement — can be analysed, while this process itself effects a transformation in the socio-political scene. If, when speaking of other social movements, the subjects are often considered as already constituted (peasants, workers, and so on) the category 'women' poses the urgent need from a conceptual and empirical point of view to study the process of constitution or development of the social groups and identities, starting from the practice of participation itself and mutual recognition in the course of action.

History and memory
It is now recognized that there is an urgent need to retrieve historical memory in order to bring to light what is missing at the level of power. In effect, history which is a history of power leaves out issues relating to women and to reproduction. It is, therefore, crucial to build up a micro-history based on the retrieval of popular recollections and the recollections of the actors themselves and of their own movements, which has so much to do with the process of establishing identities. Because of the absence of women in the public sphere and, moreover, because there are few written traces from the past concerning women from the popular sectors, reconstruction of history through personal testimonies is a priority. Collating life stories and comparative recollections to build up history not only yields data but also sets in train a process of research and reflection.

The dynamics of women's participation in social movements
In various places and different historical situations, two aspects of women's participation have been identified as important. These are the degree to which movements are institutionalized or organized, and the degree of continuity they manifest over time. Given the organization of the family and the sexual division of labour, which impede women's public participation because of their domestic responsibilities and the ideological burden of femininity, it would seem that women participate more frequently in protest movements which arise at particular critical moments than in more long lasting, formal and institutionalized organizations, which involve greater responsibilities and commitment of time and energy (as well as opposition from their male partners). In turn, an analysis of the process of participation over time also reveals a lack of continuity in women's participation, which, if it were to be researched, would make it possible to discover the ways in which women engage in politics and how these could be extended and transformed.

Organization of this book

The chapters which follow comprise different case studies of the forms of collective action and women's participation in social movements. The range of studies and cases is wide, as is the variety of focuses and methodologies used by the writers.

Chapter 1 takes up the story of how a poor neighbourhood in Lima was established and of the central role played by women. Through their life stories we follow the women's migration to the city, establishing a family and their search for housing, resolved in this case by settling in a newly-established poor neighbourhood on the city outskirts. Throughout the life cycle of these women, and throughout the political changes in Peru in the period between 1950 and 1985, women's practices are subject to change. They resort to mutual-aid networks among neighbours then withdraw into the family, and then surface once again in organizations started by people from outside the community and, more recently, promote substantial changes in the pattern of community organization and other democratic practices.

In chapter 2 Teresa Caldeira analyses how women from six popular neighbourhoods in São Paulo experience their participation in the public world. The reasons they give to justify their participation are made explicit, and are based on their traditional roles as mother and housekeeper. But their role of defending family and community well-being in times of crisis (their class position) cannot fully explain their efforts to participate. These are also partly explained by the fact that the women begin to establish a space of their own in which to develop an identity based on gender. The women are demanding their rights and establishing an identity simultaneously.

Chapter 3 presents an overview of three forms of women's participation in present day Argentina. Feijoo and Gogna analyse the human rights movement, neighbourhood movements and the feminist movement. The history of participation in each of these is presented through the ties with the country's political process. Political instability and the brutal experience of dictatorship in Argentina, from 1976 onwards, are exceedingly important factors, which have a decisive influence on the shaping of collective practices and social groups. Although distanced from politics in the conventional sense of the term, the actions comprising these three different examples of participation are based on the politicization of the private sphere, which requires a reformulation of the meaning of politics itself.

Chapter 4 presents an extreme case in which Gálvez and Todaro analyse both the presence of women in the Chilean labour movement and their absence. In a climate of repression and recession, is there any space for the presence of a new protagonist in organizations which themselves are being persecuted and are on the defensive? Furthermore, the type of participation they are studying is, according to our general view, the least likely to involve the collective action of women. They are formal organizations, tied to social roles as workers in the formal employment sector, which traditionally women have been less involved in and usually as a secondary activity, since their traditional domestic and family roles have tended to predominate. In this situation, which in many senses is extreme, the possibilities for women's presence are obviously very limited.

Chapters 5 and 6 refer to the experience of Bolivian women, especially in the rural areas. In chapter 5 Rosario León tells the story of how the Bartolina Sisa Federation of peasant women was founded in 1980. She outlines the Federation's forerunners and origins, the occasion that prompted its founding and its subsequent development, all the time linking this process of organization among peasant women with the development of peasant organizations and with changes in the country's political circumstances. The author traces the tension between the various identities — class, ethnic group and kinsfolk — that leads women to join men's organizations in a subordinate position. The growing identity among women on the basis of gender constitutes the organizing theme of the story.

In chapter 6, using a different methodology based on the retrieval of collective memory by employing oral history techniques, the Andean Oral History Workshop reconstructs with the women themselves the story of women's struggles. Cultural practices intended to resist the advance of *criollo* culture are thereby retrieved and revalidated.[5] While it is not possible to gain from this chapter a global overview of the practices adopted by the community to resist the erosion of their culture, or of the role of women in these practices — indeed that is not the purpose of this work — this methodology allows a much deeper examination at the level of significance and meaning for the participants. Moreover, in reconstructing this history through research work, a collective identity is also constructed in the same process.

In the final chapter, we attempt once again to take up the analytical issues that have been put forward, resume and revise the empirical material from the case studies and draw some comparative conclusions. This involves making some abstractions, since it is not our intention to make comparisons between the cases we observed. Our aim is rather to draw up some more general propositions that can be applied to situations in which questions emerge concerning the position of women and changes in their situation arising from their own collective actions. These examples do not embrace the whole of the Latin American situation, nor all countries. But they do illustrate a range of experiences. We hope that the propositions we put forward will stimulate more profound interpretations and further empirical studies in this field of enquiry and social change.

Notes

1.There is no precise English formulation of the Spanish phrase *sectores populares*. Working classes is an inadequate translation because regular employment in waged work is not the norm and unemployment is high. The translation 'popular sectors' is therefore preferred. In broad terms the popular sectors in Latin America are synonymous with the urban poor, who are largely disempowered citizens in their own societies. While most have secured the rights and duties of political citizenship (often suspended during periods of military rule), the majority of Latin American people cannot claim to be full members of the economic community. They do not have the right to a decent livelihood, being incorporated into the economy at the very lowest levels. Most of the popular sectors are physically segregated in enormous neighbourhoods of poor people's housing, usually in distant suburbs far from work. (Translators)

2.In this, Evers' logic is impeccable: if we detect new social movements in societies with very diverse political regimes, how can we attribute to them political causality and finality? The author suggests that perhaps their emergence is linked to the logic of capitalist social organization. But (and here I depart from Evers' argument) are not similar movements to be found in non-capitalist societies? Does not the emergence of social movements have something to do with industrialism and the complexity of the processes of institutional differentiation and specialization, which at some point require overall reconstruction of segmented identities?

3. Civil society refers to the relatively autonomous space that is not wholly controlled by the state or the corporate sector, in which citizens can develop their own social relations and actions for mutual support and survival. This includes networks of friends and relatives, women's centres, neighbourhood organizations, church groups, trade unions, and so on. (Translators)

4. The relationship between the conceptualization and interpretation of action on the part of the subjects themselves and of the observer is a problematic one in the history of social sciences. From establishing true external parameters, which allow one to speak of 'true consciousness' or 'false consciousness', to the identification between observer and actor that accepts uncritically everything the actor does and says is true (both extremes render the analysis impossible, turning the research into an act of faith), these all constitute recurrent themes with no single solution.

5. *Criollo* culture refers to the dominant culture of the oligarchy or elite who were non-native people mainly originating from Spain during the colonial period. They administered the colonial state and accumulated considerable economic power. Their non-indigenous culture still predominates. (Translators)

1.   Establishing an Identity: Women Settlers in a Poor Lima Neighbourhood

Cecilia Blondet

Introduction[1]

The following chapter relates the story of a number of individual women who, sometime between 1940 and 1960, migrate from their place of origin and manage to become popular housewives, establishing a physical and social presence in a poor neighbourhood in the San Martin de Porres district in the city of Lima.[2]

This slow and as yet unfinished process suffers setbacks as well as achieving progress, and takes place in a context of poverty, which at times limits the women's capacity to choose and forces the story's protagonists to resort to a number of strategies involving negotiation and conciliation in order to survive. Uncertainty and insecurity are part of this construction process. Strength and courage, the attributes of heroines and saints, are therefore essential to the women, if they are to successfully develop urban social roots.

The women are engaged in a continuous struggle to become individuals in a precarious environment, where conflict is a daily fact of life. During this process of becoming an individual and establishing the family, collective efforts are crucial. A dynamic is thereby established between the individual and the collective, between people and institutions, which, in practice, gives rise to their new social identity as women settlers.[3]

The story takes place in recent decades at a time when Peru's agrarian structures are breaking up, a time which also coincides with the country's post-war industrial development. Both phenomena give rise, among other things, to mass migration to the cities. Lima becomes the main point of attraction and, since the 1950s, it has undergone enormous changes in its configuration. New neighbourhoods have been established as the enormous influx of migrants seek to make a place for themselves in the capital.[4]

This process of establishing new human settlements is tinged by the different cultural traditions of the men and women involved. A new social identity is slowly created in the recently built shanty towns, as a product of the fusion of these traditions and people's common experience. This social identity is rooted more in the experience of migration and in the ways in which the new urban space is appropriated than in the peasant origins of the settlers.

We shall observe a number of fundamental changes taking place throughout the lives of the migrants at the personal, family and social level and between the generations. We believe that these changes, which express a shift from servile status to that of citizen, are tied directly to the life cycle of women. This decisive relationship between personal and social aspirations defines the type of social participation engaged in by women at different points in the ebb and flow of the neighbourhood movement.[5]

In the early years of the settlement, women's lives are organized around domestic affairs, which are crucial for building up the neighbourhood. The activities they undertake in the private and public spheres are complementary. The family, and the woman who is responsible for it, needs the neighbours in order to survive: the individual needs the collective. The uncertainty and the fragility of the situation demand determination. There is widespread participation by women in efforts to mobilize the inhabitants to join in building-up their own neighbourhoods and in providing support for the neighbourhood organizations that demand the urban services they need as households.

Subsequently — perhaps ten years or so after people arrive in the neighbourhood — the domestic unit begins to establish itself, its members increase and less outside co-operation from neighbours is needed. Work or income is contributed by the children, and others close to the family, such as friends and relatives who arrive from the same native province, assist with the domestic tasks.

This situation has two important effects. First, it liberates the woman from some of the domestic chores, allowing her to take on other work and to extend her strictly reproductive role to activities outside the home. In order to contribute to the family income, she goes out to work in service jobs (domestic service or street vending) and family life revolves around such activities.

Second, as the domestic space begins to close in and become privatized, there is less need for mutual-aid networks among neighbours, and there is less and less need for collective work and actions. At the same time as daily life becomes organized on an individual basis, there emerge new initiatives such as mothers' clubs which are sponsored from above and which build on the women's earlier experience of participation. They introduce vertical, patron–client type relations between the members and the bodies that sponsor these organizations. The leaders, who take on the role of intermediaries, are generally women who do not need to earn money due to their relatively better economic situation compared to the others. A special kind of clientelism is introduced, permeated with reciprocal and close parent–godparent relationships between the leader (patroness) and the members (clients), who for their part carry out their activities in an increasingly collective manner, leaving behind previous interpersonal relationships.[6]

The third phase, which corresponds to the period from the late 1970s to the present, has been one marked by crisis and recession. The trends in organization and participation have therefore changed. While in the first period daily life revolved around the domestic space and in the second around the economic sphere, in this third period the emphasis is once again on the domestic sphere, due to the crisis, the tight labour market, high prices and scarcity of food. But it oscillates between the private family domestic sphere and the public collective domestic sphere. Perhaps the most important characteristic is the movement between the one and the other.

The growing independence of the domestic unit with respect to the earlier collective organization becomes threatened by the increasing difficulty of achieving reproduction at the family level. Two measures are therefore resorted to. First, the extended family and groups of relatives begin to act together, not only as a consumption unit but also for production purposes. The small business of an individual family member becomes a family affair, thereby generating income and 'resolving' the unemployment problem. These small production and consumption units are also a source of employment for relatives and others originating from the same region of Peru.

Second, family consumption is organized on a collective basis, especially in relation to domestic tasks. This is done through new organizations such as family and popular kitchens and dining rooms, which save time for other work or for providing the women with training.[7]

In this respect, the clubs and the earlier experience of organizing provide a favourable basis for collective action. Food is channelled through the clubs and participation is therefore necessary in exchange for a share of the food. In turn, new women (young and old) come on to the scene and question this type of organization and begin to establish a new participation model which, with some difficulty, they try to link to the neighbourhood organizations and social movement.

In practice, making domestic tasks public and visible seems to begin to widen consumption capacity beyond the narrow reproductive confines of the domestic unit. The same is the case with respect to multi-family strategies, though there is a difference, in that the popular dining rooms serve to legitimize the collective and public nature of the organization.

We believe, therefore, that these social organizations can be considered as potential political institutions in which women, through their daily practice, become defined as collective protagonists on the social scene. In the process, they establish more democratic relations among themselves as participants and with respect to other institutions, thereby transforming the nature of women's participation.

Methodology

The backdrop to this work, which comprises a case study of a Lima neighbourhood, is the story of how this neighbourhood is built up. But, above all, this chapter takes up the story of how the women involved become social subjects or protagonists and it describes the principal landmarks that line the route followed in this process.

We have tried to place all these stories, which represent ways of internalizing reality, in the context in which they unfold. They are part of a dynamic, complex process, characterized by a permanent dialectical relationship between the individual and the community. These are personal stories that express the history of a social group, in which the testimonies convey the values, beliefs, moral principles and customs that are part of daily events. The women's testimonies provide us access to this social representation, and allow us to retrieve their popular meanings and logic, as well as the women's perceptions of themselves as social protagonists in the local and national context.

Our work is therefore located on the frontier between the personal and the social domains and is intended to take the form of a 'choral' history with many different contributions, which are interesting not solely for their faithful reconstruction of events but above all for the way in which those involved have internalized their experiences and the way they remember them. This provides us with some insight into the values, ideas and changes in life styles of the population being studied. Participatory observation, backed up by interviews and written sources, which were very few in our case, give our evidence a greater factual underpinning.

Our evidence was collected following a general census of the population from which a sample of informants was drawn, taking into account sex, age, place of origin, level of education and occupation. Thus the different cases roughly correspond to the varied personal situations to be found in Cruz de Mayo.

A knowledge of the patterns of settlement in the city of Lima indicates that this district is an example of one, fairly frequent type of expansion to be found in the city. Hence, despite its limited scale, this study can throw light on the urban popular sectors in Lima, especially on the migrants who live in the so-called 'young towns' that sprang up as a result of land occupations.[8]

At the same time, it is necessary to make clear that this is an *exploratory* study only, due to the enormous number and heterogeneity of the popular sectors in Lima and to the lack of studies on popular culture and generally on urban history and anthropology. We hope that it will suggest new ideas for deeper analysis of this theme and approach, which we consider to be of crucial importance if we are to understand better the urban popular sectors and their evolution in recent decades.

The neighbourhood[9]

The Cruz de Mayo neighbourhood established during the regime of General Odria (1948–56), is located in the District of San Martin de Porres, to the north-east of Lima on the right bank of the River Rimac. The enormous expansion of the district occurred in the second half of the 1950s and in the 1960s. Once the population begins to settle, the suburbs begin to develop and new waves of migrants go to other areas skirting the city of Lima. The land invasions, which have continued to occur in the district in recent years, are not on the same scale as in previous decades.

Perhaps because it emerged in the period of industrial expansion in the 1950s and 1960s and also because it is situated between two large industrial areas, the district has one of the highest percentages of manual waged workers in metropolitan Lima. But the proportion of workers declines from 37.2 per cent in 1972 to 29.5 per cent in 1981, which gives an indication of the impact of the crisis experienced by Peru in this period.

By way of final information on the district, we should mention the existence of a massive number of grass-roots organizations, which either have peasant origins or arose during the process of urban expansion. Likewise, we should point out the changes in the politics of the district which are similar to, though more accentuated than, the situation in other popular districts in the capital. From being a bastion of the Odristas in its earliest days, it went on to elect a left-wing mayor in November 1980 with 28.18 per cent of the vote. The same leftist coalition — *Izquierda Unida* — (United Left) won the municipal elections again in 1983.

Within this district, the Cruz de Mayo neighbourhood proper started to become populated from 1959 onwards and at the beginning it experienced a number of very tough invasions. Due to the fact that this was one of the areas nearest the river, it was always more exposed to floods and therefore was developed only relatively late and in a somewhat precarious fashion. The inhabitants had to confront endless problems and this led them to set up institutions that would help them to move ahead together and install themselves on what was very harsh terrain.

At the present time, Cruz de Mayo houses between 115 and 125 families in two blocks that face on to three different streets. A census that covered 87.5 per cent of the population in Cruz de Mayo included a total of 74 dwellings, occupied by 105 families totalling 629 people. On average there are 1.4 families and 8.5 occupants per dwelling. The majority of the dwellings consist of one floor only and two bedrooms on average, which reveals a high degree of overcrowding. In one extreme case we found four families in a single dwelling.

A first estimate of the population surveyed shows a male to female ratio of 95.95 per cent. Most inhabitants (72.5 per cent) are under 30 years of age. The proportion of inhabitants between 15 and 29 years of age is higher than for those between 0 and 14 years. This is due to the fact that there is still a small inflow of migrants, especially of young people aged between 15 and 30 who come as 'relations' to live in relatives' dwellings and who remain unmarried or have just set themselves up as a family.

The figures also indicate that it is a relatively old neighbourhood. The young arrivals who helped form it are now adults and mainly to be found in the 30 to 60 age group, and their children were almost all born in Lima. (Most came from the Peruvian highlands and some from the coast, including some from Lima itself.) Of the population aged between 0 and 14 in Cruz de Mayo, 92.3 per cent were born in Lima and 10 per cent are from the provinces. On the other hand, more than half of those over 30 years of age are from the highlands, the percentage rising with age.

Stories of migration, poverty and progress

The women who migrated between 1940 and 1950 were mostly born in the highlands and they have a key feature in common: the fact of being uprooted as individuals or as families from their place of origin. This largely explains their departure from the highlands. Many factors give rise to this uprooting, including the onset of what became a progressive deterioration in the agrarian sector, affecting both the large estates and the communities, with the result that the poorest families were unable to survive in the rural areas. In other words, what propels people to migrate is a sense of no longer belonging to local society.

In such circumstances, the extreme but nonetheless frequent situation arises in which many families with a large number of children, or with only one parent, reduce the cost of maintaining their daughters by handing them over to better-off relatives or neighbours. Domestic work is done in exchange for food, shelter and, in some cases, schooling. This is the case with Marta from Catacaos (a peasant community in the Department of Piura in northern Peru), who at eight years of age was handed over to her godmother to help her out with the housework, and also with Valeria, who relates how she was given to another family on the death of her parents. Similarly, Estela who came from Tumbes and who founded the neighbourhood, was made her godmother's responsibility when her parents died. She had to work for her and, although she was allowed to go to school, she suffered real exploitation:

> I had to leave everything ready before leaving the house at eight in the morning to go to school. I used to get up at three in the morning and at four thirty had to go and buy milk from the cowshed. I bought the bread and left the breakfast ready, because my godmother served breakfasts. When I got back from the market I had to start again, sweeping up, making the beds . . . almost everything. Then I had to get myself ready to go to school, but sometimes I couldn't do it all because I couldn't wake up, because I was young.

Five of our interviewees had been obliged to work in truly miserable conditions from the time they were very young. The excessive work-load and the violence meted out to them, combined with the impossibility of getting a school education, led them to migrate. Behind these apparently individual decisions, lies a social phenomenon — uprootedness and the impossibility of surviving — that expels peasants from their place of origin. This phenomenon manifests itself in different ways according to geographic region, characteristics of the family and the actual migrant, resulting in different modes of departure.

The first mode is characterized by a rupture in individual relationships, which results in the person fleeing from their original environment. The main factor that prompted Estela and Isabel into taking such a momentous decision was the feeling of not belonging to anyone or anything. Under such circumstances, migration is an act of assertion and a positive approach to life.

Estela recalls the situation as follows:

> I was fed up, simply tired of so many beatings. I'd say my family was perhaps
> neurotic, because I was a girl who did everything, I didn't deserve this sort of
> treatment. I couldn't understand it.
> *Where were you going to?*
> Well, I went by stages. From Tumbes I went to Zorritos. I wanted to know,
> just get to know, I didn't want to turn back.
> *Did you have any money?*
> Where from? You didn't need money to leave, you worked your way, you
> see.

Isabel explains:

> I had an older sister who was let down by a man and the same happened to
> another sister. I was 14 years old and my mother said 'What do you prefer —
> to be deceived or to get married?' She said that this man was going to make
> me marry him. He had a lot of mules. Sometimes he'd come on his mule and
> talk to my mother about marrying me. I was frightened of [him]. I'd run
> away. I didn't want anything to do with it. Ugh! My mother used to hit me
> and my brothers did as well. They wanted me to marry because they had
> everything, just everything and they didn't suffer at all. 'Oh no!' I said, 'I
> don't want to get married, I'd rather the earth swallowed me up than marry
> this man.'

Another type of departure, occurring in less violent and dramatic cases,
similarly demonstrates the break-up of the family nucleus and the social
uprooting, which leads to the search for progress, money and education. These
women also migrate alone, though in these cases the decision to migrate is a
family one or the family is agreeable to the idea.

While in the first cases, it is rejection of their situation in the village that
drives the women to leave, in the second type of case, both for the women and
the family that remains behind, the attractions of the city, reinforced by the
spread of the commercial economy, become a stimulus to migrate.
Nevertheless, the common factor is that all of them took their own individual
decision to go. As Pilar says:

> Well, I came after many many arguments with my mother and my father.
> They weren't at all happy with me. So I was going to go away and find work.
> They had wheat, maize, everything there. But no money. And as my
> brothers were younger, they needed to study and needed someone to help
> provide the money.

Pilar, who is the eldest daughter in the family, 'sacrifices' herself for brothers
who had to study. She is a mother to her brothers and looks after them as she

will with her own sons later. Girl 'mothers' is a frequent phenomenon and, later, in the city, this gives rise to women's participation in social movements reinforcing the traditional roles of women.

From the outset the women struggle and work, because in Lima they cannot rely on a supportive structure comprising family members or others from back home, which would ease their entry into urban life. Even those to whom such support is available prefer to manage without it so as to avoid being treated as servants and, even though this means going without the domestic servant's miniscule wage, they at least enjoy the somewhat insecure freedom of not living with their relatives. Pilar herself, who was determined to come to Lima, does not use the family as a resource:

> I was always proud of not going to the house of my uncle and aunt, because I thought they were going to say 'you have come to our house'. That's why I decided to work to send money back to my family.

Pilar's pride, or rather her fear of being both rejected and used, is a feeling found frequently among adult migrants. As yet the migrant networks are not very developed and people are not used to migrating, lodging with relatives and studying. Later, as the number of migrants increases and the distance between the capital and the provinces is shortened, migrants from the same area or region begin to form mutual-help networks, comprising clubs among people from the same province or their own extended family. This affords them some protection as they establish themselves in the large city.

The third group reveals a different migration pattern. Although there is the same 'push' factor caused by uprooting in the place of origin, migration occurs on a family or group basis. The whole family or a large part of it migrates, such that the whole process is dealt with collectively, from deciding to leave to settling in Lima. It does not, therefore, require of the children, particularly the young women, an individual decision that carries such high risks. This fact distinguishes the way this category of migrants inserts itself into city life.

Once the decision has been taken, the actual act of migrating varies according to the reasons which gave rise to the decision. But, in general, there are three main migration patterns. There are those who leave alone, willing to look forward, breaking relations with their family or godmother, and who migrate in stages according to the suitability of the work they find. As Estela explains:

> In Zorritos I worked in a house, a very nice house. But I don't exactly know what it was they said but I left. I went back to Tumbes, but not to my godmother's house. I didn't want to see her. I went to the house of a captain, who I know. He went with his wife to Sullana. So I came as well, as I was wanting to leave. After a while I left this woman's house because she was really rotten. I left her and went to Piura, and from there I came here [to Lima] with a friend.

And in Isabel's case, her departure is an act of desperation in that her mother and brothers and sisters wanted to marry her to a wealthy man:

> I left at nine in the morning on the eighth of August, without taking even a step back. And I walked and walked, night and day, night and day. I kept on going for three days, and what I went without — the food ran out at night! And my mother and brothers were coming after me. Yes, I came over the mountain-tops where nobody ever goes.

From then on, Isabel, Estela and others who were running away began to know their way around, working and, by force of circumstances, learning to survive on their own, in a continual struggle to acquire a place for themselves in society.

Another pattern involves travelling with employers or godparents, the female migrant shifting around according to the movements of the families who employ them. In such cases, they generally come to Lima directly, spend a time with those employing them and then look for better working conditions elsewhere. Finally, those who have family or regional connections *en route* or in Lima come with introductions and recommendations, so they do not find themselves in the totally unknown. The adventure in these cases begins not with the journey itself but on their arrival in Lima.

Lima

Arrival in Lima is regarded as a very special moment. Ever since life in the village the migrants have had an image of the city, woven from stories and comments from neighbours who had been there and from their own expectations. For one person it seems the land of promise:

> Well, where I lived I did think about Lima, because it was the capital. I always thought it was better than where I lived, much nicer because it was the capital. Of course, where I come from it is light but it is rather overcast, not like here. This is a very nice city. (Milagros)

For others, Lima seemed to symbolize damnation:

> I never wanted to come here. I've lost so many good jobs. As soon as they mentioned Lima to me, I'd say 'I'm not going to Lima', because people said that when you got there the men abused you and all the women were prostitutes. The men are bad. 'Oh no' I said. Well when I came here I came married. Nobody brought me to Lima unmarried. (Estela)

In Lima all agree about the tension between the pain of departure and the fear and loneliness in the big city on the one hand, and the fact of being dazzled by the bright lights, and on the other, the bustle of city life and the thousand-and-one opportunities the city affords to actually achieve their aspirations. Depending on the situation in which they arrive, the stories of some put more emphasis on the violence and fear, others on the attractive, overwhelming aspects. The existence or otherwise of social networks into which the women can be absorbed helps define their image of the city and the possibilities it offers, in the same way that migration, either alone or accompanied, puts its own stamp on the migrant's introduction to urban life. Thus, for example, those who arrive with employers or godparents are in a somewhat exceptional situation. Seeing the city from the houses of those they are accompanying and enjoying a certain measure of protection, they see Lima as orderly and accessible though still rigid, in a hierarchical structure that since then has become fractured:

> When I came to Lima everything seemed so lovely. It was different. When I arrived bread was cheap and the people here behaved as people in Lima did. Some were easy to get on with. Others no. They were rude. It depended. Because I was a young girl I couldn't go out, I was with my godmother's sons. I used to take them to the park. (Mireya)

These women do not go hungry or feel afraid because they do not know where they will spend the night, and they are less vulnerable to the more sordid and aggressive aspects of the capital, unlike others for whom Lima is a mixture of dream and disenchantment.

> I didn't know anything. I came here but I kept on crying, I wanted to go back. I had heard of the big city. I heard about it when I was small — Lima and Ica. And I said 'Where are they going to stay?' When I arrived, the place seemed very sad to me, I didn't like it at all. I cried because I was frightened. I sang *huaynos*, and I was choked with anger and kept crying. I kept remembering things and I'd cry, until bit by bit I got used to it.[10] (Valeria)

Valeria arrived at her brother-in-law's house and, instead of taking her, her husband and small daughter in as lodgers, they are literally taken in to live with them:

> We came here to my brother-in-law's. It was really dreadful. Even with my three-year-old daughter, I wasn't allowed out at all, not even into the living room. It was only a small house they had. The road passed on the outside and inside there was a small alleyway. There we were, in just a corner.

This experience of meagreness and poverty prolonged her experience as a poor peasant woman. Therefore the perception of life held by abandoned peasant women — the so-called Valentinas — does not alter. To become accustomed to Lima therefore means having to continue to face gratuitous violence, except that this now occurs in an unfamiliar context, which makes the situation even worse. Valeria, who frequently complained about the bad treatment she put up with back where she came from recalls:

> It's all very nice, the weather there. They had plenty of everything, cheese,

milk, but not now. So many people have come here and they have killed many others. How can that be? It was nice then, the village was very healthy, the people were good there.

Her first images of her native land come back to her — a pretty, pleasant and healthy place, while the city of Lima belongs to others. The sense of uprootedness which she experienced in the village becomes even worse in the city. In her homeland, although she was a poor orphan she recognized the meaning that governed social behaviour. From her very inferior situation as a poor orphaned girl, Valeria could see an order in her village. Lima, on the other hand, symbolized disorder, chaos and evil. Without a doubt this relationship with the city will change as the migrant settles in a job and a particular place. Despite the differences in their perceptions all the women migrants face the unknown with enormous insecurity. And they are aware that only by dint of hard work will they be able to turn into reality their intuitive plans for a different future and their wish for a better life which, in the last analysis, is the driving force that keeps them going in the desperate search for ways of adapting.

City life

The migrant women's images of the city come sharply face to face with reality when, during their very first days, they have a taste of the awfulness of urban poverty. The bustle, the bright lights and illuminated publicity and Lima's grey sky all have an impact. At this point, they experience fear of the unknown and anxiety. But they are certain of their capacity to work, of the urgency to find work and the need to find a place to settle and to adapt, since in Lima they have to achieve something better — their aspiration for greater personal fulfilment.

Few of them say they have come to stay. Nevertheless, after 30 years few in fact have left. Apart from the pressing need to work, life in the city opens up a new world of friends and people from the same rural area, with whom they can go out and about in the little spare time they have. Although narrow, this social world is important because it facilitates sharing the learning experience in relation to urban life, 'socializing' the knowledge of those who came earlier for the benefit of those just arriving.

Such knowledge ranges from how to get around, where to eat cheaply or get together to reminisce and share memories, to recommendations as to where work can be found and how to earn an income. Curiously, they do not as yet refer to these reference points for migrant workers living in Lima as clubs (Altamirano, 1984). They are still informal networks among provincials which only later begin to be formalized into institutions. For the time being, the women gain access to these provincial circles through relatives, work colleagues and people from their own area who are already settled in Lima.

Work: the pivot of life

While the women recognize that work is the only way to subsist in the city, they discover that the possibilities are very limited. Their low level of education results from their peasant background in which, due to the effects of the recent commercialization of the economy, preference is given to male labour while girls and women are kept away from school. In rural areas education involves the family in heavy investment and results in the boys being better qualified and hence better paid, which brings future compensation for the efforts made. The girls do not attend school, having to help their parents either with agricultural tasks or domestic chores so that their brothers can go to school. Thus women's social place in rural areas is principally a domestic one, if we exclude the agricultural skills they develop, which are of no use to them in the city.

Having few qualifications but many domestic skills, the work prospects for migrant women are limited. If the need for shelter and food is also taken into account, it is clear why domestic work is so often resorted to as a source of work. Pilar provides an interesting example, illustrating the doubts and then the choice made in this respect:

> In Orrantia, my uncle said 'Look here, my girl, if you go to work in this factory, they pay a pittance, they pay weekly but it's a pittance. A friend of mine is manager of a cotton ginning plant. This gentleman is German and foreign families are more responsible.' Well, I wasn't sure. I had always dreamed of working in a factory because you have Saturdays off and every Sunday. But in this other sort of work you only got a rest every fortnight. Then I said to myself that it was better to at least be sure of getting my meals, so I'll try my luck in this, and I accepted it.

Another key feature with respect to the migrant women is the need to put themselves in a sort of patronage situation, whereby they get a sense of order, security and affection in exchange for doing menial work and being loyal. Entering into clientelistic relationships as a means of adapting in the first place and later as a means of achieving social mobility is crucial in this process of inserting themselves into urban life.[11] During this initial period they do not have the benefit of protective horizontal relationships. Employers and godparents are pillars of strength, making possible both material and spiritual survival. We therefore find different types of clientelistic situations. There are good employers who do not try to make them lose their Indian culture and who take them as they are, as Pilar explains:

> After a time I became quite used to it all. I started rearing animals, everything. They took notice of what I said. They used to say I could make *patasca* — a dish from my province — with whatever ingredients I needed and make it my way.[12]

There are, however, bad employers who abuse, mistreat and humiliate. Isabel:

> My life was a tragedy. I wanted to study and I asked him to show me how to study. 'No', he said, 'you are not going to college. I got a girl so that she would work'.

The day off in the city

Once a week or fortnight, the resident housemaids leave the very elegant neighbourhoods where they live and go to the more popular neighbourhoods where their relatives or other people from the same province live. The day off is spent visiting or helping relatives, walking about or shopping. The whole of their social life is concentrated into this one day, so what they do or do not do involves choices, though these are not necessarily carefully thought out. Their future life might be determined by such a day off without them really having thought about it.[13]

Little by little they make new friends in the city — mostly men friends who are employed or work near where they themselves are employed. The concierge, the presser at the dry cleaners, the ice-cream seller or the ticket collector at the cinema, begin to see them and invite them out on their day off. Or it might be the mini-bus driver, the lorry driver or other young men from the same region (though not necessarily the same town) who are attending the festivities held in Lima in celebration of their region's feast days.

They all recall having had many suitors, including some from social classes above their own. Nevertheless, when it is time to start thinking about settling down, they all choose someone who is their social equal. Pilar's own reminiscences illustrate this:

> What I liked most about him was the way he behaved. You mustn't think that I would have married the first one I fell for. No, no no. As I say, as a girl I had very curly hair and I had lots of admirers and I had another one called Pepe Aguilar from some ministry or other in Avenida Salaverry. He was very . . . how shall I say . . . it seemed he wanted to be unfaithful to me, sort of deceive me, I don't know.

For Pilar, marriage was not a means of climbing the social ladder but the meeting up with a partner who would struggle alongside her in order to conquer some space in the city for themselves. Thus, when referring to her partner she says: 'Well, because the highlander was a very well mannered sort, wasn't he? They say that sometimes those city types who are not Indian are very forward.'

The sense of 'being equal' does not only relate to the common regional origins of the migrants in Lima. It also refers to the community of interest and objectives they share, which will determine both their futures. In other words, there is a shared conviction of the need to work to build a place for themselves. So, after a time, they join up together in the Cruz de Mayo neighbourhood.

Marriage: the key ritual in establishing a new urban identity

Following a period of between five and ten years employed in domestic service or as workers, the women migrants again disturb the somewhat precarious stability they have achieved through employment and knowledge of the city, in order to continue the process of establishing roots — a process that began when they arrived in Lima. The original purpose of leaving home was to seek a better life: education, to be treated well, to have money for the family. At a certain point the first stage, which involved migration and the early days in Lima, reaches its limit. Pilar explains:

> Well, I went around quite a lot and like others I also fell in love and my husband, well of course, he's from Ayacucho. So I said, 'I'm going to set up home because I haven't been working and working just for nothing. Never.' So, while working I bought my blankets, some sheets — things for the house. I stopped sending my mother all my money.

The women who want to achieve personal fulfilment, who want 'to be something', to be part of a wider social network, to establish a family, know that they cannot do this on their own and that it is necessary to go through the next stage accompanied by someone else. Utopia and reality come together, with the next phase seen in terms of 'coupledom'.

Being part of a couple is crucial in the woman's life cycle. This is as much because it allows her to have children (which is probably the most complete expression of her notion of personal fulfilment, of possession and imagined or possible future) as because a partner brings with him relatives and other people from the same region. The network of social relations is thereby extended, providing a new context for reproduction of the family. Marriage is not, therefore, associated with the idea of romantic love, but rather with the possibility of being liberated from the family and employers who have hitherto controlled the woman's life, and it is associated with the idea of beginning to establish her own family.

> Sister, get married. What would you rather be — a slave for those shameful people or a slave in your own home?

But not everyone manages to achieve the two-parent model of family, either because of becoming single mothers or because of being abandoned. Many of the women interviewed in this case study manage to remain as part of a couple only at great sacrifice to themselves throughout married life. The fact that the majority of women in the neighbourhood who migrated in the 1950s has a partner indicates the importance of the couple. It represents a landmark in the history of change, in which many factors intervene, combining the need to 'have something', to build the future and to do this as a couple. Unlike in the countryside, in the city it is necessary to have a husband, in order to be considered 'worthy' and respectable. In the rural areas the man and the woman carry out complementary production and reproduction tasks. When the woman is left on her own she is integrated first into the family and then into the communal organization, and this is no reason for being considered socially inferior. The problem presents itself in economic terms and in relation to the market. (De la Cadena, 1985)

In order to ensure the success of this new family undertaking, the man must have a number of qualities. He should be honest, worthy, a gentleman and, above all, very hard-working. This is very much a prototype. But when in practice the ideal type takes on a human form, the result can be catastrophic, as in Mireya's case:

> Work, work, I carried on working until I bumped into that devil who's now dead. I came to Barranco to settle down. He was older than me. I wasn't the sort who had lots of male friends or went to lots of parties, nothing of that sort. When you don't know much, you don't have much to go by, so you slip up like a street cat, a blind chicken. He deceived me. He really let me down. I don't know what he wanted, it must have been my bad luck and that's how it was. Even now, when I think about it I still get very angry.

The sense of failure overwhelmed any illusions Mireya had, even those about being a mother.

> When I became his, I gave up work and then my child arrived. What a sad life I have. I'm a founder of the neighbourhood but I still don't have a house yet, only some pieces of wood and a bit of a roof. He drank a lot you know, a lot. And he was separated. He had been married in a registry office. He'd been married but I didn't know. He was from the north, but when he was drunk, he was like all the others — he just let work slide. Luckily I only had one child, just a boy who is the father of these grandchildren.

Valeria's case is different, however. She was handed over to her husband when her parents died, so did not choose her partner. She expresses frustration about the lack of affection, and ill-treatment:

> I and my husband knew one another back there when I was 15. I was 15 when I was forcibly given to him by this woman who had brought me up. He is older. I suffer just as much with him, just as much, not less. Ugh, I've suffered such a lot! It's always been like that. My husband was never at all loving. But he was hard-working. I've never received any affection. But I put up with it all. What else could I do?

In the end Valeria is resigned to the situation because, in spite of everything, with him she can establish a family and begin to be 'someone'. When speaking of her children, her face lights up and she admits that life here in Lima is not so sad:

> *And how is it here in Lima?*
> Well, now I have my daughter and my grandchildren, so it's more or less all right. Before, I didn't have my son, nothing, no one to respect me. All I did was cry a lot. My husband drank. He used to get drunk, so there were no children. But now we do have children. There are several of us. So I'm happy now because I've got my grandchildren. So I'm calmer now and I don't keep reminiscing so much about the highlands now either.

When children are born the conflict lessens. They are the backbone of the family. Estela confirms this:

It was so nice when I had my first daughter. I could touch something of my own, I had something. This was mine, nobody else's. I created her, she was mine. That's why being a mother is so lovely. I don't know how mothers can kill their children.

Establishing the settlement: a history of land invasions

The next step is to find a place where they can live independently. Therefore, establishing the neighbourhood is, especially for the women, also the official establishment of the family and the origin of the women's new identity as citizens and inhabitants of Lima. From here onwards, the neighbourhood will be almost the only scene of action for the women settlers, since their continual presence is basic to the settlement's development. Everything that happens to them in the future will have something to do with the group of people who arrived to live in this area with them. Daily life will teach them the importance of working collectively in order to secure their own family's future.

The story begins as they arrive two by two with their new-born children in search of somewhere to spend the night. Through relatives or contacts originating from the same rural areas, they have found out that there is space here. Or they may have been registered on the official government list, but to no avail. They are driven to occupy new areas by the overcrowding and discomfort where they lodged with relatives or by the restricted space and dark and damp of the rooms they rented. Their reminiscences reveal the difficulties, uncertainties and worries they have at this particular time. No one forgets how inhospitable the place was, or the animals, the water and other things which turned up. 'Around here it was all sand, it was like a seaside beach. Bodies used to float along in the water.' (Ernestina)

They all share the feeling that the place they are invading belongs to no one except the dead, something alien continually cornering them and trying to eject them. The river represents aggression and, though full of water, which is essential for daily life, it is also full of dirty, putrid water bearing drowned corpses. They wage a fierce struggle against this hostile environment, as described by Valeria, who had come from the mountains:

This here was all water and stone and there were corpses here. Sometimes, there was water right here. The river flowed right by here. The stream ran behind and the water here stank. The water came down here, right down here. We were here, you see, when I saw one of those corpses. People died like dogs, lots of them. The water arrived, it came in here bringing mud and rocks from the river banks. It came in here. It was full of water here, and the river was full. And the people . . . so many people died. And a woman said that the water carried a woman right back here in the yard. She was put in a pit and she rotted there. She's been there ever since and people live there now, right on top. (Valeria)

And the scene described by Estela who came from the coastal region makes it clear that they all felt equally threatened and under attack:

> Yes, this was stone and wattling and this was made of cardboard. When we first came to San Pedro I lived in what was like a pigeon house and you could see absolutely everything. It was just like a beach and people began arriving on that side over there, on the edge of the river. Awful smells came from the river and the water came right by my house. It was all so dreadful. So when they began to invade over there, well I was afraid. I said the water comes there and will sweep everyone away. One day I saw a bundle — the river carried dogs and pigs from the farms, enormous things. They looked white from here. 'This pig is rotting away', I said, 'rotting away.' One day the vultures started eating it. Oh dear, the pig. The water level in the river dropped so the boys went to play there and they were rolling all over the place. So I went to look. It was all in bits and only a little finger was left, a finger. But it was a woman's finger! I saw the dogs eating her. Only bones were left. We put them back over there — we made her a grave and we threw the finger in with everything else.

Thus, during this period the struggle was not mainly against the state or those appointed as adjudicators, as it was later when they had to confront one or other group in order to put down permanent roots. The main recollections relating to this period are of the struggle against the elements.

But a time comes when those attempting to take over the land win their struggle and manage to make what was someone else's their own. One night, when the river once again threatened to overflow its banks and demolish their wattle huts, a piece of wood is retrieved from the river and made into a cross as a sign of peace.

It is said that since that night the river has never overflowed again. The filthy water that brought death and darkness became the water of goodness, life and light. The piece of wood was the sign that they could remain and that the environment had now begun to accept them. 'Bit by bit they were able to channel the river. I can see it, but it's hard to believe.' (Estela)

Stories about construction: one for all and all for one

The decision to invade and occupy part of the dry sandy areas bordering the river Rimac demonstrated once again the migrant women's strength and courage. If, as Figueroa (1981) indicates, risk avoidance is a key peasant characteristic, another side to the peasant character is revealed when the decision to leave the place of birth is taken. It requires courage and willingness to take risks to build a family and a home in the city. In this respect, women play a very important role in that they never tire of encouraging efforts to invade and occupy a piece of land in order to possess it and call it their own.

The history of women's collective participation in the neighbourhood now begins. Up to this point the struggle to stay alive in the city was basically one of individual efforts in isolation. The migrants' new social environment now comprises the couple and subsequently all the inhabitants.

Early days: just try getting me out!

Well, to be honest we did everything, especially the women, because the men went off to work. And we women had to struggle for everything, those of us who were always up at the front. Because, when it came to co-operating on housing, the husband wasn't there. But who was? The wife. And they had to talk to her — it has always been the wife. So that's why I tell you that women have such an important role. Whether they recognize it or not is another matter, because the men are always saying that they own the home. If the men don't do the washing, the cooking or the sweeping and aren't even here, I don't see how they can be head of the household. Owner of the street yes, but not of the house.

I don't know, the men are more cowardly. They like the small details, legal matters but they don't take risks. Very few of them look to the home, or fight for it — they don't dare. Along comes another and tells them it is his and they just let them have it. Women don't, because we cling on by our teeth or whatever else to the very stones themselves. Just try getting me out! Why? Because we think of the children. (Estela)

As Estela says, women are the ones who are there, so it is they who face the new life from a wholly precarious position and who manage to make the sandy stretches and the river their very own.

In this first stage of the occupation, the women's actions are carried out both in and from the domestic sphere. This is a very complex situation involving the private and the public, the individual and the collective at one and the same time. Their tasks include cooking, washing and giving birth as well as organizing collective work to build roadways, lay pipes or install cables. These typically domestic activities are geared to establishing the family and the community unit both in physical and social terms.

It is, however, possible to distinguish different forms of women's collective participation. One form of participation revolves around daily life, such as organizing production in the domestic unit. In order to begin consolidating their situation, communal efforts are required, such as mutual help networks and the fictive kin system of *compadrazgo*. Establishing a family needs outside collective support and it therefore becomes a context that provides apprenticeship in interpersonal relations and horizontal exchange. These new horizontal connections do not replace the initial clientelistic relationships, which are crucial for establishing oneself in Lima. Rather, this first stage of settling is accompanied by a process of gradual recognition of the importance of collective initiatives to achieve satisfaction of the needs they all share. This gives rise to the subsequent transformation of the traditional patron–client model and, later, of other forms of social participation.

In order to carry out tasks they cannot manage individually the women organize themselves into mutual support networks. For example, daily shopping in the market, queueing up for water, getting vaccinations or medicine for their children, all require women to leave their wattle shacks and abandon their small plot. If they have other young children, these are left in the care of neighbours while they are out. In one way or another they can identify with Milagros' memories:

> The neighbours were good. We lent one another a hand in taking care of things. When we had to go to Lima, I left her in charge of my house because, being little huts, they weren't safe. So one asked — neighbour keep an eye on it for me! And if someone came, one asked who they were and who they were looking for and whether they wanted to leave a message. We neighbours helped one another.

And, as in Estela's case, a godmother lent her a hand when, being on her own with two daughters, she fell ill with typhoid fever:

> God is merciful. You know, a woman brought me food, washed the nappies and so I told her 'Victoria, I have enormous respect for you.' I tell my daughters that, whatever else happens, this woman from the highlands has done us a favour which no one else, not even the family, has done.

The women get to know one another like this and build up relationships which, to a certain extent, substitute for the supportive relationships offered by kinship and the extended family, though most do not have the benefit of the latter. As a result, we find that the *compadrazgo* system is very widespread, because these spiritual bonds help consolidate the mutual support networks. There is no longer an attempt to find a godmother or godfather with a better social position with whom to establish a client-type relationship. Instead, they tend to choose couples with whom they can collaborate on equal terms. Moreover, in times of difficulty or serious illness, the reciprocal help between women, especially godmothers, fulfils a key function in the reproduction of the family unit. If either the mother or the father falls ill, close neighbours, who themselves have been helped out, will take on the responsibility of feeding and caring for the children, until the situation returns to normal and the mother can take over again. To make this possible, the rest of the neighbours make collections of money or food. Sometimes, when the mother dies, the same godmothers take on full responsibility for the children in an informal sort of adoption:

> The woman sold bits and pieces and the little boy — her son — came here to collect the money because she let me pay weekly. That's the sort of friendship we had. Then, when she died in childbirth and I went to buy something, the little boy came up to me (he'd have been about 11 years old) and said to me 'Family woman, my mother has died'. And he put his arms

round me. It had a big effect on me didn't it, because I was an orphan and, well, I couldn't help telling him that now that one mother had died, here was another. It's as if the mother had said 'Here, I'm leaving you my sons . . .' So I had to take on the kids . . . Marita, Socorro, Meche, Julia, Maco, Lucho, Segundo . . . (Estela)

But in a situation where the conditions are so extremely difficult, uncertainty and insecurity reinforce individualism and give rise to problems and conflicts. Jealousies abound in the midst of poverty but there is solidarity as and when it is useful in achieving the primary aim of survival. They are constructing something for everyone because they are building up something for themselves and, to this extent, agreement and arguments are complementary parts of one and the same process.

There are other types of collective participation that relate to the public domain and concern not just daily life but above all the consolidation and construction of the neighbourhood. These need organization among the settlers in order to demand services and infrastructure from institutions outside the locality, particularly from the state.

Once more the public and private spaces intertwine: the women participate by virtue of the fact that as part of a family they are asserting their possession. They demand urban services to improve the conditions of life for their families by taking part in mass marches and demonstrations to defend their piece of land and demand that the river be properly channelled and the banks strengthened.

Both men and women — we have woken up floating in the river, because suddenly it overflows. So we have been to the Palace, all of us together, to the Government Palace, to insist that they channel the river.

We left my small son to be looked after, while I went to Lima. We women were there at dawn . . . such a lot of people. (Valeria)

While the women participate *en masse* in such mobilizations, it is possible to distinguish between different types of participation. In the type of mobilization and organization among neighbours just described, involving a direct connection with the public sphere, women participate on an *ad hoc*, temporary and unstructured basis. The women do not take up positions in the organizations or assume responsibilities, since these are predominantly male functions. On the other hand, in other activities linked to neighbourhood development that take place in the immediate locality (which can be considered an extension of the domestic space since there is no clear delimitation between the private household and the public space comprising the neighbourhood) women take on more active roles in the participation process. It is the women who, each weekend, organize the work necessary for the collective construction of the roadways and footpaths and lay out the cables and pipes.

We ourselves made the connections from the mains to our houses. We wore

our finger nails right down. I scratched out that track which used to be made
of stones in order to lay the foundations for the trench so that the water
could be connected here at the front, because the water came from this side.
(Ignacia)

But irrespective of whether the women's participation is active or passive, it
is channelled through the neighbourhood support organization. Mass
participation by men and women in the process of constructing the
neighbourhood is perhaps the most striking feature of this period. They are
aware that if they do nothing no one else will and those who do not participate
do not have the right to ask for anything later on. In order for each one to get
what they want they have to co-operate and work collectively. The dynamic
between the individual and the collective is crucial to understanding the
neighbourhood movement, the family in the popular sectors and women's
participation. Thus the sense of unity is loaded with personal and social
pressures.

As Isabel says:

In this street we have all been united. Those who aren't, oh well, they have to
go without water; so whether you like it or not you have to work together if
you don't want to remain without water.

In this process each partner's work is complementary, in that the domestic unit
requires both work in the home and money if it is to function. In this sense they
therefore occupy separate spaces.

The private space — the domestic one — is assigned to the woman, and the
public sphere, considered the productive one, belongs to the man. At this stage
women do actually operate according to this principle, because to maintain the
cycle of family life they basically carry out domestic and reproductive
functions. As we saw, however, in so doing they move continuously between
the private and public spheres, without this altering their principal role as
wife–mother. In any case, this participation within the imposed limits is
important for these women's apprenticeship in citizenship. (Feijoo, 1984; Jelin,
1984)

Self-built housing

Of course my husband gave me something but it wasn't enough. Everyone
was building their house and I was still living in a hut, so I went and did
domestic work like I used to before. I left the children behind — they were
already getting quite big and they were going to school. I did half time and
then came home. I joined a lottery-savings group and with the money I
bought bricks and cement for the foundations. Then I went and set up a
kiosk on Argentina Avenue where I sold snacks. I worked hard and now I
have a roof over my head. (Estela)

Subsequently, about ten years after arriving in the neighbourhood, the domestic unit becomes the central focus. They now have a plot of land and a shack; the neighbourhood has recognizable boundaries and the children have grown up and now go to school. Now they set about constructing their own house. This requires considerable investment in terms of effort, time and money, both for the schooling of the children and building the house. Migrants consider education of the children and having a house of their own to be their greatest assets, both being the concrete fulfilment of their dream of putting down urban roots. Once again it is possible to see how the cycle of family life, the relationship between work inside and outside the home and consolidation in the city and neighbourhood coincide. (Feijoo, 1984) In order to help establish the family, the women go out to work as washerwomen, cooks, street vendors or sewing ladies in private households. Their work is generally in services in the informal sector, because with few qualifications and, normally, many responsibilities in their own household, they are limited as to what other types of employment they can obtain. (Barrig, Chueca and Yanez, 1985)

They also have their own domestic chores but, unlike during the early years when it was almost impossible to think of regularly leaving their plot, in this second stage a routine has been established in which the woman is no longer alone. Other family members, especially the children who are now growing up, and relatives and other people from their native province, who are close to them who come to the city, share the domestic chores. This reduces the time the housewife has to spend looking after the household, making it possible for her to go out to work. Thus feminine roles multiply and the women become organizers of the household's daily life and also wage workers.

During this period, mutual help among the women is less crucial although in very difficult situations they continue to cultivate their relationships with their children's godmothers. This institutionalization of co-operation is maintained and respected.

As family life becomes more closed and private, daily life becomes organized on an increasingly individualized basis. Domestic activity becomes more and more independent of the neighbourhood mutual support networks that operated among women during the early period at the domestic level and also more independent at the public level, since the neighbourhood organizations also begin to disband, having to a certain extent achieved their aims.

The relative stability at this point can be related to the overall social situation of the country. Velasco Alvarado assumed power in 1968 and introduced a number of reforms, which in practice increased the space for social participation by the popular sectors and increased their civil rights. This set in train a considerable transformation of the overall political scene. The shanty town residents organized themselves and, to a considerable extent, their grievances were heard and they were provided with infrastructure, since the economic crisis had not yet made itself felt. From 1975 onwards, the limits of action begin to be redefined and popular organizations resort to confrontation and violence in the pursuit of their objectives. (Cotler, 1985)

The situation of the migrants who arrived between 1950 and 1960 is somewhat privileged, in that a certain social stability prevails which they will not experience again.

Towards the end of the 1960s mothers' clubs begin to emerge. These are new organizations, promoted 'from above' by Christian or governmental aid agencies, whose aim is to manipulate the mutual-aid networks in order to gain their political support.

Mothers' clubs — promoted from above
Ever since the Odria government (1948–56), the popular neighbourhoods began to feature on the national political scene. But, due to the paternalist nature of the government, their presence was somewhat mediated by others.

It was during the first Belaunde government (1963–68) that the neighbourhoods became potential bases of political support for political parties. Belaunde began his presidency with a reform in municipal law, which meant that mayors were no longer to be designated by the government but elected by popular vote. (Collier, 1978) This decision transformed the scene in these outlying neighbourhoods, where the enormous mass of migrants arriving in the city since the 1950s had settled because they could not be accommodated in the already urbanized areas.

It is an interesting place for party political activity. This situation became particularly acute after 1967, as the time for a change in government approached and the opposition parties, as well as the party in power, began their election campaign. The desperate search for popular support increased political activity. (Menendez, 1985) In the neighbourhood we are studying mothers' clubs were opened, aiming to gain electoral support for political parties in exchange for benefits and promises. Social workers and even Señora Cruchaga (first lady in Belaunde's government) arrived to organize, with the help of the National Welfare Council, contests and competitions between the women belonging to the mothers' clubs. The prizes were sewing machines, cookers, beds and first aid kits. The winners were the women whose houses were best kept, who had the cleanest yard and the cleanest and tidiest children — in other words the most devoted, thorough, attentive and grateful housewives.

> In Señora Cruchaga's clubs they gave cookers. Here too. But there were disputes. The one with the most points got a good cooker and the one with low points won the last one, so one way or another there was something. Instead of bringing unity the competition gave rise to division, and the mothers' club was closed because they withdrew Belaunde's wife. So you see what people were like . . . no? (Isabel)

During this first stage, when the mothers' clubs emerged, clientelism was rampant. It reinforced both the female domestic and reproductive role and the individualism that began to develop during the construction of the neighbourhood and the privatization of the family unit.

The mothers' club leaders are women who do not need to go out and find work. Women who, because they work, do not have so much time available are excluded from leadership roles. (Saralafosse, 1985) As a result, the organic structure favours one group of women settlers above others, revealing the deliberate intentions of the sponsoring organization whose policy is one of winning 'clients', by using the social heterogeneity that exists in the neighbourhood. It is a governmental choice, showing whom they wish to work with and how they intend doing this.

The women settlers, for their part, accept this new phenomenon which has landed in their midst and extract the maximum benefit. After all, for the women who are materially better off, clientelism offers the possibility of social mobility; and for those women abandoned by their husbands or without a family network to embrace them, it is an answer to many of their problems. It is a means of seeking the sort of protection which, in any case, the women had experienced in their previous employment as domestic servants. So this 'invasion' seems attractive to all of them, albeit for different reasons.

Conversely, bearing in mind their history of participation in the founding of the settlement, the women recognize the importance of collective action to resolve outstanding issues in the community. Thus, different needs come together in the mothers' clubs: the need to join together again to find a collective solution to problems such as rubbish collection or children's health and other more individual needs, such as once again creating a space for women's meetings and for women to receive training, similar to that which existed during the early years and was gradually lost. There is an ambiguity in the mothers' clubs, which embrace both political proposals for organization and more personal objectives of sharing tasks, reminiscences and aspirations. This ambiguity is a reflection of the ambiguity of the women settlers themselves. On the one hand the women are demanding, active and engaged in struggle. On the other, they are submissive and long-suffering, in accordance with the model of women and femininity imposed by this society in the urban setting. In practice, this model is incongruous for women from the popular sectors but to date it is ideologically invincible.

There does not exist, as yet, a political practice that supports the structuring of these new organizations, since the political parties do not recognize the women's potential as political protagonists, nor do the women aspire to such a role. There is no interest that they should be politically 'militant'. Their importance lies in the fact that they constitute a source of mass electoral support and in this respect it is enough that they are organized in mothers' clubs. The experience of the women inhabitants in the public sphere has been centred basically on the defence of their plot of land, on their activities as a mass support base in the neighbourhood organizations, on mutual support efforts and on developing spiritual kinship among themselves. This experience, which demonstrates very precise limits, makes it difficult for them to consider and develop clearer political objectives. In the last analysis, their participation in the neighbourhood movement has been from the standpoint of consolidating the family unit and not as militants. In other words, they were not opting for social change but for their integration into urban life and for better living conditions.

In this initial period, therefore, the mothers' clubs are organizations which have nothing to do with 'neighbourhood organization' in that they make no claims or demands of the state or their sponsors and do not stand up for their rights. Rather, their attitude is one of grateful recipients. They are examples of 'meeting', strongly influenced by a clientelism largely imposed by the sponsoring bodies. A sense of almost explicit manipulation marks these organizations from their birth, both from the side of the sponsoring bodies looking for popular support among the women and from the women themselves who need this patron–client relationship.

The women's leaders are key persons in this process because they articulate the actions and intentions from above and below. Isabel's case is very eloquent. Towards the end of 1966 she set up the neighbourhood's first mothers' club and here she explains what prompted her to do so:

> When I came to this site, this place, I didn't feel friendly towards anybody. For a long time I really suffered here, being on my own, not joining in with anyone. I was afraid. Then later we began to help one another. It was my idea to establish a mothers' club in the Sixth Zone so that we could pool our ideas and problems and see how we could help each other out. Besides, we can do a lot for our health and personal defence which benefits the household, and also help one another out with the children — you know the widows and the men who are sick — everything, help with everything in the community.

As in melodrama, this is a combination of episodes from normal daily life, which is both personal and social, with more epic actions that evoke the founding of the neighbourhood. The extent of identification among the women is therefore almost inevitable. In a way it is a 'message' of salvation, starting with the initial solitude and isolation followed by the hope that all this suffering will be relieved by joining forces and by the collective efforts of the community. In sum, it is a complex interplay between the individual and the collective, between the personal and the social.

Isabel continues her story, explaining how she had to go from house to house convincing the neighbours of the importance of the club, until one day she achieved her aim:

> It was very nicely set up. All the important people came and all the neighbours — it filled up very nicely. We still didn't have a roof, we still had nothing. Around this time INAPROME was in existence (before that it was the Social Welfare — the National Welfare Council of Pueblo Libre). So we asked ourselves who we could invite so that they would give us paper and rubber stamps. Then my husband said why didn't I also invite the woman who was the top director. And so I did — I got her to come and the priest too. He is the Club's founder. Afterwards I brought along a woman called Niñon Aguilar from the National Welfare Council and I asked her whether

as a social worker she couldn't visit me here because I was going to set up a mothers' club and we might need something, so perhaps she'd consider it. They came. There were four of them and all us women. The ceremony began and the priest began to address them. None of us spoke because we were not at all left-wing and we didn't know a thing. Well, we said the Club would be established because we needed it, we needed the company of our neighbours, we needed to communicate among ourselves and to help one another. This doesn't only depend on money — if there is money, that's all right. But all the more so if there is no money, we would all pull together and establish a fund and help one another out.

Isabel brought women along and invited others and established her club, in the presence of the authorities from the neighbourhood and where possible from the city. Participation of the notables is crucial both from the point of view of lending the occasion an air of distinction and also with a view to getting them committed to the club's future. Thus *compadrazgo* or patronage relations are entered into with the authorities and subsequently become transformed into an openly clientelistic relationship. From now on Isabel and the club's management have every right to request a meeting with any of these invitees to ask favours for herself or the club's members. This places Isabel in an enviable position *vis-à-vis* the members, because from now on she becomes someone special in the neighbourhood, assuming a new status.

For the leaders, the mothers' clubs are a means of climbing the social scale. This is something achieved only by those who hold a privileged position compared with the rest of the women, in that they do not have a job and thus have time to carry out the various formalities and bureaucratic procedures involved in obtaining the donations. The formal proceedings of the founding ceremony and the weekly sessions are fundamental. Furthermore, the Andean presence in the neighbourhood, as far as reciprocal relations between equals are concerned, gives a particular meaning to the clientelism in the clubs, reproducing the type of relations between *compadres* combined with submissiveness to the landowner. (Cotler, 1968)

Forming a club is not a simple process. Isabel assumes an almost motherly responsibility towards the members and the other authorities, taking *compadrazgo* very seriously. In future, Isabel will take care to ensure that the club is considered to be in the same mould as the clubs belonging to the National Welfare Council and that it receives donations of games, cakes and Christmas cakes. She also ensures that it is she who distributes these donations to the women, in other words she is the intermediary between the powers that be and the base.

This situation leads the club leader to develop a proprietorial attitude towards the institution and the women members. This even expresses itself in apparently irrelevant aspects such as holding club meetings in the homes of the leaders or considering it only natural that a sewing machine donated to the club should remain in the possession of the president. Women who do not have a house cannot become president and the woman who does become president, because she has a house, acquires higher status, which puts her under an obligation towards the members. Thus, this local power they acquire is often maternal. But it is also arbitrary and vertical: any member who does not agree with the policy decided by the leader and who begins to get support for opposing views is expelled. Estela, who for a long time was the president of the San Jose club, states the extreme case:

> I removed her from her post democratically, thanking her for the help she had given and telling her that now she had no supporters among the members. Or rather, I sent her the vote of censure and told her to withdraw in a dignified manner.

Furthermore, many jealousies and rivalries develop between the women and between clubs.

> A very competent woman came in. She used to talk with Señora Cruchaga and, because she knew how to speak and express herself, she got elected. In the Sixth Zone people joined, they came from every zone, no one stayed in the corner at home. They all came to the competition to win the prizes. That's not right — yes or no? Well me, I was against that, quite against it. I regretted having brought along the woman from the National Welfare Council, because the next year, along with the Señora Cruchaga de Belaunde in came this Señora Chiguan, as I said. And because she knew how to speak and expressed herself better she got the presidency. There were two factions in the mothers' club: one against the competition and another in favour, and the group in favour had more on their side and won the vote. Those against the competition lost. (Isabel)

This rivalry is rooted in the struggle for the power, privilege and prestige involved and, at a more individual level, for the concrete benefits it brings. The organizational structure of the clubs during this first stage benefits the individual (firstly the leader and then the members) rather than favouring collective work, service to the community or training in how to organize.

Velasco and the 1970s
On the fall of Belaunde and the assumption of power by the Armed Forces Revolutionary Government headed by General Velasco in 1968, interest in the mothers' clubs began to fall off. Local neighbourhood clubs came to life again, the National Office for Young Towns (ONDEPJOV) was created, and later, through the National Support System for Social Mobilization (SINAMOS), new channels of participation were opened up.[14] The women inhabitants retreated and many of the mothers' club leaders responded to the government's call for them to participate. There was a change in government discourse and in the kinds of organization used to try to reach the popular urban sectors. The clubs did not become involved in the political process — instead they declined.

From the second half of the 1970s onwards the situation began to change, with the onset of a period of unprecedented economic crisis, which hit the urban popular sectors very hard.

One characteristic of the mothers' clubs is their temporary nature, which is explained by the fact that they are promoted from above. Since they live on the benefits provided by clientelistic entities, they are active when donations are available but languish when there are none.

Faced now with economic crisis, the women are forced to look for new ways to supplement their family income. But this time they do not return to work in domestic services or to their old occupations. Instead, the actual neighbourhood and, in particular, the mothers' clubs, present themselves as appropriate areas for collective work.

Due to the stage in life they have reached, women between 40 and 50 years old who have a considerable number of children cannot return to their earlier work because no one will employ them as manual workers or as domestic servants. Nevertheless, with the increasingly widespread existence of food aid programmes and organizations to help women, the practice of collective work amongst women has begun to assert itself. As the crisis bites deeper and unemployment increases, the women have to contribute to and, in many cases, assume sole responsibility for the economic reproduction of the family. The neighbourhood offers them almost their only opportunities.

From 1978 onwards, such institutions as OFASA, CARITAS, ONAA, and PIBA among others and Popular Cooperation itself during the second Belaunde government (1980–85), increased the distribution of food as part of the government's social welfare policy to tackle the economic crisis. These subsidies, clearly tinged with a welfare connotation, are no solution to the problems but they help palliate the situation. Such food distribution programmes are carried out by private or religious bodies, often based overseas, or by the state apparatus itself. They generally work through the mothers' clubs which, in return for food, get the women together to carry out communal tasks. Considerable physical effort is required to carry out these tasks, which include cleaning up rubbish dumps, school premises and health centres, carrying earth and stones. They involve a full day's work every day. (Barrig, 1982)

There is a massive response on the part of the women to this type of programme. Valeria, and many women like her, approach the mother's clubs in order to obtain these food gifts.

> Yes, I went to Isabel's but since last year I haven't been back. I went for sugar, we didn't have any then. We got into an argument and Doña Isabel vetoed me and I haven't been since. Now I go to a literacy group. That's nice. It's not Isabel's. It's not much, but it's OK.

So the women shift from one club to another, attracted by the food hand-outs, but without being very conscious of the meaning of collective work or the social services the club provides to the community, or the sort of courses and requirements of each programme. Valeria continues:

> Yes, it was very hard. Here we first made baskets and did knitting, then after that we worked last year, but not this year. We also transported stones in exchange for food. They call it a programme. We carried a lot — it hurt around one's waist and stomach. But you had to do it if you wanted to get something. Yes, women are stronger than men, using a spade all the time. First we worked scrubbing floors using brushes with soap powder and water. You get very tired. Last year we also made dolls for children. After that I once helped by bringing eggs, egg whites. Then I gave out milk. A bit at a time, for everyone. That's nice. We made *cachangas* and gave them out.[15] We also did cleaning. You had to put in a lot of hard work to get it really clean. Over there all the young grandchildren are drinking milk.

Any task is undertaken if food can be obtained in return. So there is a considerable rise in the number of club members who begin to ask the club for increased material benefits, training for work in other activities and concrete solutions to the problems of hunger and survival in general.

The only clubs that survive are those which manage to adapt to new circumstances. From the point of view of the presidents, their ability to obtain more provisions to distribute in exchange for attendance on courses, or communal work influences whether they are able to consolidate their formal position in the club. Unlike in the clubs' early years, when the leaders enjoyed unlimited power — being able to decide what should be done and how — they now have to prove their efficiency as 'mothers', resolving the problem of food shortages.

In the same way that the leaders build up their prestige, not by demonstrating loyalty to institutions or parties but by manipulating them in order to obtain the maximum benefit from each of them, club members now respond with a similar attitude. They do not remain loyal to their club. They no longer accept passively the leader's decisions but assume a more demanding attitude and change from one club to another according to where the best benefits are obtainable.

> Señora Zoraida's club still exists — they still get supplies. Before there were lots of women in the club. But now that Señora Zelada has joined up with OFASA, they get food provisions and, due to the situation, people go there more than ever before. They go out of necessity to get provisions. They teach them to weave straw there and they also have literacy classes . . . yes, there are lots of women there. I think that the women go there for the food. Most of the women I have spoken to say they are given rice, three litres of oil, then cornflour, soya, wheat. It's mainly for this reason people have begun to drift away from here. (Catalina)

The clubs also begin to serve as a sort of agency for knitting and sewing work done at home. Once the club has 15 to 30 mothers, it becomes particularly attractive for contractors who provide raw materials such as wool or cloth to be cut and then collect the finished 'handmade' goods for export or sale in the shops.

> You know, what with this problem and that, I'm almost finished. They say I'm not like I used to be and the work is so hard, because we knit jumpers for sale abroad. There's a workshop called Vipol and they get us to knit alpaca jumpers. For example they give us the wool, the alpaca, and we women in the club knit the jumper and they tell us the style they want. Well, that's what we do, with various women here in my neighbourhood. (Ana)

This work differs from the food exchange programmes in that there is an individual cash relationship with the employer. But there is a lot in common since in both cases the club offers a space where the women can organize to work more efficiently and fill the orders.

New generations on the scene

Parallel to this process, other institutions, such as the parish, the local council and the popular education centres introduce a new progressive discourse and a new social practice. This alters the meaning of the mothers' clubs and of women's participation in them.

As the clubs begin to assume a different outlook, new content and massive membership, new demands begin to surface among the younger club members for greater democracy and participation in decision-making and for more rational management of the organization. They begin to question the power of the leaders. The latter are accused of not sharing power, not training the other members and of monopolizing the knowledge derived from leadership and restricting the membership's participation to a passive level, thereby preventing the development of a social consciousness in line with the current national political message and economic reality. The young women insist on democracy, training and production. One young woman comments on her club as follows:

> The president did the organizing. She was everything in the club, did everything. She did this, she did that; she was secretary, treasurer, everything. There was no support from the grassroots, no formal work to be done or anyone to teach us. I used to say that we had to work in something, so that we could produce, so that the women could take something home, without having to go out on the streets. Women can do a job now. They can give their children some economic help and can educate them. They are not going to be poor and illiterate like their mothers were. Maybe mothers aren't going to go to university, but at least they are going to study something handy, like knitting all these things. (Tadea)

The women leaders are now caught between two different phenomena. On the one side the membership now tends to stray off elsewhere and, on the other, the young women now insist on change. Furthermore, this is a generation nourished by a different discourse, which is born in Lima, which is studying and which has not had the same experiences as the older women. They have a different preoccupation: they cannot find how to integrate themselves despite all these differences. Moreover, with the neighbourhood's infrastructure already in place, they do not consider this a victory because it does not involve them in struggle and confrontation. Their struggle, as mainly marginalized women, is to claim the leadership to which they aspire. Though significant, this is not a widespread phenomenon because many of the young women do not even participate in the new organizations that develop.

Training courses for leaders multiply, and also workshops to discuss mothers' clubs and their commitment to the community and women's participation in the neighbourhood movement. Other sorts of short courses appear that train women for working at home, making clothes, toys or giving injections which, although limited, increase women's skills.

The relationships with many of the welfare bodies that provided food also change. This helps prevent the perpetuation of the former traditional clientelistic relationships. In some cases food starts to be given to a group and new forms of organization thus emerge, such as the new infant lunches and popular kitchens and dining rooms.

The significance of participation in the mothers' clubs and in popular women's organizations begins to change. What brings women together is no longer the fact of feeling lonely, the search for company or the desire to learn something, no matter what. The motives for participating become much clearer, in particular the recognition of the need to work collectively in order to cope with the crisis:

> I have had the opportunity to talk with other friends who were in the club and who are still young, younger than me. And they say no, no they didn't learn anything there. They wanted to discuss, that's the case of the president herself. But I don't know, it's a nuisance. It doesn't give them any alternatives and that's why they don't participate. Before coming here I just happened to be talking to a woman who told me that she doesn't go to the club. But if one day they set up a workshop, then she hopes they will consider her because she is having a very bad time and she's not allowed to do anything but sit there and produce nothing. Also she's fed up with so many activities for nothing, no output of anything at all. It's the same with most of them. We are quite a big group which is thinking of becoming active. In fact the only thing we lack in order to set up a workshop is education and to get ourselves trained. (Tadea)

Once more collective work as a tool for survival takes on new life. But, unlike previously, it is this time geared to economic, productive aims and puts emphasis on the skills needed by women for this work. The scope for women's collective action thus widens and the nature of participation continues to change. From private domestic organization to organization promoted by outside agents, there is a change to these new types of association based on the achievement of very concrete aims, like solving the hunger problem, but that bring with them new forms of participation through more democratic practices. (Jelin, 1984)

With the popular dining rooms and the milk distribution networks, which involve organization and collective work, areas of common concern develop. These begin to regroup the fragmented community, once again converting what was an individual domestic concern into something collective and social. In a period of conflict like the present, which derives from the precariousness of daily life and the almost total impossibility of knowing what will happen the next day, the popular dining rooms are developing new but still fragile expressions of grass-root solidarity, which are the seeds of new organizations in the process of creation.

Through these new organizations and with very precise aims in mind, such as reducing the cost of food ingredients and getting help from several sources, the women begin to build links with trade unions, local neighbourhood organizations and political parties. Thus, recently, a new collective actor has begun to emerge on the public scene, one that is beginning to make demands upon, control and negotiate with other institutions, thereby legitimizing collective domestic work and making the domestic role of women socially visible.

This process is neither clear nor straightforward. The women embark on a new struggle for the recognition of their organization, especially in the Federation of Young Towns. One illuminating experience is that of the women from the neighbourhood and district during the most recent Federation congress:

On the occasions I have been able to participate, sometimes there are these problems, differences and insults. We were invited to the Departmental Federation of Young Towns (FEDEJUP) and we had the opportunity to see the left intent on winning a dominant position only in order to get power. The people who were struggling — none of that mattered to them. For example, those of us who were there to represent the mothers' club were insulted. They treated us very badly. They said that we shouldn't be there or have a full vote because we were only a mothers' club and concerned with milk distribution. Go back home and get on with the cooking and washing — what are you doing here? This is not a dining room congress, it's a congress of the young towns. So I answered one of them. I said if this is a young towns' congress then we have a right to be here because it's not only men who live there, women do too. And if it wasn't for the women there wouldn't be any men either. So everything has to be made compatible, both the men and women. And the majority of the FEDEJUP leaders are on the left — the united left — and they were provoking these differences. They were promoting disharmony, they were devaluing women. (Tadea)

Finally, we believe this apprenticeship in interpersonal democratic practices could be an important step towards the continued transformation of clientelism, assuming that these new organizations still need donations in order to subsist and be efficient in achieving their aims. Learning the discipline of working alongside one's equals, learning to work in shifts and at certain hours and, in particular how, as a group, to relate to other institutions in society, such as the Council, the parish or the District Federation, are all undoubtedly an important part of the apprenticeship in public affairs.

Concluding thoughts

Throughout this study and through the life stories of these women, we have seen the slow, complex transformation process by means of which the women move from being isolated individuals with no social position in the city to forming families among the popular sectors originating from the provinces and becoming integrated in the urban social structure of Lima. The migrant women experienced uprooting but have now established new roots. As migrant women they have thereby established part of a new social identity as urban inhabitants.

Two factors are crucial in this process. The first is traditional clientelism, which provides a mechanism of insertion during the early days, and by means of which interpersonal relations of the patron–client type can be used and a certain position can be achieved, within the limits imposed by this model. The other is the family as a domestic unit, which serves as the nexus for integration of the individual into the network of the wider social structure.

Both clientelism and the family undergo changes as a result of daily practice, to the extent that the individuals themselves change. The initial content becomes richer and more dynamic relationships are created, which assist the integration process. The domestic unit thus operates in an increasingly complex space in relation to the management of family reproduction. In turn, interpersonal client-type relations begin to be replaced by a new form of clientelism that the clients start to define in a collective manner.

This is the context in which women's social participation takes place. The duality of the 'woman–domestic unit' is the key to understanding the process of women's participation, which is prompted by the problems of daily survival. Individualism and solidarity are thus linked to the development of the family unit.

The women involved in this process experience a transition from the individual to the collective, from clientelism to family autonomy. This process is nevertheless complex and often ambiguous, involving both advances and setbacks. The life cycle is crucial in explaining each instance of their participation.

Finally, the women who began this process on setting out from their place of origin are now housewives belonging to the popular urban sectors of society. They have learned their rights day by day as citizens in San Martin de Porres. They have a house, a husband and children with whom they live the present and they being to project a different future for themselves, belonging to them.

The women have learned about the city, about organizing and about urban poverty. Nevertheless, their participation does not go beyond the limits of the family. They struggle for better conditions of life for their loved ones, without as yet organizing themselves as a social and political force which demands a change in their subordinate status in daily life and in women's work. It is therefore necessary to consider these organizations as channels for collective action, including mechanisms for legitimizing social movements and the role of the new protagonists, thereby transforming the nature of popular participation by women.

Notes

1. This work forms part of the research on 'Urbanization and the Working Classes in Metropolitan Lima' carried out by the Institute of Peruvian Studies and, in particular, constitutes part of the project on 'Urbanization and Popular Culture in Metropolitan Lima', in which Carlos Ivan Degregori, Nicolas Lynch and myself took part.
I would like to thank the people along with whom I learned about the adversity and the courage involved in the process of women becoming citizens. In particular, I would like to thank the women of San Martin de Porres, who are the leading characters in this research in the history of the neighbourhood and in the movement involving women settlers in the popular neighbourhoods of Lima. We shared many hours of conversation and life with these women. I would like to mention Marisol de la Cadena and Julio Cotler for their continual encouragement and thoughts on the subject, Carlos Ivan Degregori for his valuable suggestions and many corrections, and Elizabeth Jelin and Amparo Menendez for their invaluable comments. In addition, I would like to thank Nicolas Lynch, my research and discussion partner and also *Alternativa*, the Centre for Popular Education in San Martin de Porres and Patricia Oliart and Rosario Murillo, who were involved in many stages of this research. Finally, my thanks are due to Aida Nagata for her efficiency and patience in making this manuscript readable.
2. 'Popular housewives' here refers to housewives who belong to the popular sectors of society. See Introduction by Elizabeth Jelin, note 1.
3. The Spanish original refers to *pobladoras*. Although *pobladoras* can mean female inhabitants and residents, the word carries an additional meaning in this context. It conveys the notion that the women have founded the settlements, in this case in the outlying dry barren areas around Lima, which are referred to later in this chapter as neighbourhoods or shanty towns. (Translators)
4. These new neighbourhoods were established on the outskirts of the city, on land to which the settlers had no title. They were therefore squatter settlements. Initially, no urban services were provided for these settlements which contain thousands of families. They are in effect shanty towns but will usually be referred to as 'neighbourhoods' to reflect the more social dimensions of the Spanish word *barrio*. (Translators)
5. The Spanish term *movimiento barrial* refers to a movement involving the residents of a neighbourhood, district or suburb. In Peru, however, *barrios* and *barriadas* refer to the poor neighbourhoods which are in fact often squatter

settlements or shanty towns. *Movimiento barrial* is therefore translated as shanty town movement or neighbourhood movement according to the context. (Translators)

6. *Compadrazgo* refers to the status of godparent (*comadre*/godmother and *copadre*/godfather) which has special significance in Latin America. The *comadre* is the godmother seen from the point of view of the child's godfather or parent. Thus, if I am the child's godfather, *mi comadre* is 'my fellow godparent' and, if I am the child's parent, *mi comadre* is 'my child's godmother'. This is the basis of a fictive kinship system that plays an important role in social relations in Latin America. (Translators)

7. *Comedores familiares*, *comedores populares* in the Spanish translate as family or popular dining rooms or restaurants. These describe efforts by poor women in the poor neighbourhoods to pool their scarce food resources and their labour to provide, on a collective or co-operative basis, meals more economic and nutritious than could be done on an individual nuclear family basis. The meals are also often consumed communally. (Translators)

8. Young towns (*pueblos jovenes*) refers to the extensive shanty towns described in notes 3. and 4. above. They are mostly located on the outskirts of Lima but have also grown up around other towns and cities. (Translators)

9. Information in this section relating to the neighbourhood and its inhabitants is part of the research entitled 'Urbanization and Popular Culture in Metropolitan Lima'.

10. *Huaynos* is an indigenous dance with a happy binary rhythm. (Translators)

11. *Clientelism:* Clientelism, clientelistic and patron–client relations are referred to frequently in this and other chapters and a brief explanation is therefore in order. The institution of clientage is perhaps one of the most basic forms of social relations outside kinship. The patron–client relationship is characterized by inequality between the superior patron and the inferior client or client group. The client groups, in this case poor, neighbourhood women, develop patronage relations with individual, more powerful women; and the formation and maintenance of the relationship is based on reciprocity in the exchange of goods and services, albeit of a different kind. The women 'clients' will receive material assistance or other forms of practical help in times of need and in return the 'patroness' will receive less tangible resources such as deference, esteem, loyalty or personal services. (Translators)

12. *Patasca* is a dish made from boiled maize.

13. The same is the case with very many women in such circumstances. At times they build up their hopes, believing and relying on promises of love and marriage, and then become pregnant. As a result, their ideal plan crumbles because they dreamt about having a partner, of having a family with a man around. But, although it seems paradoxical, they are not discouraged or frightened and they continue with their motherhood which, while somewhat overwhelming, also gives them strength, because the child is an investment as well as a burden.

Thus, while the ideal is to join up with another to build a home together, because this is the alternative to the patron–client type relations which they face as domestic servants, having a child on their own is part of the uncertainty in their lives. Because this constitutes a set-back, this decision involves continuing with their employers in an almost irreversible dependency or alternatively relying on the extended family.

14. See note 8.

15. *Cachangas*: pancakes made of flour and fried in very hot, shallow fat or oil.

2.   Women, Daily Life and Politics

Teresa Pires de Rio Caldeira

Anyone who has followed the development of social movements in the city of São Paulo since the 1970s either directly by observing daily life in the surrounding shanty towns, or indirectly through the newspapers, will know that these movements are in the main constituted and led by women. It is women who form the mothers' clubs and who are the major participants in the Christian Base Communities (CEBs).[1] They have mobilized around specific demands[2] such as health care, nurseries or the needs of the shanty towns and it is women who go around these popular neighbourhoods collecting signatures in support of different petitions. It was women who thought up, implemented and in the main directed the Cost of Living Movement. And basically it is women who make up the demonstrations that leave one or other of these marginal neighbourhoods almost daily for the Town Hall[3] to express some protest or demand about the precarious conditions in their neighbourhoods. Likewise, it is women who regularly go to the regional administration offices to press for and obtain public services for their communities.[4]

With all the evidence available in the recollections of the participants, from researchers familiar with these movements and from what has appeared in the newspapers,[5] it is incredible that information on women's participation is absent from the analysis in almost all studies on these social movements. In the majority of cases the protagonists of these movements are described using general categories, such as the 'inhabitants of peripheral areas', the 'popular classes', the 'people', the 'poor', and so on, with no reference whatsoever to their gender. It is sometimes mentioned that the majority of participants are women but they are never taken as a specific object of study.[6] It is true that there are some studies that focus specifically on the 'woman's question' and which look at their political participation.[7] Nevertheless there have been no serious attempts to incorporate these studies into the debate on social movements due, among other things, to the particular divisions existing among research fields in Brazilian social sciences. Although the area of 'women's studies' is accepted as an academic subject and has gained space within the universities, research centres and scientific meetings, work produced under this heading is not taken into account in discussions in other fields. Indeed, it is seen as a somewhat distinct subject. Studies on 'women' involve a discussion of their role in the trade unions, the family, political parties, literature, schools, social movements, religion or wherever. The most diverse themes are covered when the 'woman's question' is discussed. But when the discussion is centred on a particular theme such as political parties or education, there is a tendency to use general categories and to forget about the specificity of gender.[8]

An analysis of women's specific role is essential, however, not only to describe but also to understand the characteristics of these social movements.[9] To focus on the nature of these movements from the perspective of women's participation rather than that of the 'popular classes' allows us to reconsider themes that have been linked repeatedly to these movements and which risk being considered as common ground before being sufficiently explored or understood.

The majority of studies insist on using the term 'new' to characterize the social movements that emerged in Latin America in the 1970s. Frequently the novelty lay in some form of locally based egalitarian grass-roots organization created out of an awareness of needs. This organization would be democratic in its internal running and based more on consensus that on the representation of interests (and therefore differences). In general, the characteristics of this form of organization are expressed in the notion of building a community.[10] The novelty would also seem to consist in the ways in which these organizations related to the state and to institutional policy. By voicing their interests autonomously and identifying their rights, these popular organizations confronted the state directly (the state being seen as the entity responsible for delivering these rights) by presenting their demands but never petitions. They did not engage in the practice of political mediation, so beloved by traditional politicians, and they also turned their backs on the political parties, which were considered incapable of representing the local community. Finally, the form of political expression adopted by these movements was also new. Ignoring the risk of repression they put emphasis on maintaining a collective and public presence in all situations of political confrontation, by means of assemblies, marches, public events, demonstrations, and suchlike.

Although there is consensus on the existence of many of these characteristics in the social movements and on their enormous political significance in a country with a long tradition of elitism and authoritarianism, much still remains to be clarified. One indication of this is the disagreement between different studies on which aspects to emphasize in order to highlight their novelty. There are at least two ways of conceiving their central features. One type of analysis of these 'new forms of politics' — probably the dominant tendency — emphasizes the more political aspects and the relationship between these and 'outside' movements. In other words, the accent is on the question of autonomy, the authentic expression of interests, the absence of intermediaries and representatives, the recognition of rights and pressures on the state. Besides exaggerating many aspects, such as the spontaneity and autonomy of the movements,[11] this approach runs the risk of making wide generalizations from a particular local experience. It is assumed (or hoped) that there might be an almost automatic and more or less direct path between the insistence on the right to running water, voting for the opposition and the demand for a change of political regime; and from the community movement, to the trade union movement, to the political party. The results of research on electoral patterns have already cast serious doubts on this automatic transition and shown how disruptive and problematic party membership can be in the context of social movements.[12] Further doubts are raised by the analysis of women's participation.

In the other tendency that can be observed in the analyses, emphasis is put on day-to-day experience within the local movements and associations. Here, more weight is given to new forms of socializing and collective identity, to experiences of equality, which are seen as part of the process of creating a community. This perspective has tended to move away from the field of political considerations, and characterizes the movements as essentially social.[13] To examine the possible formation of a new women's identity within these movements is thus an important way of contributing to this discussion.

In short, an analysis of women's political participation allows an evaluation of several themes raised in a discussion of 'new forms of politics'. Above all, identifying the participants' gender and the ways in which this influences the organization of the movements offers a more accurate description of the situation and allows criticism of the use of general categories, whereby political phenomena tend to be related to the 'class situation' of the participants.[14]

Furthermore, an analysis of the forms this participation takes and the insertion of the movements into daily life, allows us to re-evaluate the two tendencies mentioned above. Consequently, we shall attempt to describe the different ways in which women participate in local associations and activities to press for their demands and to capture the essence of daily experiences in the work of these movements. We aim to try to understand the political significance of this participation (which is manifested through the way these movements perceive relationships with the 'outside') as well as the implications for the organization of daily life, interpersonal relations and the development of a vision of society. We also hope to show how these movements, while generating new forms of external confrontation, are internally creating new forms of socializing and changing the patterns of interpersonal relations and social roles, especially of gender roles. In doing this, we focus on the cultural context in which political activities are carried out. Here, greater emphasis is given to those aspects that lead to a transformation in the particular ways of organizing life and which go beyond the expression of interests in relation to the state and dominant groups. Changes in political ideas and values and changes in the forms of collective organization of daily life are seen here as inseparable dimensions of the same process.

With these new perspectives on the relevance of daily life we might be able to reach an understanding of women's enormous participation in the social movements. Our focus therefore moves away from debates that concentrate on politics, or categories that use the 'class position' to define these movements, although we do not totally disregard them. By posing different questions on the relation between politics and daily life, we might be able to understand more about these new movements, whose autonomy and authenticity are much praised and in which are vested great hopes for social and political change. They are the result of the actions of women who, imprisoned by their gender, were always defined and identified as alien to politics, which is seen as a sphere of life beyond their capabilities. By observing the actual roles of each gender in the context of a political activity (which is defined in its function of its relation to the state in defence of specific rights) we might gain knowledge of the real changes taking place in practice within the social movements themselves. Perhaps in this way we shall be able to specify what is 'novel' about these movements.

A very mixed universe

We were involved with the inhabitants of six neighbourhoods on the periphery of São Paulo from September 1981 to 1983.[15] During this period we observed their daily life and tried to register all existing forms of organization and participation in collective activities. In addition, we collected a great number of testimonies and interviews from those who were not involved as well as those who were. We also held a series of collective meetings (involving between 10 and 50 women) in all the existing groups and associations. We then individually interviewed all the women who had attended. We discussed forms of participation but we mainly talked about the women's life histories, the neighbourhood, the city and its problems, children and family, television, work, football, in fact everything that makes up daily life.

The first thing to which we would like to draw attention is the invariable presence of local associations and forms of participation in the neighbourhoods we studied. But these were extremely varied and clearly differentiated from one another. When we began the field work we had decided to include at least one neighbourhood where there was no type of local association or focus around which the inhabitants organized, but it was only after a long search that we found such a neighbourhood. In the first three months of research we witnessed the formation of three associations of disgruntled residents and the organization of a number of demonstrations on specific issues. These popular demonstrations were widespread and the forms they took varied enormously, therefore it is necessary to begin by establishing their differences.

Not all the neighbourhoods had the same type of association, as can be seen in Table 2.1. Furthermore, even when similar institutions existed, such as the Society of Friends of the Neighbourhood (SABs) and the Association of Shanty Town Dwellers,[16] the way in which they worked was completely different, as they ranged from more 'clientelistic'[17] to 'authentic' types of grass-roots organization. Only some of the forms of participation corresponded to the idea generally associated with the 'new social movements' which we attempted to describe above. This type of participation was found in the organizations of the Catholic Church (the Christian Base Communities — CEBs — and their different pastoral working groups and associations for mothers or youths and so on) as well as in what we term 'local movements' (illegal squatters, shanty towns, transport, nurseries, urban services and so forth) and in some of the SABs. It should be noted that there is an important distinction between the SABs and associations of shanty town dwellers, and the CEBs and local movements. While the first have a formal hierarchical structure, this has been rejected by the latter who promote the equitable participation of those united by common needs. Therefore it is to these groups rather than the former that the concept of 'novelty' is most frequently attributed.

Of the six neighbourhoods studied, at the beginning three and by the end two, had no type of social mobilization that could be identified as 'new'. But this did not prevent the latter neighbourhoods from obtaining urban improvements through the initiatives of people acting individually. Pressing for demands is not synonymous with social movements or the organization of the people. It quite often involves presenting petitions and, of course, putting pressure on public bodies, but this can be done by one single person with initiative, generally a woman. In addition, the type of procedures used — obtaining letters of support from politicians, sending out petitions, for example — are not a new departure. Traditionally, they have been among the methods used by the popular classes in their relationship with the authorities. People acting on their own could be found in all the neighbourhoods, sometimes working alongside social movements, and on other occasions side by side with various churches and branches of political parties. In summary, in every neighbourhood we found various types of association and actions competing with each other and on many occasions working simultaneously for the same objective. Demands were taken up by one or other and, as each group or institution had its own style and conception of politics and of how to fight for demands, it was not uncommon for there to be conflicts and arguments among the participants or 'clients'.

It is important to bear in mind this heterogeneity in order to understand women's active participation. There were women activists in all the neighbourhoods and they were not restricted to those spaces created specifically for them, such as the mothers' clubs and women's groups.[18] They constituted an absolute majority in the CEBs and local movements, with the exception of the groups of illegal squatters, which are generally considered to be a male domain. Although women are less active in the SABs, one of those we studied was led by a woman. Women participate in almost everything, in fact they are the minority only in the party committees and wards, as this overtly political space is considered to be masculine. To understand how the women see their activism in the public arena, what they think of politics and what joining in politics means to them, we must differentiate the women in our study according to their form of participation.

The group of women in which we are most closely interested is the clientele of the local associations and social movements. That is, those who join in efforts to build democratic grass-roots organizations through sharing the same situation (or because of the same felt needs) and who have identified common interests. They are members of women's groups, mothers' groups, CEB and

SAB, the renewed Neighbours' Associations, and the whole range of local movements. Generally the women who make up these groups participate in more than one association and nothing prevents them from becoming involved in other types of action, especially those promoted by women acting on their own initiative. They are mainly married women, housewives with children, and very few of them work outside the home. Their numbers varied in each neighbourhood but never exceeded fifty.

In all the neighbourhoods studied, we were told of how, when they began building up the neighbourhood 'it was just a jungle' and only after some time and as a result of their demands and struggles did urban improvements start to be made. They all told the story of one or more women who, without belonging to any institution or movement, drew up written petitions (perhaps obtaining a letter of support from a known politician) and took them either alone or in the company of a few neighbours to the Town Hall, the Regional Council, the headquarters of the electricity company or wherever else necessary, but always to public institutions, some of which already received the public directly without the need for intermediaries.[19] These women were not interested in organizing people and they did not necessarily want to obtain benefits for the whole community. In many cases they were quite content to get some improvements for the immediate area or streets where they lived. There were always one or two such women in each neighbourhood, all married with children and generally without a job outside the home.

In all the areas studied the initiatives of these women co-existed — not very harmoniously, we should say in passing — with local movements and institutions, such as the CEBs and SABs. Innovative or traditional, client orientated or not, these institutions generally function in the name of the people and their discourse expresses the demands and is focused on the interests of the neighbourhood as a whole. Their conflict with women acting on their own initiative is greater, the more actively the institution or movement concerns itself with organizing or uniting the community as a whole and with developing political awareness, that is when it approaches most closely the 'new' model defined in the literature. But it is important to say that the conflicts with these individual women activists are more frequent among the leaders of these bodies than with the participants, who readily approve of anyone trying to obtain improvements for the neighbourhood.

We found various other types of women community leaders. Firstly, are those linked to the Catholic Church, who are the majority. They are leaders of street groups, mothers' clubs and other groups involved in all kinds of pastoral work and struggles for specific demands. They are always concerned to organize people and raise their awareness and they generally participate in organic church structures, such as sectional and regional councils. Secondly, are those who are normally called 'external agents' who do not live in the neighbourhood and are generally linked to organizations with a wider structure, such as political parties (which until 1985 were illegal) or feminist groups. These women organize movements pressing for health care and nurseries, feminist movements, shanty town movements and other related

Table 2.1
Institutions, movements and activities in support of specific demands in the selected neighbourhoods — 2nd semester/1982

Institutions Movements and Activities	Selected Neighbourhoods					
	Jardim das Câmelias	Jardim Miriam	Jardim Marieta	Jardim Peri-Peri	Jaguaré	Cidade Júlia
Independent Activists	X	X	X	X	X	X
SABs or Dwellers' Unions	1	2	1	1	2	3
Local Movements:						
Illegal squatting	X					X
Health	X				X	
Women	X	X				
Shanty Towns		X				
Transport					X	
Nurseries	X	X				
Urban Services	X				X	X
Catholic Religious Organizations:						
Workers		X				
Youth	X	X				
CEBs	X	X				
Mothers	X		X		X	X
Other religions						
Brazilian Church		X				
Umbanda	X	X	X			X
Assembly of God	X	X	X		X	X
Other Christian religions	X	X	X		X	X
Seicho-no-ie				X		
Sports Clubs or Samba Schools		2	2	1	2	2
Committees or Wards of Political Parties	PT PTB	PT PTB	PDT PDS	PDS	PMDB PT	

areas. They see their work in a somewhat similar way to the first group. These two types of leadership, when they exist, together usually have about four or five women in each neighbourhood. Thirdly, it is also possible to find, although in smaller numbers, women who are leaders of the SABs. The membership of these societies, as we have already pointed out, is almost totally masculine. We did meet one female SAB president who, as we shall see later, in spite of speaking in the name of the community, had no intention whatsoever of organizing it.

Finally, we turn to women's participation in the political parties. This is quite limited, as political parties are considered to be a male domain. The women we met who were involved in the parties participated in two ways but none held important positions in the wards or committees. On the one hand there were women working individually, paid to canvass for votes, who were generally linked to a politician or a ward but worked on their own to canvass support for their candidates whether in the Brazilian Democratic Union (PMDB); the Brazilian Labour Party (PTB); Democratic Labour Party (PDT); or the Democratic Social Party (PDS).[20] Many of these women did this political electioneering in addition to activities in support of specific demands undertaken on their own initiative. There were a maximum of three women in each neighbourhood active in this way. On the other hand, we also found women in some areas who were working as canvassers and who were members of a ward or committee linked to a local group with a more permanent role than that of election campaigning. This type of work was generally carried out for the Workers' Party (PT) and the few women involved were leaders but not clientele of the church or other local social movements.

Having established the heterogeneity of women's participation, we shall now analyse its significance for those women we have described as the clientele of the local social movements, or as the subjects of the experience of democratic participation in the CEBs or some SABs. We have chosen to emphasize this group for an obvious reason: though they are not mentioned, it is these women and the role they play that form the basis of all the comments and conjectures formulated in the literature on social movements. We shall also refer to other contrasting types of women's activism, characterizing and explaining the significance of the women's participation.

Making up for lost time

The first group of women we shall consider are as anonymous in their public presence as they are ignored in the literature. They make up the banner-carrying crowds that fill the squares and public administration offices. Rarely, however, are they the spokespersons of these demonstrations.

As well as accompanying the women on their demonstrations and in their daily work in the neighbourhoods, we also collected testimonies about their lives and participation activities. A notable feature was the way in which these interviews developed. The women spoke openly and at length about themselves, their families, children, daily life in their neighbourhoods, the struggle to survive on little money in such a precarious place, their constant involvement (what the meetings were like, who went, what they did, what they liked, and so on). On the other hand, they were reticent and spoke with difficulty about the current and, in particular, past political regimes. So, unlike when relating at length their personal life histories (monologues marked by the emotion of stopping and thinking and evaluating their own lives) their replies were a confused string of monosyllables when the interviewer urged them to talk about the more political themes on the agenda in the election campaign — about those in power and their actions, the elections or amnesty, the political opening, strikes, the military, foreign debt, and suchlike.[21]

To ask about politics was to hear the reply 'I don't know', 'who can say', 'I don't get involved in that', 'I don't understand politics' and similar responses. If it was difficult for them to talk about the present, it was almost impossible to do so about the past. Their memories hardly registered that world considered by the popular classes in general and women in particular to be 'on the other side'. In her book about the recollection of neighbours, Eclea Bosi states that, 'only personally significant events are retained'. (Bosi, 1979:384) What was important for the majority of the women whom we met were the things that had happened in their private and family lives. They 'didn't get involved' in 'history', especially political history. Their political recollections lacked dates and almost always names; they remembered some events and personalities but did not link them together or see their inter-relationships. Their recollections were fragmentary and mentioned only as if to satisfy the curiosity of the interviewer who insisted on asking about them. There was nothing in the past that stood out, not because events were irrelevant but because people 'cannot see why it would be useful', they do not 'seek to know' or to 'study a bit'. Events that were observed and stored in the memory related to important episodes in their own lives and it was these that dictated their memory. For instance, one woman remembered that Getulio Vargas had died when she was a girl because that day was declared a holiday and she did not have to go to school. Another recalled that 'in the time of Medici things were fine, everything went well' and others recalled what happened 'when I was twenty', 'before this baby was born', 'a month before I was married'.[22] Their domestic space and daily life was what mattered to them and what they wanted to talk about in the interviews, which they regarded as a distraction and one of the rare occasions on which they could direct attention towards themselves.

One woman, with whom we talked for more than three hours, expressed her dissatisfaction at the persistence of the political themes half way through the interview and right until the very end:

> This interview is all about politics, but I don't understand anything about politics. I just don't know, it's something that doesn't affect me. I don't know, I thought my interview would be completely different . . . I thought our conversation would be like women's talk, like the one you did with Mrs J. and it never entered my head that it would be all about politics . . . I don't understand anything about politics.

In the final half hour the researcher decided to respond to the interviewee's expectations and went on to ask her about her daily routine at home, her children and husband. Towards the end she seemed to have already forgotten the disagreeable beginning and commented:

It is so pleasant to chat among ourselves. It doesn't seem like an interview, no. Huh! an interview is something more serious.

(V., housewife, three daughters, participated in the CEB, in the campaigns for nurseries and health and in a number of marches to the Regional Council and Town Hall, member of the women's group.)

This polarity between 'women's talk' and 'political things' also came up in other testimonies, although not in exactly the same words. It is not only a matter of what they do or do not like to talk about, it also indicates the spaces or spheres in which women include, or from which they exclude, themselves. In these terms, their participation in local movements — always stressed as something positive — is situated in the sphere of 'women's talk'. Generally, these interviewees, who are anonymous participants in the social movements, do not see their activism as political activism.

These two spheres need to be further defined. The positive and female side can be seen in their replies to the questions about why they were involved in these movements, or why they liked or thought it important to participate. The answers were very clear and almost identical in all the interviews:

At that time I was really ill, depressed because I felt alone here, I think I'm scared of being alone . . . So, I felt alone and I felt sick, maybe it was an illness or perhaps loneliness, I don't know. Then my husband said to me: 'It would be a good idea if you went over to help that sister' [the nun who was organizing the local CEB]. So we began to work there in the Community.[23] I think that friendships are a good thing. When you see someone with problems quite often just a word helps. It also takes you out of yourself and resolves your own problem too. That's how I started having plenty of friendships here. And there one begins to move ahead.

(A., housewife, six children, ex-member of the CEB, participated in the campaign for nurseries and health, in the squatters movement, in the SAB and member of the women's group.)

Another explained it like this:

One gets to know people and find out about the problems of others in the neighbourhood . . . Yes it's a healthy thing to get out of the house to be with lots of people, each talking about their own problems. Getting to know about others' problems you forget your own. Getting out, mixing with people, with different neighbourhoods, but mainly in the struggle . . . one learns, one even learns to talk a bit better, by sharing with others you also find out about many things you don't have here.

(R., housewife, two children, participated in the CEB and in the campaign for nurseries of which she was the neighbourhood representative on the regional committee.)

Participating was important for all the interviewees, particularly because they learnt something. They met others, made 'friends' in the neighbourhood, but above all they settled any doubts they had, shared and solved problems and found guidance. As well as learning, there were two other benefits. On the one hand, it made them feel less nervous or as they put it, 'they lost their fear'. On the other, they gained self-esteem from learning how to talk in public, they were respected and felt more secure in the world outside the four walls of their homes.

The idea of participating and learning would therefore seem to be the antithesis of isolation at home. A woman who stays at home 'doesn't know much', 'doesn't develop'. On her own she 'doesn't learn', is barely alive, is distressed and undervalues herself. Participating is good because it gets women out of the house, puts an end to the routine, loneliness and isolation, and helps them find company. Participating means an opening to the world, in other words, learning your way about the city, going to different places and dealing with public organizations.

On examining the references women made to the amount of time they had available, further dimensions of the significance of women's participation in the various social movements become apparent. Firstly, it is women and not men who are involved in this type of movement and they attend the CEBs more frequently because they have more time. Since in general they are housewives, their time is more flexible and they can adjust their housework to the timetable of meetings and activities, which would be impossible if they had a fixed job outside the home.

Women are thus able to participate because of the flexibility and availability of their time, but it is these very same factors that also create a need for them to participate. Participating means breaking with monotony and unstructured time, which would otherwise be filled only by housework. Events and meetings imply regular breaks from the excesses of daily routine, the chance of giving meaning to time that otherwise would invariably be spent on others. Time for meetings was clearly time put aside for themselves.

Note the following dialogue between two participants of the CEB, both housewives with children:

M. Women . . . need a chance to go out once in a while, it's better than staying at home.
Z. If you just stayed in on your own doing the cleaning you'd go mad.
M. Because housework is never-ending, you're the one that is finished . . . At these meetings you get a bit of a break. It's a chance to have a rest and to learn.
Z. Sometimes you can go to the door and have a chat with the neighbour. But the thing is that this is just for a short while as there is always something you've left inside that needs finishing. And if you go out and go to a meeting, you get a bit more time to yourself. So, it seems to me, that it is important to participate because, let's say we get ten women here at the meeting, we learn more than if we were on our own or with one other person. Because it seems to me that it's an exchange of experiences and for those who, let's say, didn't

get much chance to study, then we can learn like this, by exchanging experiences and learning things about life through practical experience.

M. And you also enjoy yourself.

Z. Yes, you also enjoy yourself because if you didn't you'd stay locked in at home by yourself.

M. Time flies and you don't even notice.

Z. And it's as though you've stopped in time . . . If you go out you develop a bit.

The dialogue is clear and precise: participate and learn, gain experience and develop, in order to make up for time lost in the home when they did not study or develop, a time in which they were getting 'left behind'. Far from a few women complained about having 'woken-up' so late, of having lost so much time among the dishes, nappies, the pots and pans. Besides, participating is enjoyable, it means having one's own space, a wider social life, fun and time for themselves. Furthermore, by breaking up and labelling their time it becomes more visible, because there is now a sense to it. Participation leads to an awareness of time, or more precisely of events in time, rather than time affecting someone who has been standing still.

In short, women enjoy participating and make the effort to do so because the experience of daily activities in the movements and the structuring of their time offers them the possibility of learning, coming out of their isolation and opening up to the world. Given the meaning these women attribute to participation we can understand why, for instance, the majority of women involved in the nursery campaigns in the neighbourhoods we studied were not thinking of finding a job outside the home or placing their children in one of the nurseries for which they were campaigning. Or why, when a number of women in one of the neighbourhoods left the CEB because of a difference of opinion with one of the nuns who directed it, they immediately began to look for some other type of activity, saying that they could not 'stand still'. In this case the political dimension of what they were going to do or not do was clearly secondary, as was the practical use of the nursery for women who did not intend to use it.

These aspects, which the women we interviewed indicated as being the most important and determining reasons for their participation, are not only ignored in the literature on women's social movements but are even contradictory to what this literature generally emphasizes as the characteristic features of participation. These works give particular emphasis to two types of experience: 1) distinguishes the class situation where women's awareness of poverty and injustice is what forms the organizational basis of such social movements and motivates their participation; and 2) the emphasis is on experiencing a new political activity, defined by egalitarian and democratic practice, and a new way of confronting the state. These elements are certainly not absent from the literature, but apart from the fact that they need to be qualified (for example, do the experiences of equality and mutual recognition of which our interviewees spoke have the same meaning as the experiences of equality referred to in these other analyses?), there are no grounds for considering them to be more apt than others in defining participation in the social movements, particularly participation by women.

To understand more about these elements implies, among others things, investigating the type of political vision that is being generated in practice. We should not forget that in the first testimony the interviewee did not see her participation in the local movements from the perspective of 'political things', from which she distanced herself, but rather as falling within the sphere of 'women's talk'. Examining the elements emphasized in the literature means finding out which type of experience is counted as more important by those participating in the movements. It is generally assumed that the experience of class is a key factor. The evidence we gathered would, however, seem to indicate that it is living as a poor woman (tied to the home and housework with no possibility of studying) that the participants themselves emphasize and which at the same time is being modified. Women in a position of equality, talking together about their problems, looking for common solutions, learning, trying to recover lost time, all this would seem to indicate that women are experiencing changes — although small — in their role, and that this is becoming more outward orientated. What is at issue is their identity as women rather than as workers or poor people.

It is not a conscious process on the part of the women, although it is clearly exemplified by two leaders of one of the neighbourhoods. They were able to break away from the CEB to which they belonged to organize a women's group independently of the Church; the latter institution imposed many limitations on exploring women's issues more deeply. As one of them said:

... in the Women's Movement, I discovered myself as a woman, as a being, as a person. I hadn't known that women ... have always been oppressed. But it never occurred to me that women were oppressed even though they had rights. Women had to obey because they were women. 'She isn't a man'. 'I'm not a man, so I must obey orders'. It was in the Women's Movement that I began to identify myself as a woman and to understand the rights I have as a woman. I've learnt a lot of things to pass on to other women. (P., married, housewife, member of the Women's group, the nurseries campaign and the CEB.)

This interviewee, who is a leader, expresses more emphatically and clearly than other participants in the social movements why active participation has an innovative meaning for women. This obviously does not exclude references to the class situation. If for no other reason, activities centred around specific demands are legitimized by the perception of social inequality and lack of recognition of the rights of the poor. But the discourse that legitimizes participation should not be confused with the underlying motivations for action. All the women refer to their class position in order to claim their rights, but this is a way of legitimizing a practice that has other connotations and other forms of legitimization, one of which is the appeal to the role of mother, to woman's traditional role, as we shall see later.

In summary, it can be argued that women's active participation in the social movements brings to light aspects not emphasized in the literature, namely the experience of woman's situation. Clearly, the elements normally chosen to describe such participation should be looked at more closely. In this sense, it is worth reconstructing the way our interviewees link their experience of 'opening to the world' with their experience of the class situation, the traditional role assigned to women, and their conception of politics.

The good of some versus the interests of others

Being active in the various movements in pursuit of their rights and claims and in institutions such as the CEBs and the SABs is generally described by the women as 'struggling for one's own good'. This means opposing discrimination and social injustice, demanding 'one's rights' because everyone pays their taxes. On the other hand, it also means fighting to improve their housing and their possessions, and for the good of their families and above all, their children. It is not uncommon to find participation associated with explanations such as: 'when I saw my children arrive home at night, in such darkness, then I realized I had to do something and I began to collect signatures for the petition'.[24] Finally, in the case of some leaders of social movements and the CEBs, it can also mean fighting for the rights of people in general, of the poor, and of the oppressed.

Of all the possible meanings it could entail, the category 'fighting for one's own good' is the one mentioned most frequently as referring to the women's own families and neighbourhoods. It is in this sense that the traditional role of mother is associated with participation in a movement for specific demands. When women have to justify to someone the fact that they are going out of their houses and changing the domestic routine to go to meetings, or when they have to legitimize themselves before the authorities, the administrator, the press or public opinion, it is common for them to appeal to their situation as mothers. As long as their families live badly or their children are in danger they cannot be satisfied and stay at home waiting for the impossible, namely that the services they need will be provided without having to fight for them. In this sense it can be said that the role of mother is expanding into the public arena. Struggling and participating are activities beginning to be seen as part of the duties a responsible mother is obliged to carry out in a city such as São Paulo, where the urban life is precarious and the public authorities act only under pressure.

Within this context, the literature on social movements has insisted that women's participation occurs because such movements relate to the reproduction of the labour force, the domestic sphere, to aspects that have always formed part of women's universe.[25] In general, this type of argument has been considered sufficient to explain the female presence in social movements, though in fact it gives rise to a distortion and a deficiency. The distortion consists in considering female participation as more conservative than it really is, and the deficiency lies in not perceiving the ambiguity of women's participation, which in spite of being carried out in the name of their most traditional role, involves going out and leaving precisely that sphere used as a means of legitimization.

The category 'fighting for one's own good' is also apparent in other contexts. It becomes a central element in defining what the women interviewed consider as 'politics' and is the basis for the development of dichotomies such as: 'women's talk' and 'political matters'.

As evidenced by the structure of the interviews mentioned above, politics is something that women feel distant from for various reasons. Unlike the women leaders of the Worker's Party (PT), of the CEBs and local movements, women who simply participate do not generally have a wide vision of politics. For them life is not politics nor is politics all-embracing. They make a constant effort to define a space for politics which they try to 'steer clear of', a space they have no desire to find out about. It is a space of 'ignorance' as opposed to the way in which participation in local movements and in the CEBs is presented as a space of knowledge.

An analysis of our interviewees' comments regarding their lack of party political participation makes this clear. We are insistent on this matter because we notice that none of the women who participated in any of the neighbourhood movements joined a political party, not even when encouraged to do so by the people who prompted their participation in the local movements. If these movements have become a female universe, the parties in turn, just as the unions, are clearly masculine worlds.

In general, when we asked the women why they did not participate in political parties, they replied: 'because their business is politics'. What, then, was the difference between their participation and what went on in the parties? The replies brought out the contrast between their personal experience of participation on the one hand and what they imagine about politics on the other:

Party meetings are largely political discussions and those of the health clinic are about other things. I think the discussions of the Workers' Party are more about politics and that of the clinic isn't political, it's about the lack of facilities, about how it's working . . . I don't understand anything about politics. Now, there in the women's group meetings, I feel more sure.
(S., housewife, three children, participant in the CEB, in the nurseries, the health clinic and squatters campaigns, member of the Women's Group.)
When you join a struggle and go to the Town Hall, do you think you are mixing in politics?
No! I don't think it's political because what we are fighting for is for the good of the people . . . I think that politics . . . who knows . . . It's a debate they have between themselves there, isn't it?

There was obviously a distinction between what the interviewees did and what they classified as 'politics', that is between 'our' immediate interests in the neighbourhood and something remote and foreign to the neighbourhood. As has already been mentioned, members of the popular sectors conceive of politics as something remote which goes on in another sphere among 'those out there', something that does not inspire respect, something unknown and generally regarded as a mystery. As one of them said:

> There are many hidden goings-on that neither you nor I know about, only those in there know. It's because they do things differently, so that neither you nor I can understand anything. (R.)

But it is not always a complete mystery, and in spite of the remoteness some ideas are formed. In general, there is agreement among women that politicians speak another language, different from that of the popular movements and their interests. It is also quite often considered that what takes place there is confusion, arguments, unintelligible goings-on (because of the remoteness, and the different language used). Sometimes women state clearly the opinion that what motivates people in the parties is personal interest and the struggle to out-do one another, that is, the struggle for power. It is thus that many of the interviewees drew a distinction between the 'struggle for one's own good' and the 'fight for personal interests'. For example:

> It seems to me that there [in the Workers' Party] in the debates, it must be political. . . . There you're on your own . . . you look after your own interests. Logical, isn't it! So, who knows. They're rich, so why start fighting against other neighbours on their account? Then troubles are stirred up . . . Here we are struggling for something that is for our own good. (V.)

> In the party it is easier to participate out of self-interest. And in the community, I at least believe that in the community it is not based on self-interest, but in the party it is interest-orientated . . . Because in the party people want to get to the top, and nobody can change my ideas about that . . . But in the community no one is above or below the other, it seems, in my opinion, that everyone is equal.
> (L., married, six children, dishwasher in a company, member of the CEB, participated in the nurseries campaign.)

The idea that the community is a place of equality must surely be one of the most important notions associated with the new social movements. The struggles and local associations are frequently built on the basis of certain shared characteristics, such as being settlers of a neighbourhood, all women or all poor, and suchlike. This sense of shared experience and identity are what sustain the movements, and in this sense, their *raison d'être* sets them apart from political parties. To take a party line is to break this sameness, introducing differences of opinion and interests. For this reason, during the 1982 election campaign all the local movements we were studying proclaimed their neutrality instead of committing themselves to the electoral contest, as was generally hoped by their leaders and the politicians.[26]

But even in cases where the community is not necessarily perceived as a place of equality, the women make a clear distinction between a struggle in which the weak can fight for their own or their families' interests and one made up of a different type of people (politicians are professionals, activists in the social movements are not). Here, the struggle concerns other interests: it is so that they, the politicians, can get to the top; they are the outsiders, from another class. It is ultimately a matter of collective as opposed to individual interests, a distinction between us and them.

This distinction assumes a different character when the 'us and them' are associated with gender differences. Here on this side — the side of the neighbourhood, the family, the struggle for one's own good and that of the community — is female. The other side — that of politics and of political parties — is masculine. Many women do not join the party simply because 'there are only men there' or because 'they get involved in politics there and women shouldn't get mixed up in that'. Others have a more developed argument that explicitly links aspects of gender and a view of collective versus individual interests.

> There are more men in the party. Men are like that, they are more interested in personal things. That's my view. And women, like in the community, do it because they want to. I think that all people involved in the community do it without self-interest. (L.)

In this way the circle closes, separating not only popular activism from party activism but also specific demands from politics, women from political activity, and women from men. There are several points to make here. Firstly, some women complain that they do not participate in political parties because they have not been invited to do so by either the leaders or their husbands who have, however, encouraged and called on them to participate in the CEBs and specific campaigns. Thus, it is the actual leaders and members of the parties themselves who appear to be responsible for keeping their masculine world, together with politics, in a separate sphere.[27] Secondly, it is important to observe that far from impeding participation, space for action identified as specifically female in counterposition to the exclusive sphere of politics actually facilitates such participation.

A good part of the literature on social behaviour considers that the explanation for the presence of the popular classes in the social movements is extreme poverty. This presupposes a direct and automatic relation, or even an evolution, between the perception of need, public action and campaigns to remedy this need, and the elaboration in political terms of the unjust social situation. What we are trying to show, through an analysis of the participation of women in local movements and in the CEBs, is that the reality of the situation is more complex than this. Participation can arise out of a variety of circumstances, which may differ from the arguments given publicly to justify a struggle (the lack of public provision, social injustice, and so on) and also in the meaning that the leaders confer on the movements; the leaders see these struggles and community participation as political activities. In the case of the women who form the clientele membership of these movements, participation is linked not only to a number of meanings relating to the domestic and female universe (the home, the family, children, disinterested work for others, co-operation, among others) but also to the creation of a semantic space that separates their action in pursuit of certain demands from politics, as well as to living a new experience as women.

This latter point is extremely significant, as our interviews indicate. In the meetings of local movements, CEBs and women's groups, not only are problems resolved and 'friendships made', but women also discuss specifically female problems with other women. They talk about their relationship with their husbands, and domestic conflicts. In two of the neighbourhoods we studied, the women involved in the mothers' clubs decided to begin meeting independently in order to discuss sexuality and birth control — matters of particular interest to them but practically prohibited as topics for discussion within the Church. In short, parallel to the struggles to which they are committed, they begin to define a space for the treatment of topics of exclusive interest to women.[28]

In this sense the separation between the female universe of participation and that of politics is not only useful in reinforcing a traditional separation but also helps to establish a really new experience, perceived as an opening-up and liberation. A new space is being created, not only to enable women to share the equally pervasive oppression and to identify common problems but also to construct an agreeable alternative. Within the social movements women are creating a new identity, as the discussion of their own distinctive topics acquires legitimacy.

This construction of a new identity deserves to be carefully analysed. But first it should be stressed that we are not implying that the women who participate in local movements in the neighbourhoods we studied are 'feminists' or that they identify in some way with 'feminism'. On the contrary, these women have the worst possible image of feminism, partly as a result of the influence of the Catholic Church and militants from illegal political parties, who have managed to transmit their preconceptions — the same as in the literature on social movements — that associate feminism with the middle classes, and treat it as something spurious.

We have already seen that this new identity contrasts with two other experiences: that of the traditional housewife and that of the man of politics. The situation of the housewife enclosed within the four walls of her home, frozen in time, totally dependent on the man — obviously a negative characterization — is offset against an 'opening to the world' achieved by participating in local movements and associations such as the CEBs and SABs. Thus, women's new identity is established through the practices of these movements, which contrast with the traditional; they encourage women not to stay alone at home all day but to go out, to learn, to participate.

But it is important to see the way in which their leaving the home is legitimized so as not to generate too strong conflicts. In general, women who participate do not work outside the home and on several occasions we were told how they were prevented from doing so by their husbands, alluding to all types of masculine and feminine stereotypes. Their participation in the community or in campaigns for specific demands, however, is neither disapproved of nor prohibited, although it can cause domestic problems, and this is because the space for the new experience has opened precisely on the basis of a widening of women's traditional and legitimate role. They are responsible mothers and housewives, participating in a space for women only, which is thus not considered dangerous. Preserving participation as a female space (in contrast to the masculine space of politics) can therefore be considered as necessary to the strategy of legitimizing activism in the public world without creating excessive conflicts in the private sphere.

But although conflicts are avoided in the private sphere this does not mean that it remains intact. In the same way as a new public space is opening up for women, their relations inside the home begin to change. Firstly, women are absent more often, they leave some chores undone to go to meetings and they begin to accept as natural attitudes that from a traditional point of view would be considered neglectful, and would disqualify them from their traditional role. Female qualities are now beginning to be judged more in terms of the struggle in which women are involved rather than by the perfect shine on the floor tiles at home.

Of course, acceptance of this change is neither unproblematic nor complete. For example, when there are conflicts in the neighbourhood one of the first weapons used in the daily intrigues is to emphasize that the women who are involved are 'abandoning' their homes and children. Despite this vulnerability and the conflicts generated inside the home, however, there appear to be grounds for confronting this challenge:

> My husband doesn't like me to participate. Ah, but even if there's a fuss, I go. I don't know, he seems to think that I go out too much, that I stay out too long. He thinks that if I get too stuck on Church things I'll become a fanatic. At least that's what I understand from him. But I like it, so I put my foot down and go. Sometimes, when I have the chance to go and celebrate the liturgy, when I get back there's a row, a fight. But he's the one that causes it, I don't want to get involved in arguments, and the following day I'll go again. He'd have to tie me up to stop me . . . It seems to me that men prefer to see women at home washing clothes, cooking, I think that's what it is. If he goes out that's all right but if the woman goes, she'll see what happens. Women must do something they like: I like it so I do it . . . You make friends in the local groups, you make contacts and it opens women up, little by little things become clearer; let's see if we can overcome this fear we have of our husbands. (L.)

In some cases the changes within the home would seem to have gone further. This was the case for two of the leaders of a women's group, who spoke at length about the changes taking place in their homes, not without having to confront resistance from their husbands.

> I had a lot of activities in the Church but at home I couldn't break away from a load of things I felt were my duty because I'm a woman, a mother. I just couldn't break away. I began to be aware of this through the women's group and I said to hell with it all because it wasn't me who should be doing them! . . . At home it was like this: when my husband and children had a bath I would get them towels and lay out all their clothes for them to dress. That was my obligation . . . Suddenly I realized that it wasn't just me, everyone had to change . . . I had thought that as a woman, a wife, it was my duty to do all these things for my husband. Then one day I saw that it wasn't so. What I mean is that in connection with housework, I think — or rather I thought, that I had to make the meals, clean the house, control household expenditure, pay the bills, it was up to me. Now we divide everything between us . . . it's much better, because I don't feel I'm being oppressed by anyone . . . When I discovered myself as a woman, that I have the same rights as everyone else, my relationship with my children changed, everything changed and our relationship improved one hundred percent. My relationship with my husband got better, I mean it was as if we had just met now, three years later. He wouldn't accept it at first but in time he began to see that it was a need, my need. At first it was like this, a lot of fights, separation . . .
> (I., married, housewife, ex-member of the CEB, member of the Women's Group, participant in the nurseries campaign.)

Conflicts are part of the process. Woman's individuality is not built without cost. The process is long, not only because of domestic conflicts but also because of a lack of the necessary practical conditions, especially economic, which would allow a poor woman to have a more independent life. Wages are very low, there is little chance of living without male financial support, and besides, the prejudices that face a woman with an independent life are enormous. When changes do occur, it is those women who have already managed to change or who know how to fight who go out and explain things a bit to other women, in the certainty that there will be a favourable reception. Although they might not immediately manage to change the other women to the extent they themselves have changed, they do help them overcome some of their fears, or at least help them look critically at the situation in which they live. As one of them explained:

> Women don't need to learn anything, only the men. Women, I don't know why, women are always left behind. And I don't know what defect women have that we aren't allowed to do anything. I really can't explain this.
> (E., married, housewife, five children, member of the CEB, participant in the nursery and health campaigns.)

Besides contrasting with their traditional role, this new identity for women is formed taking the male world of politics into account. As we saw from the analysis of the interviews, women try to set themselves apart from politics, and to set their community and egalitarian experience and the struggle for the common good against the individualistic interests of politics. In relation to this point the hypothesis can already be formulated that this separation is maintained precisely in order to allow changes in women's role. Because it is so difficult to leave the home and legitimize their participation, because the restrictions on entering the job market — identified as masculine — are very great, it is understandable that women attempt to separate their new public activity from a sphere considered to be eminently male, competitive, preoccupied with individual interests, and where images of manipulation, dishonesty and corruption weigh heavily. There is no doubt that women's absence from the political parties does limit their personal transformation in the public arena. But neither is there any doubt that it is this limitation which is enabling them to change.

This last point relating women to politics leads us to make certain observations on how women involved in the movements perceive their activity compared with women who fight on their own initiative, and those who work as electoral canvassers in the more traditional sense.

Politics as a vocation

Those women who launch activities in pursuit of specific demands on their own initiative, like those who participate in the social movements, resolved to become publicly active because they perceived a need 'to fight for their own good'.[29] In the case of the former, however, this fight refers more to personal and family interests, since they are not linked to any institution. Furthermore, their participation is not perceived as 'an opening to the world' in the same way as it is with participants in the social movements.

Women who campaign in isolation are more concerned about the problems of urban infrastructure (such as water supply, drainage, paved roads) than they are about the lack of nurseries, health centres and so on. For them, leaving their homes in search of solutions to these problems is an attempt to preserve their families' and children's welfare but also their property. They know it would be difficult for them to move from where they live to better areas, so their objective is to 'improve what they have'. Their motivation is personal and very often the demands they pursue through public bodies are very restricted, for example, limited to the paving or lighting of a street or area of a neighbourhood. Women who are active in this way have as a reference point a limited vision of the urban space in which they live. For the majority of the settlers we interviewed in the peripheral areas, the space of their neighbourhoods is not only differentiated but also hierarchical: all comments on the neighbourhood included references to 'the other side', the 'part up there', to 'the other side of the shanty town', and so forth, each part being evaluated as good or bad. The social movements and associations such as the CEBs and SABs do what they can to break down these divisions and speak in the name of all the inhabitants of the neighbourhood. In this sense it could be said that the social movements tend to promote change in accordance with the manner in which space of the neighbourhood is represented. The opposite happens with the women who campaign alone, who not only act along these divisions but also tend to reinforce them by obtaining benefits for only one part of the neighbourhood, thus accentuating the physical differences and the rivalry between the inhabitants.

As much as their motives and the range of their demands are restricted, however, the individual campaigners cannot express them in this fashion. They know that the solution to their demands is never individual but collective. It is thus essential to collect signatures from the neighbours and to have the support of some of them to present these demands to the authorities. It is when they have to legitimize their struggle to the neighbourhood that the personal qualities of the women we interviewed stand out.

Above all, they see themselves as people with initiative who are willing to work for the others.[30] They are different from the average housewife in that they spend part of their day drawing up plans and collecting signatures.

> I'm very like that, as they say. I spend my time imagining . . . so, I began to imagine, to prepare a draft . . . I was the first to go and talk to the Mayor. (EV., married, housewife, three children, presented innumerable claims to public authorities, has various political contacts and is an electoral canvasser.)

As well as having initiative, which is generally considered positive by their neighbours (thereby converting the campaigners into benefactors deserving of victory laurels), these women consider themselves to be popular and therefore capable of obtaining the necessary support to push for their demands.

> I got a petition going there with many signatures. I got at least six hundred names. (C.)

> In two days I got three hundred signatures . . . I felt proud and am pleased by the prestige I have in the neighbourhood. (EV.)

Furthermore, they are women who sacrifice their housework in order to go to public bodies, putting up with long waits and unreliable transport. Of course, the same can be said of the women in the social movements, the difference being that the latter regard sacrifice as something given on behalf of others and not in terms of a personal victory.

There is also a difference in the way the rewards are conceived, although there are some points in common. Women who campaign in isolation may or may not obtain water or paving, but they always win some prestige inside and outside the neighbourhood and 'get to be known'. Contrary to the attitude of the participants of the movements, for whom 'knowing' is an experience between equals, what matters to the isolated campaigners is their relation with the powerful. They are not so much concerned about leaving the circle of the family and neighbourhood or making new friends, but principally interested in meeting important personalities, receiving attention, being flattered by politicians, manipulating acquaintances in the bureaucracy and public bodies, and knowing how to use the mass media.[31] While the participants of the social movements present themselves as equals and in solidarity with all the neighbourhood's inhabitants, the individual campaigners try to differentiate themselves, claiming greater intelligence, more information, greater capacity for action: in other words, their solidarity is directed towards the higher echelons.

From a political point of view, residents of the neighbourhoods recognize that the efforts of these campaigners acting on their own behalf is limited, precisely because they lack a vision of the neighbourhood as a whole, a wider political assessment, and because they are motivated by private interests. But for the women themselves, it is others who are limitations on their effectiveness: the difficulty in uniting the 'weak', the 'people of the neighbourhood' — a population they consider to be too much at ease and in some cases ignorant, a condition they put down to the lack of formal education.

> And because all my brothers have had an education I go to them to learn how I should communicate with the rest. The fact is I didn't finish primary school, you know? . . . talk about studying, I wanted to study for a diploma. Seriously. If I were! oh young lady I wanted to be governor . . . My God! I really would like that! (EV.)

> I'm like that, I don't know, I forget a lot you know? Sometimes I talk about something and then I can't remember anything . . . I only regret not having read much, not knowing . . . I didn't have any education, you know? I didn't go to school much and . . . I would like to have the education that my daughter has, because I don't think I would have stayed put, no, if I had studied I would have got a post . . . I would have wanted to work, because that is really nice!
> (A., housewife, married, two children, made various requests for the neighbourhood to the local authorities, participates in the SAB, is an electoral canvasser.)

The fact that they do not have an education prevents these women — who, unlike those who participate in the social movements confess to a liking for politics — from advancing in their careers as leaders. They do not lack the other necessary qualities:

> *Did you feel that you had the ability for this?*
> I don't know if I felt that, I didn't think about it. I'm an extrovert, very communicative. I can form friendships on the bus. But . . . did I have the ability? I don't know if it's ability because this is how I am normally, you know. (N.)

All the individual campaigners credited themselves with more or less the same characteristics, which guaranteed them popularity in the neighbourhood and the ability to deal with politicians. These characteristics are not only necessary for the negotiation of petitions for the neighbourhood, but are also required for the work of electoral canvassing and they use this to negotiate with the politicians.

> I spoke with Dr Joaozinho, Secretary to Adhemar de Barros, I felt very satisfied, I didn't reckon on the prestige that I have in my neighbourhood . . . I said: 'I wasn't counting on that prestige, but look, eh! The elections are about to descend on us!' (EV.)

Popularity appears to be a basic ingredient in drawing up petitions as well as in negotiating future work as electoral canvassers. The relation between the two activities is so close that almost all of the individual activists we met worked as canvassers for known politicians during the 1982 election campaign.

The party did not matter very much, since what counted was personal relations, although none of the women was linked to the PT, which really has another form of political work. The women would try to take advantage of those who valued them most when choosing which candidate to work with and frequently they did not commit themselves to work without previous bargaining.

The women we met who were only electoral canvassers described themselves in the same way as the individual campaigners. Some were communicative and popular with a passion and liking for politics. In all, they possessed what one of our interviewees defined as a gift:

> I always liked politics, you know? . . . Even as a girl I found it easy to make contact with people. I was never a quiet girl . . . I liked conversation, to make friends. I don't know if that has helped me . . . getting on with people, it's probably true though, isn't it? . . . I have a gift for politics. But I never studied and that's why I never had the nerve to get more involved with it. How I like it! Politics, work, I do both. But I feel I wouldn't be capable of being a governor, or even a councillor . . . If you have a gift for something, you need to study for it . . . to develop and perfect this gift that you have. Because having the gift isn't enough on its own.
> (R., married, two children, president of a SAB.)

This interviewee manages to express her liking for politics and the qualities required to practise it, things which the other interviewees indicate in a less articulate way. She is someone who has achieved more in her career: she is the president of a SAB. She has some characteristics that enable us to distinguish her vision (which approximates to that of men) from that of other women who campaign on their own, although the differences are by no means great. Given her institutional position, she does not have an individualistic discourse, nor does she support the defence of personal interests. She speaks in the name of the people and struggles for the neighbourhood as a whole. But her method of work is not very different. Because she is the president of the SAB, she does not need petitions to legitimize her access to public organizations and, therefore, she generally acts alone. She feels that things are obtained through skill and insistence, by knowing how to ask, and never through pressure. It is totally beyond her to organize the residents of her neighbourhood to put pressure on the authorities; she prefers to use her gift, her skill and knowledge. This is clearly incompatible with the activities of the movements that make demands, not requests, on the state, and which use their collective presence and pressure to try to obtain services.

These peculiarities in our interviewee's ideas concur with the characteristics of all the women who campaign on their own, whether they are canvassers or not, and lead us to a comparison with the women who participate in the social movements. There is very little similarity between the two forms of action: the behaviour of the first can be associated with clientelism or with the traditional way of engaging in politics, and that of the second with what is new and 'authentic'.

Of all the characteristics differentiating these two groups, the one that stands out most clearly is their perception of politics. While one group tries to deny its involvement, to distance itself, seeing politics as something negative, the other values it highly and states so explicitly. This contrast is notable when we consider that social scientists associate political action with the activism of women who deny any links with party politics. They regard them as more aware, more 'authentic', protagonists of a new approach to involvement in politics. Undoubtedly the forms of activism are changing but it is quite something else to think that this transformation is solely and explicitly in relation to politics.

Another point that draws our attention is the way the female experience is lived. For those who participate in the social movements this is the central meaning behind their action, but the subject does not arise for the individual campaigners. This is perhaps because being women does not appear to impose any restriction on them acting in the public sphere and carrying out an activity that is considered typically masculine. But neither this fact nor the absence of criticism concerning their situation as females imply that women's traditional role is not one of their important reference points. Besides being used to legitimize their demands, it is apparently what sustains their ventures into the public sphere. This was made clear in the reply of one of our interviewees, a canvasser, when we asked her what would happen to her after the elections, when the outcome was known:

> I'm carrying on in the same way, here at home, looking after the house, my children and . . . if he needs me for anything, to help him in some way, I'm going to help him . . . I'll be at his side whether he wins or loses. I'll be here at home. (N.)

This statement leaves no doubts regarding the security provided by women's traditional role when making incursions into the outside world. Someone who has a secure place to return to will probably size up the risks of a new experience; but we could also ask ourselves if it is not perhaps woman's traditional condition that actually facilitates the diversity of her participation. Acting in an area that is not her own, she would have less expectations of success than a man and it would not be so humiliating to return home, pretending that nothing had happened. That is, failure would not be an overriding preoccupation and would even allow space for other parallel or secondary experiments in connection with political objectives. Could this not be a viable explanation for the fact that so many women and so few men are to be found in an activity that everyone recognizes as new.

In search of novelty

As we have said, studies of social movements have basically concentrated on analysing the external aspects, the activities directed outwards. But this is just one aspect of the question. Together with the change in the way externally oriented politics is conducted, there appears to be a wider cultural change in that practices and meanings attributed to women, their social roles and ways of perceiving interpersonal relations, are being redefined. It is not only, nor perhaps even principally, values linked to political activism that are involved, but rather those which refer to a way of life. The really novel aspect of recent social movements is that as a form of engaging in politics they affect daily life and modify it.

The example of women is very clear in this respect. Women are never seen in their daily context and specific roles but are always hidden behind global categories such as 'the people', the 'popular strata', the 'settlers of the shanty towns', in other words, valued for what they represent in terms of an expression of class interests. They are seen through the very political–institutional perspective from which they tend to distance themselves. An image was thereby created that had nothing to do with the real meaning the women attached to their participation. Politics, sung in prose and verse by analysts as the central aspect of the new social movements, is rejected and distanced by the majority of women who participate. For them, the new form of activism found in social movements is considered not to be politics but a new way of experiencing the condition of womanhood.

One of the great innovations promoted through the daily action of the social movements is thus the transformation in women's situation. Women's space and attributes are being redefined and the limits of what characterizes the public and private as well as male and female are being transformed. (Perhaps these limits have always been more flexible than was thought, as participation by the individual women campaigners suggests, or perhaps they offered more possibilities than was thought.) And it is all happening in a fragmented way within the compass of daily life.

The evident ambiguity between the old and the new in relation to women is an indication of change. Women make demands on the authorities as mothers, but they want their own space and activity and to be able to leave their children in a nursery so that a professional will take charge of them. Women justify the new tasks they assume in the public world on the basis of their role in the private world. But certainly the best sign that values are changing is the fact that they are learning to share their doubts and lack of confidence with others in the movements: 'why is it that women always have to be like this?'; 'why is it that women always have to do that?'; 'why do women have to remain in ignorance?'.

These questions had been developing for some time but had not been fully perceived. In daily life, the tendency is not to pay attention to the differences, to women. Moreover, the questions mentioned above (taken literally from testimonies) are considered as feminist and therefore middle class. They are not seen as the concerns of those who live in poverty in neighbourhoods on the fringes of the city, facing all kinds of difficulties, but rather those of bourgeois women without problems and with a lot of spare time.

If prejudice was not enough to deny poor women the possibility of reflecting on the problem of their specific condition, we need to remind ourselves that we live in a society in which what concerns one social group affects the other. The feminist movement as such did not penetrate any of the neighbourhoods that we studied, but their discourse did. This probably happened mainly through the Movement to Fight for Nurseries, which was the most direct bridge between the feminist movements and the neighbourhood movements.

For example, the fact that the movement for nurseries was one of the most important there has ever been in São Paulo must have had a considerable impact on the criticisms voiced against all these 'women's issues'. It was centrally co-ordinated and grew from links formed between the neighbourhood and feminist movements during the First Congress of Paulista Women in 1987. Except for the Cost of Living Movement, it was the movement that managed to diffuse most widely throughout the city. Moreover, together with the Health Movement, it was one of those that the authorities legalized most rapidly, adopting the movement's demands as achievements of their own.[32] This privileged position, and the considerable attention that the movement gained, must surely have had a part to play in the speed with which access to nurseries became considered as an almost natural right and, by extension, in the fact that leaving children in someone else's care and with professionals was now considered legitimate, even when the mother was not working outside the home. The acceptance of these values so alien to traditional ones, can easily be related to the various themes linked to women's rights, such as the right to know, to go out, to have one's own life, and so on.

But the importance of the Movement to Fight for Nurseries and the influence that militant feminists might have had in the neighbourhoods, should not be exaggerated. It is also necessary to bear in mind that the ideas generated within the feminist movement did not remain locked in but were diffused, even by the mass media, and thus stopped being the exclusive property of one organization. They became available references and, as such, elements to be appropriated, adopted, rejected or transformed in a wide variety of situations. Feminist ideas are being discussed today as much on the 'Eight o'Clock Soap Opera' as in right-wing groups. It has already become a legitimate and accepted 'global pattern' to separate from a husband who refuses to understand that a woman must have her own life. Similarly, in relation to family planning, the 'right to choose' is a constant refrain sung by the military and right-wing politicians concerned about population policies.[33]

The CEBs and other local movements are spaces in which the issues generated by the feminist movement develop easily. They constitute an environment of collective discussion, one that encompasses a 'community' and which legitimizes the politicization of the private sphere in defence of individual rights, which is the basic way to arrive at the notion of defending civil rights. Thus, these associations and movements are fertile ground for redefining and criticizing sexism, racism, authoritarianism and intolerance in the heart of society. They are, as Durham (1984) rightly noted, spaces for public appraisal of the individual. By means of their participation in social movements, working-class women, who had previously found a space only in the domestic sphere (and even that was precarious) for the recognition of their individuality, freedom and dignity, are now able to find this recognition in the public domain. This experience, which is translated into the notion that participating represents personal enrichment, is especially significant for women, since they have always been deemed to lack political will and to be invisible (even when carrying out an important public role), their habits and image being silenced by the privatization of their space.[34] In this respect, the experience of these social movements is not very different from that of the so-called liberation or minority movements. In both cases the personal is politicized, and recognition is given to a hitherto silenced experience, thus opening up the way to change.

All that has been said about women's participation would seem to indicate that what is happening in the social movements is a much wider cultural transformation that what we at first presumed, and which we have tried to express in the discussion on the new forms of political activism. The points of reference for the analysis should thus be others.

These other references are just beginning to be formulated in the social sciences. Examples of such efforts are the works of Touraine (1978), Castells (1983), Lechner (1982), Karner (1983) and Evers (1984). Although these works cover a range of different perspectives, and are often of a tentative nature, they are all attempting to build a new conceptual field for analysing social movements. They all agree that the categories and the concepts available to social sciences to date are inadequate for taking account of these new social phenomena and that it is necessary to find others.

In this search for new points of reference it must be realized that politics has changed, that public activism does not only, nor even primarily, revolve around the state; that daily life is a space in which changes are taking place without a general revolution; that the explanation for these new movements is not the economic situation; that experiences are fragmentary; that there is no reason why different experiences involving identity should converge at some point, and so on.

We do not seek to resolve here any of the theoretical questions raised in these works. Through the example of women, however, we have tried to show that by observing all aspects of the problem encompassed by the social movements themselves, one can see evidence of their capacity to transform — if we cast aside the old models that give priority to class, structure, the party, and general categories. These do not reveal the specific, and it is from the specific and less perceptible within the framework of the old models that the novelties are emerging.

Notes

1. The Christian Communities developed out of the philosophy of the Theology of Liberation in the late 1960s, which saw the role of the popular Church as taking the side of the poor and working for social reform by promoting among the poor a sense of community and collective action for change. (Translators)

2. There is no exact translation of the term *reivindicar* or *mujeres reivindicadoras* as used in the original text. The essence is that of pressing or campaigning for a specific demand on the basis of a perceived need or of expressing a grievance. (Translators)

3. The *Prefectura* referred to in the original is translated as Town Hall which is the British term used for the headquarters of the local authority or local government offices. (Translators)

4. The Municipality of São Paulo is divided into 17 regional administrations, responsible for the provision of services at a local level but with little autonomy in decision-making. Despite this, given their proximity to the residential areas, many local residents' demands are directed to them, especially the most trivial (requests for rubbish to be collected, a machine sent to repair a rain-damaged road, or similar) and that in general, demand little mobilization. It is common, for instance, for some people to go personally to the regional administrative offices; nevertheless, there are also collective actions.

5. For example, in the section 'Society Facing the Crisis' of the newspaper *A Folha de São Paulo*, specialized in reporting matters relating to the popular organizations.

6. Lavinas and Le Doaré (1982) and Massolo and Díaz Ronner (1983) also noted the absence of women. Among others, this absence from the analysis of social movements is an expression of the wider tendency to exclude women from historiographies. Cf. Blachman (1976) and Paoli (1985).

7. Alvarez (1985); Blay (1980 and 1982); Cardoso (1983a).

8. Maria Valeria Pena made some observations in this respect during her presentation to the meeting of the working group 'Sociology of Women' at the ASESP Congress, São Paulo, 1983.

9. The term 'social movements' is used generally in relation to a heterogeneous range of local associations and forms of political demonstration. This general term will be used in the introduction but in the following section the differences among them are explained in detail.

10. For a critical analysis of the meaning for the social movements of the ideal of 'community', see Durham (1984).

11. For a criticism of the emphasis on autonomy and spontaneity and an analysis of the role of the so-called 'external agents', see, for example, Grossi (cf.).

12. Cf. Cardoso (1983b); Durham (1984); Caldeira (1984b).

13. A typical example of this tendency is the analysis by Evers (1984).

14. See Cardoso (1984) for a criticism of how the concept of class is frequently used in analyses of social movements.

15. The data presented here was collected during the course of the research project 'The Periphery of São Paulo and the Context of Political Action', carried out in the Brazilian Centre for Analyses and Planning (CEBRAP), and co-ordinated by Ruth Cardoso. The field work was carried out by Antonio Flavio Pierucci, Antonio Manuel T. Mendes, Celia Sakurai, Helena María Sampaio, María Cristina Guarnieri and myself. The neighbourhoods studied were: Jardim das Camélias (East Zone); Jardim Miriam and Cidade Júlia (South Zone); Jaguaré and Jardim Peri-Peri (West Zone); and Jardim Marieta (municipality of Osasco, metropolitian region of São Paulo). The neighbourhoods studied each have a population of around 5,000 inhabitants, except Jaguaré where the figure is double. The period in which the field work was carried out coincided with the campaign for the election of State Governor, the first direct elections held for 20 years, during which time the incumbents of executive posts were designated by the Federal Government. In the 15 November 1982 elections occupants of legislative posts at the federal, state and municipal levels were also elected.

16. In general, public authorities recognize and take cognizance of the differences between the SABs and the Unions and Associations of Shanty Town Dwellers. The *Prefectura* of São Paulo officially recognizes the Society of Friends of the Neighbourhood as the representative of the inhabitants' interests, providing the Society adopts a model statute approved by the Town Hall and is registered with the Notary. Only the associations that follow this pattern are named SABs. Entities denominated Association or Union of Shanty Town Dwellers were generally set up by the inhabitants as a matter of expediency to escape the ties and rules imposed by the public authorities, although it was also used by traditional politicians and political groups who had been removed from the pre-existing organizations. At present, however, following a process of renewal in the SABs' management since the beginning of the 1970s (severing the patron–client type relations with the public authorities and establishing a more confrontational and oppositional relationship), it cannot be said that the SABs are linked to the state whereas the associations and unions are not; this difference is only in relation to their origins. To distinguish the two different types of SABs the adjectives 'renewed' and 'traditional' will be used frequently in referring to those that define themselves as independent or otherwise from the public authorities and that maintain or do not maintain clientelistic ties with politicians.

17. See Chapter 1, note 11.

18. The difference between these two types of organizations is: the mothers' clubs are organized by the Catholic Church and the women's groups are independent, although many of these have developed due to disagreements in the mothers' clubs. In some of the women's groups the influence of militant feminists was felt.

19. Cf. Cardoso (1983c); Jacobi (1983).

20. Five parties contested the elections in 1982: the PDS, the government party and successor to the old ARENA, which supported the military government; the PMDB, which comprised a heterogeneous opposition front, successor to the MDB,

the only opposition party allowed during the military regime; the PTB, which claimed the labourist heritage, as organized by Getulio Vargas since the 1940s and which served as a base for populism in the 1950s and early 1960s; the PDT, also claiming the heritage of labourism, led by Leonel Brizola; and the PT, that arose out of the new union movement in the 1970s, closely linked to the new social movements of which it claimed to be representative, presided over by Luis Ignacio da Silva, known as Lula, the most important union leader to emerge in the country in the 1970s.

21. This position in relation to politics, and this pattern of structuring the interviews, are far from exclusive to women who participate in the social movements, being extremely common among women in the working classes. Cf. Caldeira (1984a).

22. On the political recollections of members of the Brazilian working classes, men and women, see Bosi (1979) and Caldeira (1984a). A determining factor in the ability to recall political matters and events seems to be active participation in parties, election campaigns and unions, but not in movements for specific demands. Among the men interviewed by us and those who speak most articulately of the political past, are party militants, and the oldest, especially those who participated actively in public life in the period of redemocratization (1945 to 1964).

23. 'Community' is the way 'Christian Base Communities' are referred to in the majority of cases.

24. The same type of justification is also used *vis-à-vis* going out to work. The married women we interviewed, however much they considered working outside the home totally justifiable when 'for our children's good', considered their work when single in an extremely negative light — as a waste of time.

25. For a debate on these lines, see Evers et al (1982).

26. Cf. Cardoso (1983b).

27. This pattern was very clear in one of the neighbourhoods we studied: when the leaders of the social movements wanted to create a branch of the Workers' Party (PT) they called on the men specifically (many of whom had never participated in the movements) and not on the women. Furthermore, they arranged the meetings for Saturday night rather than the afternoon, which made it difficult for women to attend.

28. Moreover, a very 'feminine' way of running meetings is developed and promoted. In these there is a certain feeling of complicity between the participants, a spontaneity when approaching 'intimate matters' and a frankness when expressing feelings, which can lead just as easily to laughter as to tears. The women in one neighbourhood adopted the habit of taking tea and cakes to the meetings, or of preferring to use the space of their own homes for meetings instead of the community hall.

29. All this analysis concerning women who campaign for demands in isolation is based on a research report produced by Celia Sakurai (1983).

30. We also found some men who carry out this same type of activity and whose discourse is very similar to that of these women campaigners. But they were all linked to institutions similar to the SABs, this institutional basis legitimizing their action.

31. An interesting aspect in relation to the social movements is the space they were given in the mass communications media. Most of the radio and television networks report on them and for residents to telephone radio and television stations requesting a reporter each time an important problem arises in their neighbourhood is becoming more frequent.

32. On the Movement Fighting for Nurseries, see Alvarez (1984), Blay (1980 and 1982) and Gohn (1983). Gohn's work reflects a typical attempt to detract from the gender aspect of participation in the movements by concentrating on the concept of class. Given its importance, the Movement for Nurseries is generally referred to in analyses of the social movements as a typical example of attempts by public authorities to manipulate a movement with electoral ends in view, and of the capacity to express a movement's interests in an autonomous way. The attempt at manipulation failed, but it did prove that the state's efforts to manipulate this mobilization by women was an extremely effective way of giving credibility and legitimization to the mobilization and of implictly recognizing the justice of its claims.

33. Cf. Alvarez (1984).

34. In this respect see Paoli (1985).

3. Women in the Transition to Democracy

María del Carmen Feijoo and Mónica Gogna

Rebellion against the rule of 'The Three Ks'

Introduction

The task of analysing and describing the characteristics of the women's social movement, and the transformations it underwent during the period of transition from dictatorship to democracy in Argentina, must be seen as part of a process that developed in 1981 and continued until 1984, when this transition began to be consolidated. But this process cannot be analysed without reference to a longer period during which the movement gained in significance. This period witnessed a shift from democracy to authoritarianism, and back to democracy once again. Like all historical junctures, the moment of transition interconnects various times: both the long historical sweep and a time made up of particular incidents, of events. If we avoid the type of history that Braudel (1968) calls *événementielle* it is possible to place ourselves in a longer period of time in which the crossroads, the old determinations that become new events, and repeated, familiar, and outdated events take on new meaning, although unless they are placed in the appropriate context they become trivial anecdotes. From the point of view of the specific social protagonists, the dynamic of these different times becomes interiorized and is articulated through the thread of individual and collective memory that provides both the frame of reference, which enables us to recognize the old and the new, and the set of values used to judge new situations. Memory, together with dynamic, changing frames of reference in each actor, have the versatility to vary their content and the capacity to change the protagonists themselves in their condition as subjects.

This introduction aims to avoid the risks involved in analysing the role of the women's movements ahistorically. Rather it suggests the need to describe their actions, analyse their meaning and discuss what we understand by them, within the context of a longer-term analysis, less punctual and which talks as much about women as about society. Events leave their mark, and it is the search for these strands of memory, these events recounted over a longer period of time, that enables us to reconstruct the social context in which these phenomena took place. By placing what has been remembered into context we also avoid dangerous comparisons of 'signs', which can be analysed incorrectly if removed from the global context in which they were produced. Similar 'gestures' can have contrasting meanings if we are unable to comprehend the full context in which the sign is emitted.

Such cautions are also valid from the perspective of the social scientist. In this field, in addition to the above warning regarding the problem of time, one must also take into account the effects of changes that have taken place in knowledge stemming from contributions such as that of feminist theory, and which have led to a redefinition and relocation of old problems into different fields. We refer to conceptual and methodological changes that necessarily alter the traditional models used to examine reality and indicate the areas in which the different problems are situated. Thus, within the map of knowledge there is a shifting of content and a concern to find new explanations. Take, for instance, the struggle for divorce or family rights, which ten years ago we would undoubtedly have considered women's struggles because of the gender of the instigators. Could we consider them to be strictly women's struggles today? What are women fighting for today? Are these problems related only to family rights, or do they have broader scope and repercussions, and should they be studied in the context of wider analytical frameworks? Is it reasonable to differentiate analytically between so-called women's struggles and those in which women appear as protagonists, a differentiation not generally made? In our day it would seem very difficult to make progress in the task at hand without dealing with this type of issue. This theme will, therefore, be taken up repeatedly in the course of the present study in order to be able to consider the problems of women as a group within society and to analyse the role they played in the transition to democracy, as well as the existence or otherwise of the feminist movement in Argentina.

History, memory, awareness
From a historical perspective, feminist, feminine and/or women's struggles date back — with differing character, composition and objectives — to the end of the 19th century and beginning of the 20th century. (Feijoo, 1982a) Their objectives included a complex bundle of demands, centring alternately on problems related to civil, political and labour rights, though not necessarily in this historical order. These struggles were fragmented, dispersed and conjunctural, and they left a more or less permanent and diverse impression on women's memory. We know little about them in terms of scientific knowledge, but more from personal experience and self-examination. This relative permanence within the subjects themselves combines with the 'public' absence of these struggles when it comes to research, analysis and retrieval, as feminist historiography has so often shown. (Feijoo, 1982b; Rowbotham, 1976) They are struggles that have been forgotten, but somehow remain present and operative in women's memory, in determining the basis of their identity, and in the collective imagination. Not everyone remembers the same milestones. For some women, the memory is of Evita Perón proclaiming the passing of the law for female suffrage in 1947 (Navarro, 1981); for others, it is Cecilia Grierson entering the Faculty of Medicine dressed as a man to begin her studies at the end of the 19th century. Finally, for others it is that of anonymous working

women, sexually harassed by their supervisors in the industries set up in the capital city at the beginning of the 20th century: sandal-makers, textile workers, match-makers, hat-makers, seamstresses. These varied contents, fixed in our memory, surely form the fragile thread of identity that makes us Argentine women, taking our different places in society, especially in terms of class.

The reappearance of the women's movement on the political scene between 1981 and 1984 must by necessity refer back to these issues. The idea of reappearance, however, by no means suggests an automatic return to developments of the past or the simple retrieval of known political behaviour. In reality, it is a 'new' phenomenon, although this assertion should be made with care. In order to understand it, the analysis should go back to at least 1975, to the birth of the situation used by the 1976 military coup to legitimize the intervention. It is also necessary to make some reference to the policies adopted by the Peronist government in relation to its position regarding women and to measures principally affecting women, in order to understand the characteristics of the movement's re-emergence and its capacity to play a relevant role in the process of overthrowing the dictatorship.

The crisis of the last Peronist government, the coup and women

There appears to be no general agreement among the various authors regarding the severity of the crisis suffered by Argentina in 1975. (Landi, 1978) This crisis affected the whole of society, and each sector under attack responded to it according to its capacity. In this context, the situation of women was not viewed as especially critical. Women had participated vigorously in the pre-election campaign of 1973 and had succeeded in gaining a significant parliamentary representation compared with the number of women participating in the previous parliament: 17 elected legislators in 1973 against one deputy in 1963. (Casas, 1982) The majority were Peronists. Since the death of President Perón in 1974, his widow and Vice-President, María Estela Martínez — popularly known as Isabel — had taken over the Presidency of the country. There is little need to point out that having a woman in this office did not guarantee *per se* implementation of policies to improve women's situation. Furthermore, the Peronist movement, in spite of all it had achieved for women in previous periods (1946–55), took what, to say the least, can only be called an ambiguous stance on women's issues during the 1973–76 period. Some of the measures taken did reflect their concern for the situation of women in the popular sectors. The law on neighbourhood nurseries was passed in 1973 for women's benefit but it was never ratified and therefore never implemented. There were also measures changing the basis for access to social services and social security, such as extending those rights available to legitimate wives of affiliates to the scheme to cover common law wives, whom we prefer to call *de facto* partners. This meant they were recognized as wives with full rights, at least for the purposes of social security. These measures were consistent with a certain tradition within Peronist governments that led to substantive progress in the situation of women. The law on women's suffrage, passed in 1947, the law giving equal rights to children born in and out of wedlock, and the brief period (from 1954 up to the military coup in September 1955) during which the divorce law was in force, were measures aimed at improving the subordinate position of women in society. The figure of Evita completed the image of a combative woman committed to popular struggles.

As mentioned above, in spite of this tradition in the 1973–76 period, other measures caused astonishment among women and in some cases gave rise to veiled resistance, although this was never organized on any significant scale. We refer, among other measures, to population policies that included prohibiting free sales of female contraceptives — a measure stemming from the need to increase the country's demographic potential. Another, and one which certainly caused greater concern, was the veto from the Executive — the President herself — (paradoxically by a woman, as has often been pointed out) of the law concerning the right of both parents to exercise *patria potestad.*[1] Both Chambers had approved this draft law that constituted an important claim by women in a society in which mothers were in a frankly subordinate position within the family.

Despite the unease caused by these measures, however, women's capacity for response was limited. The feminist movement was only beginning (Cano, 1982) and in only a few cases had women's sections in political organizations been consolidated. When these groups did exist — such as in all of the popular mass organizations — they discussed the general political crisis affecting the country. Seen in retrospect, even the political organizations that attempted to develop women's sections, such as the Evita Group of the Peronist Youth, found it difficult to deal with specifically women's issues, becoming instead additional arenas for the discussion of the same issues. Though the behaviour of the Female Branch of the National (Peronist) Movement for Justice does merit more detailed examination, the summons to women within this group nevertheless did not succeed in going beyond traditional appeals.

Thus, 1975 culminated in a state of generalized crisis. Armed organizations carried out some spectacular actions — even at the very gates of the city of Buenos Aires — and indiscriminate repression, especially at the hands of para-police groups, reached unimaginable limits, such as a shooting at the base of the Obelisk itself — a monument that symbolizes the physical centre of the city. The government, under attack and with no room for manoeuvre, became weaker every day, while some of the mass media and other sectors began to work openly in favour of the military coup, which was to put an end to the disorder. The economic crisis and soaring inflation during February and March 1976 were presented as evidence of Mrs Perón's inability to govern. (Landi, 1978) Obviously, in this context of generalized crisis, there was little room for the discussion of women's problems.

The unease affecting all social sectors before the coup rapidly turned into a nightmare when the military junta's government adopted its first economic measures and put the state firmly behind the continuation of policies of terror, which until then had been carried out principally by para-police groups. The naive dreams of those who believed in military 'order' rapidly disappeared.

Almost without exception, the whole of the population came under scrutiny and women were threatened, like so many other groups. The need to reinstate 'order' was used to justify repression. (Quevedo, 1983)

The main victims of the military junta's socio-economic policies were the popular sectors. The brunt of the neo-liberal economic policy adopted — together with the consequent reordering of the social structure — hit the popular sectors in particular. The policies implemented in this process included: a drastic cut in real wages, cuts in state provision of social services for workers, the introduction of charges on health services, a reduction in state education provisions and the indexation of loans for housing and small-scale real estate. (Frenkel 1980; Llovet 1984; Feijoo 1983) Altogether these measures translated into a considerable deterioration in the living standards of the popular sectors. As has been shown (Jelin and Feijoo, 1980), in Argentina the decrease in working-class purchasing power for goods and services in times of crisis was compensated for in two ways. On the one hand, there was an increase in the number of goods repaired or replaced by home production, thereby increasing the number of hours women spent mending and making clothing and tending to vegetable plots, even in suburban neighbourhoods. The domestic unit, thus converted into the only possible palliative to the economic crisis, implied a restructuring of women's role within the unit by multiplying the number of tasks necessary to guarantee the family's daily upkeep. On the other hand, with regard to the increasing cost or lack of some basic services, it was women who had to spend more time waiting for treatment in health centres or who had to travel away from their neighbourhoods in search of hospitals that did not charge, or which offered free milk or medicines with the medical care. In either case, it was women, especially those of the popular sectors, who were doubly victimized by these policies, because as women they were responsible for reproduction and, in terms of class, they belonged to the least favoured sector of society.

In addition to these general measures, the government implemented specific policies that even further aggravated the situation of women, such as the annulment of legislation providing social services to common law wives, and upholding the population policies mentioned above.

We know much less about how the military coup affected those women involved in social production. The impact on them of anti-popular policies was certainly multiplied, since it affected them as workers in the same way as their fellow male workers, and also as women fulfilling their reproductive tasks in the home. Unfortunately, this lack of knowledge about the situation of women workers during the period of crisis is part of a much bigger gap regarding what we know about how women reacted on the labour front. In any case, we can surmise, from what we know of other crises, that they must have been the first to lose their jobs in the former sector. As Cano points out, in 1976 women's capacity to respond to these measures was practically nil. The imposition of the state of siege, repression and, in the final instance, fear, paralysed many of the attempts to respond to these injustices.

State propaganda in the mass media exacerbated all of these specific measures and helped to implant the planned neo-conservative model of society. The predominant theme was the privatization of society and public life. (Lechner, 1982) According to the government's propaganda, the dangers we were supposed to have recently eluded stemmed from society's excessive politicization, which in turn was the result of having neglected to guarantee the existence of order, the stronghold of our society. Thus the family — 'the basic unit of society' — was the refuge to which we had to return to avoid the dangers of disintegration and subversion. Naturally, this return to the family further reinforced women's subordinate position. They were appealed to as wives and mothers to become the custodian of family order (Varela-Cid and Vicens, 1984), and not only custodians but police, as shown in the propaganda that shamelessly urged parents to watch their children closely, to exercise more and more control over them. A local variant of the German 'three Ks' was proposed as the only legitimate goal for mothers suffering from hunger, injustice, fear and repression. *Kinder, Küche, Kirche* (children, kitchen, church) would have been a good slogan to define the behaviour the dictatorship expected from women. (Weisstein, 1971) In spite of official rhetoric aimed at making women's role in the home sacred, it would be naive to suppose that this saved women from becoming victims of repression. On the contrary, more perverse methods of repression were invented for them, thus linking the public world with the private. Thirty per cent of those registered as arrested or as having disappeared were women (CONADEP, 1984).

In this context women, therefore, suffered the general oppression experienced by the population as a whole but aggravated by a specific oppression, which stemmed from the old process of subsuming the needs and problems of women in the needs and problems of the 'family' — an easy transposition that affected the condition of women as 'subjects'. A 'normal' woman should never entertain desires or aspirations different from those of her family. Paradoxically, the government's attempts to privatize what was public and strengthen the family as a mechanism of social control could not prevent the family itself — now the only safe nucleus in a violent society — from becoming a refuge where opinions on the horrific situation could be exchanged and where an alternative socialization with a different discourse (both political and in opposition to the government) could flourish. (Entel, 1983) The privatization of public life thus turned out to be a boomerang.

The reaction: the old and the new
How did women react to this situation? In retrospect, it would seem that it was the military junta's very project of assuming the role of national saviour without placing a time limit on their actions, which engendered the first timid resistance. 'The process does not have time limits, but objectives' was the formula used to forge this bid for permanence. If this proposal was to be monolithic and eternal, then surely it would have to be resisted in the same way. In her study of feminist groups in the 1970s, Cano (1982) shows that in all cases groups became revitalized around 1979–80, following the paralysis of 1976. Thus, more timidly in 1978 and from 1979 onwards, some women began to

form new feminist groups which were defined as such from their inception. Others which had attempted to fight against the repression silently slowly began to reappear.

All these responses from women were preceded however, by another new, ethical response which expressed revulsion. This was the presence of the Mothers who occupied the physical centre of politics: the Plaza de Mayo. Ironically, the idea that the issue of children is the preserve of women, as indicated in the conservative three Ks formula mentioned above, was to have an unexpected outcome here. In April 1977, the Mothers began to meet in the Plaza de Mayo — the name of the square which would later be used to identify them — as their pain and sense of rebellion led them to organize themselves instead of passively accepting the disappearance of their children. (Bousquet, 1983) Their single objective was to demand to know the whereabouts of their children who had been kidnapped in the repression described above. The appearance and later consolidation of the Mothers and later the Grandmothers as a social force represented an important development in the national political scene, not only in terms of women's problems but in relation to the whole political panorama. Insulted by the press, labelled 'mad', misunderstood by some sectors, respected in silence and with fear by others, the Mothers of the Plaza de Mayo gradually became the clearest symbol that opposition to the dictatorship was not only possible in practical terms, but that it was also obligatory from an ethical point of view.

Women's responses to the dictatorship can be classified into two models: one, involving the re-emergence of organizations created before the dictatorship, but which in the interim had been inoperative; the other, involving new responses present in the creation of different organizations — of which the Mothers were typical. These included the possibility of putting forward a new basis for agreement, no longer founded on party policies as before, but on issues that united women from different political sectors and different classes. These processes culminated in 1984 in the first-ever public celebration of 8 March, International Women's Day, organized in Argentina by the Women's Multisectoral alliance (*Multisectoral de la Mujer*). This latter organization brought together different women's groups which, on this occasion, were able to iron out many of their old differences and come up with a moderate seven-point platform.

The processes that brought women together mainly on the basis of their reproductive role cannot, however, be understood without making reference to the enormous impact of the Falklands/Malvinas war, just as it is impossible to speak of contemporary Argentina without referring to this event. Planned as a means of perpetuating the regime, in reality it was the first step in the regime's rapid decline. The episode affected the various groups of the population and the diverse geographical regions in different ways. However we interpret the nature of women's problems as such, what is certain is that this episode — like that of the 30,000 disappeared people — touched on something crucial to women: the issue of progeny and the care of human life. Here, the three Ks, about which the military regime dreamt, turned into a violent reaction leading different women's groups to openly confront the regime from the standpoint of transmitters of the lives that military despotism was cutting short. As one woman said at the time:

> While the men were talking about the Exocets and how many ships had been sunk, we women were thinking 'another young boy has died, another son'; and it didn't matter whether he was Argentine or English, he was still a son. (Fontan, 1983)

Following in the Mothers' footsteps, women rebelled against conscription, an untouchable institution that had been in force for almost 80 years, proposing that it be revised. Later, other groups of parents and conscientious objectors also united in opposition to it. But, for the first time in contemporary Argentina, women were the ones to shake off fatalism and who raised voices publicly to question it. In 1982, in this context of rapid changes, feminists launched an important campaign for the exercise of shared parental authority (the law establishing this had been vetoed by the Executive in 1974) which gradually extended to issues such as divorce, women's reproductive rights, the lack of sexual education and the hereditary equality of children born in and out of wedlock, among others. In the reproductive arena, the K for kitchen, there appeared the first protests from various groups of housewives — some formed during the dictatorship, others that had re-emerged from a state of latency — which began to rebel against the rise in the cost of living, trying out new strategies of resistance.

Women respond

A section devoted to 'women' in a book about social movements automatically evokes the image of women demanding their rights. If we look at contemporary Argentine society and that of recent years, we see that this 'pigeon hole' — the struggle of women for their own rights — is relatively empty in comparison with others. In response to the authoritarian regime's attempt to define the margins of legitimacy of political action, women organized themselves in an innovative way, based on recognition of the political nature of family roles. (Feijoo, 1983) Thus, as was stated above, they mobilized to denounce the violation of human rights, they urged — after the Falklands/Malvinas war — the abolition of conscription and they protested against the high cost of living.

This section will present the history of women's struggles for human rights (specifically the case of the Mothers of the Plaza de Mayo) and for the defence of living standards (the housewives). The history of those who raised the issue of the existence of women's own interests in the period we have analysed will also be presented. We will call them 'feminists', although being aware that this label covers many diverse realities.

Although this involves dealing with different types of collective action (antagonistic, political movements and those for specific demands) (Melucci,

1980), we will attempt here to identify the possibilities and limitations of these experiences, which — besides the fact that their protagonists are women — have in common a particular relationship with politics. We will also be concerned with the links — real and potential — between different struggles.

The Mothers of the Plaza de Mayo

Brief history: The movement of the Mothers of the Plaza de Mayo was formed in April 1977, as a response to the policy of forced disappearance of individuals implemented by the military dictatorship in March 1976. The original group comprised 14 women, aged between 40 and 60 years of age. They got to know each other while going to and fro in the endless search for their children, and decided to bring their pain out into the open by demonstrating in front of the government palace and demanding that their children 'reappear alive'. Walking around the Mayo pyramid, they established links, shared their suffering and began a solitary resistance to brute power. They grew in experience and number and by July that year there were already more than 150. In October, they reached public opinion for the first time with a demand published in the daily newspaper *La Prensa* entitled 'All we want is the truth', in which 237 mothers demanded a reply from the government regarding the whereabouts of their children. (Bousquet, 1983) A few days later, they handed in a petition to the authorities with 24,000 signatures, demanding an investigation into the disappearances, freedom for those illegally detained, freedom for those detained without trial and the immediate transfer to civil courts of those already on trial. The police dispersed the mothers who delivered the petition, with tear gas and shots fired into the air, and about 300 were detained for several hours while their records were checked. In December, the organization of relatives of the disappeared received a harsh blow: several people who had been preparing the text of a demand to be published at Christmas were kidnapped as they came out of the Church of the Holy Cross. A few days later, Mrs De Vicenti, one of the founders of the Mothers, was also kidnapped. Many of the mothers were overcome with fear but they maintained their fighting spirit and renewed their struggle.[2] The football World Cup in June 1978 was another difficult time: the Mothers felt bewilderment and pain at the population's jubilation, and many no longer dared to demonstrate. But they were also aware of the possibility that foreign reporters might take photographs of their walk round the Mayo pyramid and record their testimony of pain and hope. At the end of that same year, during one of their now customary walks around the square, the Mothers broke through the police cordon and installed themselves in front of the Casa Rosada (the government house); some of them refused to go away and were taken to the police station for identity checks. The following Thursday the police prevented them from entering the square — the same thing happened the next week. They then decided to abandon the square — to which, save sporadic appearances, they would return only in January 1980 — and become officially constituted as an association. In August 1979, 20 women, before a public notary, signed the founding document of the Mothers of the Plaza de Mayo Movement.

Anticipating the problems for social movements in the process of transition to democracy, this document established that the founders — from among whom an executive committee was elected — could not join any political party. That same year, 1979, saw the visit of the Inter-American Human Rights Commission of the Organization of American States (OAS). During this period the Mothers contacted those relatives of the disappeared living in the provinces, arranged lodgings for those coming to Buenos Aires to make their accusations, and stood in queues for many hours to give their testimonies to the Commission. These contacts gradually gave a more complete picture of the scale and magnitude of the horror, if it needed to be corroborated at all. The visit, which had raised the Mothers' hopes, left them with a bitter taste. (Bousquet, 1983) In December, a few days before Christmas, they resumed their Thursday walk around the square: they demanded a Christmas without disappearances and political prisoners, objectives they had been seeking for over three years. In 1980 a 'dialogue' between the Ministry of Internal Affairs and leaders of representative sectors got underway. This period also saw a change of direction in the Mothers' strategy: they tried to persuade their compatriots to join in the protests being raised abroad. The Mothers and Relatives of the Disappeared and People Detained for Political Reasons, a human rights organization created in October 1976, which 'assumes disappearances and imprisonment as a political fact',[3] launched a campaign for national mobilization aimed at getting the list of detained–disappeared people published. They also turned to the politicians, hoping to receive support for their cause. In August that year they succeeded in publishing a public request in the newspaper *Clarín*, in which certain prominent public figures supported the demands of the relatives of the disappeared. The year 1981 saw the human rights movement shifting from a purely defensive position to one of greater initiative. The Mothers' unnegotiable rallying cry was gradually taken up by other human rights groups. In December of that year, 150 mothers staged the first 'Resistance March'. A year later they were joined on the second march by the Grandmothers[4] and Relatives, making a total of over 5,000 demonstrators.

Defeat in the Malvinas/Falklands war, an adventure that the Mothers had been the first to denounce, had accelerated the regime's deterioration. In this context, the tenacious struggle of the Mothers and the whole of the human rights movement (MDH), effectively narrowed the margin for negotiations upon which the retreating dictatorship wished to embark. (González Bombal, 1984a) The Mothers then led the March against the Law of National Peace (April 1983) and toured Europe in an attempt to gain support in the form of pressure from several governments. (Palermo and García Delgado, 1983) With politics back in play, they attended every political meeting; they asked the Multiparty Commission not to inherit the problem of the disappeared; and during the election campaign they demanded that leaders adopt the issue and demand the return of the disappeared. A month before the elections they organized the third Resistance March, with a turn-out of around 15,000, during which the streets in the centre of Buenos Aires were covered with silhouettes to symbolize those who had disappeared. Another reason for the march was to announce that 'come what may, whoever wins [the elections], their children must appear alive and those guilty of crimes against the people should be punished'.[5] Days before the constitutional government took office, the Mothers publicly declared their position in face of the new circumstances:

> In order to achieve the democracy we have longed for, we will exercise participation and criticism; we will petition and dissent and we will mobilize to obtain the legitimate rights of the people; we therefore request the newly-elected government to bring back alive those who were detained–disappeared; we request freedom for all political and trade union prisoners and that those responsible be put on trial.[6]

The strategy they proposed in order to achieve their objective was the creation of a bicameral parliamentary commission with full powers, in which the Mothers and other representatives of human rights organizations would have a voice; and the ratification by the Congress of the Law to Introduce Trial by Jury to determine the sentences for crimes committed according to the common penal code.[7] The Radical government's reply was to repeal the amnesty and order a summary trial before the Supreme Court of the armed forces of the three military juntas. In addition, the national executive gave instructions through Decree No. 187 for the creation of a National Commission on the Disappearance of Persons, made up of six legislators and ten figures from the civilian sphere, whose basic task was to receive accusations and hear evidence on human rights violations and pass them on immediately to the courts. Finally, following a heated parliamentary debate,[8] the government brought into force Law No. 23.049. The Military Code of Justice was thus reformed and it became possible for sentences passed by military tribunals (who had jurisdiction for cases of military persons tried for excesses committed in the struggle against terrorism between 24 March 1976 and 26 September 1983) to be subject to appeal before the Federal Courts. This new policy obviously did not satisfy the Mothers' expectations and on weighing up the constitutional government's first year in office they repudiated what had been done in the following terms:

> We asked him for a bicameral Commission and he [Alfonsin] gave us a national commission [CONADEP] which we did not elect. We said no to military justice and he gave us military justice. We said no to the dictatorship's judges and he confirmed 90% of them in their posts . . .[9]

The different reactions to the government's response gave rise to splits in the human rights movement (MDH). Some of these had been noticeable during the election campaign and became more evident when the CONADEP report was presented (September 1984) and at the time of the Resistance March and the march organized by the Permanent Assembly for Human Rights, in December 1984.

Questions and reflections on the women's movement: Collective action can be seen as a sign open to many interpretations. (Melucci, 1980) On the basis of this premise, we now present some reflections on women's unreported, unwavering presence in the political and social arena that flows from their concern for the situation of women. This does not mean we reject the idea that the human rights movement is an appropriate framework for an analysis of the history and driving force of the Mothers of the Plaza de Mayo. Rather, it corresponds to our view that movements basically made up of women who organize and mobilize themselves from the standpoint of their role as 'mothers', also throw light on issues such as 'women's place' in Argentine society, the relationship between women and politics and the possibility of finding links between the varying demands of social protagonists who, as women, share the same gender.

Why only women?: If, as social anthropologists maintain, rituals reflect the practices and ideas of the society in which they take place, then the Mothers' walks around the pyramid in the Plaza de Mayo every Thursday, wearing their white scarves, convey something more than just the tenacity of a struggle or the bravery of a handful of women.

The most basic question to be asked within our chosen analytical perspective is why was it the mothers and not other members of the family, who first challenged the dictatorship by demonstrating their pain and their demands before the seat of government? When confronted with this question, once the mass media began to take notice of them, members of the movement themselves gave the answer — one that refers back to the dominant sexual division of labour in our society:

> At the beginning we all went together, spontaneously. But the men had to carry on working for the upkeep of the home. The majority of us were housewives and those who were working, resigned or retired from their jobs.[10]

It also refers back to ideological and cultural factors that reveal a society in which the role of mother (as a fundamental element of women's identity) offered relatively greater security compared with other roles when faced with possible repression:

> I remember we used to tell the men not to go to the square for fear that the repression would be greater against them . . . a mother always seems more untouchable.[11]

> 'We'd better go', the women said. 'If there are only women they might not dare to intervene . . .'[12]

Those who received the relatives of the detained–disappeared as they visited the different state offices in search of information also unwittingly contributed to making the mothers the driving force behind the resistance. Thus, one of the mothers explains another factor involved in the question 'why women?':

> . . . especially when at the beginning we went to the military commandos with our husbands. They used to come out and say: 'Come on, you the mother, you can come in'. I don't know, perhaps they thought that because we were women we'd be more easily deceived. . . . That's when we began to see our own strength.[13]

Let us link this thought to another: 'we know perfectly well that they look down on us: they think of us as those mad old women'. They are treated with respect and contempt. The actions of the Mothers of the Plaza de Mayo Movement left their adversaries little room for hypocrisy, and confronted society with a sad truth: the glorification of mothers as part of our 'national tradition' has more to do with folklore than reality. Some facts speak for themselves. We have related what occurred in October 1977, when 800 mothers of the disappeared had gathered together outside the Congress building to hand in a petition (pp. 87), in October 1983, in an epsiode that could only be described as confused, a delegation of Mothers was attacked coming out of the CGT (General Labour Confederation).[14]

Female logic?: Let us return to the question, 'why mothers?' While emphasizing that it was largely a 'strategic' decision, aimed at making the most of the 'respect' for the 'traditional female role', it should not be forgotten that it was the idea of a group of women to demonstrate in the Plaza de Mayo and challenge the military junta's prohibition of meetings: 'It was the women's idea to go the square. The idea came to the women in a moment of despair.'[15]

On the other hand, besides the fact that the women themselves inisted on 'being alone in the square', the men — while supporting them — did not appear to have much faith in the plan's effectiveness:

> What happened was that to a certain extent some of the men applied masculine logic: this won't lead to anything, this won't lead anywhere, such a thing is impossible. This strange phenomenon of mothers meeting to create a kind of group awareness which gradually put pressure on the power structure did not fit into that logic.[16]

Those in power must have had even less faith in this strange logic. Thus, incredulity played its part to the Mothers' advantage in the first skirmishes to gain a 'space', an advantage they exploited determinedly.

The case of the Mothers of the Plaza de Mayo must surely resemble other women's movements which, without being concerned about changing the ideology of femininity, in fact caused a transformation in women's consciousness and the female role. (Kaplan, 1982; Swerdlow, 1982)

It could be said that the Mothers, while emphasizing global issues (justice, freedom, solidarity), challenged privatization and isolation and also put an end to the myth that women are incapable of uniting, or providing mutual solidarity. Basically, the women destroyed their image of resignation and weakness.

The members of the movement have themselves reflected on this unsought effect of their actions:

> I think one of the prejudices that exists regarding women is their supposed capacity for resignation. That is to say, the traditional 'feminine' woman is passive, resigned, with a tendency to only resort to words. I think that in this case it was shown that they can fight in a very combative way. Submission is another thing women are accused of and atavistically so because of a series of biological and historical circumstances. But in this case it was shown how they can set aside their submissiveness when they become really aware.[17]

How the experience of the Mothers has affected the image of women and their political participation at the level of Argentine society as a whole, and specifically as women, is a question we are not in a position to answer here. The obligatory references to the Mothers of the Plaza de Mayo Movement by different sectors of the community (the ruling party, left-wing parties, artists, women's groups) speak of the existence of 'some impact'. There are, however, those who still insist — perhaps in an attempt to still the cry 'the square is for the Mothers and not for cowards' — that weakness is a 'female luxury'.[18]

A redefinition of the public and private: From a certain feminist position, the struggle of the Mothers of the Plaza de Mayo can be seen as just another landmark in a long history of struggle: we are told that women have always been involved in some form of activity or organization in defence of the family.

We believe that, to say the least, this view is simplistic. Through a collective action born out of the sexual division of labour (caring for children), these women violated that very division. They left the domestic sphere and confronted the *de facto* government in the very place that symbolizes political power and, it could be said, 'naked ' power (around the square are banks, ministries and the Cathedral of Buenos Aires). In synthesis, and in the Mothers' own words: 'From washing, ironing and cooking we went out on to the streets to fight for the lives of our children'.[19]

Besides its highly symbolic nature,[20] the Plaza de Mayo was the most carefully watched place in Buenos Aires, where, as Bousquet points out, neither the General Labour Confederation nor the political parties had dared to gather their members to express repudiation of the government. But the Mothers had decided that this had to be the place, given that the junta had violated the national constitution, and consequently they rejected the police's 'offer' of other squares — Plaza Flores, Plaza San Martín, for example — in which to demonstrate.[21]

This irruption in the public world, which was both symbolic and effective, transformed all that is 'public', by drawing the ethical principle of the defence of life into its space, and radically changed the traditional parameters of political discussion.

Even though the Mothers do not explicitly redefine what is private, and are not interested in doing so, they are in fact redefining the 'traditional female role'. Moreover, they offer the image of a mother as a woman who does not sit down and cry when her child disappears but goes out on to the street and fights 'like a lion' against the dictatorship,[22] who maintains that the defence of others' lives and freedom is the best way of defending one's own life and one's own freedom, and who advises other mothers to teach their children about freedom and solidarity and basically, 'that they learn from them'.[23] This is clearly a long way from the mother stereotype that stresses only the role of passive transmitter of dominant values.

Peace as a weapon: Historical research into women's movements has shown that there is a common pattern: a focus on the issues of consumption and peace. Women's capacity to conceive and give life and, therefore, their greater predisposition to defend it, has been offered as an explanation for this recurrence,[24] a recurrence which, as we have seen, can be illustrated with several examples in recent Argentine history.

The Mothers of the Plaza de Mayo explicitly defined themselves as defenders of life, as a movement that was not 'passive but pacifist'.[25] From the beginning of its first public actions, in its first statements, the movement declared itself 'against all violence, whoever the perpetrators might be'.[26] The symbol that identified them — the white headscarf — has the following connotation for them: 'We began using that colour because it is the symbol of peace, something which unites all mothers.'[27]

Interviews with the movement's members show that their 'no to violence' stance had both a strategic and a tactical value:

We tried not to be aggressive with words, thinking of our children as hostages.

The no to violence was also a way of defending ourselves: we knew that if we were to generate violence, it could cause the opposite reaction to what we wanted.[28]

This dual characteristic defined an option that the Mothers adopted as their own distinctive trait, distinguishing them from their opponents: 'We had gained the respect of the community. Precisely because we have different moral principles including the no to violence.'[29]

The Mothers were consistent with this principle and immediately after the Malvinas/Falklands war started, they published a solitary demand urging the governments responsible to resume negotiations for peace immediately, to avoid pointless bloodshed.

The Mothers' permanent mobilization shows that their identification with peace does not imply passivity, nor does it imply naivety: their steadfast demand for 'judgement and punishment of the guilty' made Argentine society aware that justice is a fundamental requisite for the construction of a real and lasting peace.

Purely politics and 'politics which are pure': The Mothers' experience undoubtedly presents a very interesting case from two different analytical perspectives which, by chance, converge at this point. One is that of people concerned with the creation of a political scenario to legitimize the process of democratization (Lechner, 1984) and interested in 'new ways of conducting politics';[30] the other stresses the gender of the political agents.

The complexity of the phenomenon in question requires that it be approached from both these angles, bearing in mind the context in which it developed.

The Mothers of the Plaza de Mayo movement was born out of a group of middle-aged women with no previous political experience:

> There are many Mothers who agreed with the idea of demonstrating but who didn't dare to. We are not activists, it's a difficult step for us to take.[31]

But their participation — as occurred with other women in other historical circumstances — was provoked by political events that 'overtook them'. Initially a response to the brutal repression affecting individuals closely related to them, the Mothers were then to enter fully the field of the collective and the social and political space. (Palermo and García Delgado, 1983)

They became politicized, recognizing this ('what we are doing is pure politics')[32] and they valued it: generally they refer to this process in terms of growth and/or learning. At the same time, they clung jealously to their non-partisan position.[33] During the election campaign in 1983, they decided that those members of the movement who joined political parties could do so as individuals, but not as Mothers of the Plaza de Mayo.

As Offe (1981) points out, this is characteristic of any organization fighting to defend a territory (physical or moral), whose integrity is basically non-negotiable for their activists. In this particular case, their non-partisan position was certainly linked to the lack of response from political leaders concerning their appeal for the lives of their children. 'We have had very painful experiences with political leaders', the Mothers would say. They were disenchanted with politics, fearful of manipulation[34] and mistrustful when faced with the opportunism of political leaders. Coupled with this, or perhaps because of this, they proposed giving a new meaning to politics: 'we do not defend ideologies, we defend life'.

Can the struggle for human rights open the way for a new relationship with politics, to a new way of thinking and political action divorced from ideology? asks Leffort (1980) The question remains and the Mothers' action without a doubt constitutes a step in that direction. For the time being, it can be said that their political actions do not fit in with the traditional rules of the game. The President of the Mothers said in one report:

> At this point in time the position of the parties is to ask for little, or ask quietly so that many will join them. Our position has always been to ask for everything, even though few join us.[35]

They know this. 'They are aware of our insistence . . . our actions tend to disarm political activities', they would say with a certain pride.[36]

Perhaps it matters very little whether this lack of distinction between what is pragmatically effective and normatively correct is due to the fact that this new social and political protagonist is a woman (that is to say, whether it is right to see it as 'women's political specificity') or whether, as Weber would say, they are moved by the 'ethics of ultimate ends'.[37] Perhaps there is no single explanation.

What is true is that, for the first time, a voice is raised that questions the famous 'politics is the art of what is possible'. The Mothers would say: 'For us nothing is possible if there are no ethics in political decisions.'[38]

The housewives

One of the major areas of women's participation in Latin America relates to the provision of urban services and the defence of consumption. Neighbourhood associations, mothers' clubs, communal kitchens and dining-rooms are some of the expressions of this participation, which is rooted in women's role in the neighbourhood and specifically their role as housewives.

In recent years, these women's activities have become the focus of research and promotion activities, with projects that generally aim to analyse or encourage the possibility of incorporating these struggles into more global social issues; and/or aim to encourage discussion among the women involved of issues directly related to women's situation.

Thus, in an attempt to reconstruct a participatory experience, which has been ignored by studies on the 'transition to democracy' in Argentina, and in order to begin to think in terms of the potential and limitations of this action from the point of view of women's 'traditional role', we will analyse the housewives' protests in this period.

This mobilization of women took on different forms and was superseded by actions channelled through various organizations. On the one hand it included longstanding housewives' organizations, such as the Argentine Women's Union (UMA), the Housewives League (LAC) or the General Union of Housewives (UGAC),[39] and on the other it included new groups emerging at this time, the most important of which was the National Housewives Movement (MACP).

Mobilization, demobilization, organization: The housewives' protests began around 1982, when women instigated 'purchasing strikes' in several districts on the outskirts of Buenos Aires (San Martín, Vicente López, San Isidro) and organized demonstrations to protest against the high cost of living in Quilmes and the cities of Cordoba and Rosario. In July of that year the National Housewives' Movement was born in a middle-class neighbourhood in San Martín. This was made up of women who had got together spontaneously to protest against indiscriminate price rises and who launched a campaign, which later became known throughout the country by the slogan 'don't buy on Thursdays'.

The increasing deterioration of living standards and the impact of the Malvinas/Falklands war had led them to 'confront the process' in their own way: by producing and distributing leaflets inciting housewives to 'lose their fear', interesting their neighbours in the proposal, talking to shopkeepers, joining neighbourhood associations and putting up with threats from the authorities. They would say: 'the idea that you shouldn't get involved is dead and we're holding a wake for it here and now'; 'sitting on the fence is tantamount to not being anywhere', and suchlike.[40]

The housewives' presence and actions were later to become more visible in the context of the 'neighbourhood protests'. Indeed, between October and December 1982, a surprising urban protest, which attracted a considerable response, ran through the various districts of Greater Buenos Aires. An additional charge, imposed arbitrarily on top of already high taxes, sparked off a popular mobilization (González Bombal, 1984b).

Women participated in considerable numbers in these protests, which were repeated in many districts of Greater Buenos Aires and sometimes brought together as many as 20,000 people. Thus, press coverage of public protests in Avellaneda reported specifically that 'many women took part in the meeting and many of them berated the mayor with their fists raised, while they sang along with the men to football-stand music'.[41] In some cases, it was the housewives' groups or committees that called for or attended meetings outside the Town Halls (Avellaneda, Lanús, Lomas de Zamora, Tres de Febrero). In other cases, representatives from the National Housewives' Movement and the Argentine Women's Union took part in discussions with local government authorities. According to eye-witness accounts, by making their presence felt in these main squares the protesters were expressing their repudiation of a policy that, among its other defects, was bringing down the population's living standards. Whether women were representatives of neighbourhood organizations or had just turned up at the meeting, their statements followed a common pattern: they emphasized that the protest was 'not political'; they spoke of the need to dispel their fear and participate; they stressed the justice of their collective demands and voiced support of a strategy of organization and unity.

A few days after the wave of neighbourhood protests, housewives from almost the whole of Greater Buenos Aires gathered for a meeting in San Martín. They then formulated a petition demanding measures to halt the rise in the cost of living. This was delivered to the Economy Ministry after a meeting in the Plaza de Mayo at the beginning of December. Among other demands, the petition requested that the price of food should be lowered to its real price, the elimination of taxes on medicines and a freeze on the price of bread, milk and meat.

The housewives' activities declined during the summer (December–March), as did the neighbourhood movement as a whole. At the beginning of 1983, a committee of housewives and the Argentine Women's Union supported demonstrations, in front of Lanús Town Hall, against the increase in taxes and charges for services. A committee representing the Mothers of the Plaza de Mayo was also present at the meeting organized by the Federation of Societies for the Development of Lanús.[42]

In September, the Tucumán Housewives' Movement organized a 15-minute blackout to publicize their protest at the exorbitantly high cost of living. At the same time, the Movement made an appeal to the goodwill of the authorities and asked them to be flexible regarding the trade unions' demands, and entreated the latter to seek ways of protesting that would not paralyse the country.[43]

During the election campaign, the General Union of Housewives, which, in 1975, had won a vote in the Chamber for their Bill on the retirement law, requested official membership of the General Labour Confederation (CGT), as a labour organization, and quizzed the candidates of the different political parties on their interest in this law.

Once the constitutional government was installed, the housewives renewed their activities. First, they spoke to the Under-Secretary for Trade about their demand for price ceilings on milk, bread and meat, and in March 1984, called a 48-hour purchasing strike in order to press their demands. This measure, which was partially implemented, was instigated by the National Housewives' Movement and was aimed at those sectors 'which cause destabilization with exorbitant price rises while unemployment and low incomes are still rife in most Argentine homes'.[44] According to the group's statement the housewives were committed to supporting the government's major measures and, in order to do this, they mobilized and formed neighbourhood groups to monitor the implementation of the price control policy.

In May, the National Housewives' Movement and the Union of Argentine Women, together with other groups, drew up a document which simultaneously called for the defence of democracy and constitutional order with the full participation of citizens, and requested the following measures: price controls for the top 100 companies and the large meat producers, covering all stages of production, distribution, marketing and sales; affordable prices for basic food staples and with maximum limits, subsidies for bread, milk and meat; and free school dinners for the children of low-income families, in all schools throughout the year.

The campaign, whose aim was to pressure the government into calling a halt to the price rises and to gain a greater consensus to mobilize women, came to an end in October. Despite their stated intentions, the document, with 25,000 signatures, was delivered by only 100 people. This fact highlights the elusive or transitory nature of these movements, which is a common characteristic. It also refocuses our attention on the local level. What happened to those housewives' committees that emerged during the highest point of the neighbourhood movement? An initial survey shows that some of them broke up or remained in existence in name only, while others gained strength and carried on the struggle for the defence of living standards (the Housewives of Valentín Alsina, for example). There were still other organizations that went on to incorporate new demands into their activities, in addition to the initial aim of organizing neighbours for the non-payment of the additional tax levied, and to demand the provision of basic, essential public health services.[45]

An exhaustive examination of these and other examples of women's participation in the neighbourhood sphere would help progress in formulating the characterization of movements rooted in domestic roles, by looking at their duration, potential and limitations. Among the issues that need to be considered is how the process of organization developed following the mobilization and protests carried out by housewives during 'the transition'.

The case of Tucumán, where the Union of Housewives was set up at the end of 1983, fits into this category. This Union is represented in the provincial General Workers' Federation and has around 7,000 members, 'most of whom are members of the most marginalized sectors of the community'.[46] Following the example set by their neighbouring province, the women of Salta announced the formation of a union at the beginning of 1984. In July 1984, in the capital, a branch office of the Housewives' Union was inaugurated in Pompeya. This body, which announced the organization of commissions to promote the Union throughout Greater Buenos Aires, stated that it would fight for wages, social services and retirement pensions for housewives, 'the only workers whose production is not included in the Gross Domestic Product, despite being essential to the community'.[47] Shortly afterwards, the first national meeting of the housewives' Union took place in Buenos Aires, in which 230 delegates from all over the country participated. The representatives from the federal capital claimed to be followers of Eva Perón and told the press they were fighting for wages, social services, reasonably priced municipal laundries, food provisions and nurseries to enable women to participate in activities outside the home.[48] In addition, during the meeting it was decided that a national campaign would be launched for wages for housewives, retirement rights,[49] rights for common-law wives[50] and protection against all types of violence against women.

The struggle against the high cost of living. Some innovations: On the basis of this short historical reconstruction of the housewives' activities during the transition to democracy, we shall now attempt to identify the women who took part, distinguishing between the 'old' and 'new' forms of organization. We will also try to discover the effects of this type of participation on the women themselves, and on the way in which the 'domestic role' is defined (or redefined).

To begin with, it is important to point out the differences between the housewives' organizations that emerged in the period when the dictatorship was disintegrating and those that already existed. The first difference is in the characteristics of the movement's members. In the past, the struggle for these demands was led by women linked to a political party (the case of the Argentine Women's Union) or to the Church and certain right-wing sectors, as was the case with the Housewives' League. In the housewives' movement that emerged in the transition period, however, different kinds of women came together, including those with political experience, those with a background in neighbourhood actions and those without any experience of participation in political or social movements (as in the case of the promoters of the National Housewives). This movement, which was entirely new to the struggle against the high cost of living, defined itself clearly by maintaining its distance from both politics and 'charitable work'. 'Our movement is not made up of women with too much time on their hands and who do charitable work: we want to raise awareness', claimed their president.[51] They were firm in maintaining that their movement did not have political ends:

> We did not have a political platform before nor do we now . . . our movement accepts women of any ideology. We only insist that they do not use our movement as a means of imposing their ideology.[52]

This feature is common to other women's movements, a point to which we will return later.

A further aspect is the support given by the National Housewives' Movement to struggles that went further than their own specific demands, and included showing solidarity with Pérez Esquivel's fast and with the Mothers and Grandmothers of the Plaza de Mayo in the collection of signatures and on their demonstrations,[53] their representation at the meeting called by the Women's Multisector Alliance (*Multisectoral de la Mujer*) for International Women's Day and giving support to the campaign for the ratification of the Nurseries Law. In other words, while it is true that the Housewives' Movement worked for specific demands within a framework of sporadic protest during the period we are analysing, the housewives showed themselves open to issues not traditionally taken up by this sector. A period of demobilization followed the coming to power of the constitutional government.

Evaluating this experience of organization and mobilization from women's point of view involves asking what were the repercussions of this collective action on the lives of the protagonists or, in other words, what potential exists in these forms of participation rooted in 'traditional roles'. (Jelin, 1982; Feijoo, 1984)

From the protagonists' point of view the reconstruction of activities carried out evoked the difficulties of 'starting to participate without any previous experience' (fear, lack of confidence in their own potential and in the potential of the struggle to be undertaken) and also the difficulties resulting from their role within the family (lack of available time to attend meetings due to domestic responsibilities, in some cases having to overcome resistance from their husbands, and so on). On the positive side, and quite apart from the fate of the struggle itself, was the broadening of horizons resulting from collective action and learning to relate to state organisms and social groups. Such activities as preparing pamphlets, talking to shopkeepers, writing to the mayor or simply not allowing themselves to be intimidated by police threats, were all remembered as small victories.

The fact that the National Housewives' Movement was represented at the meeting called by the Women's Multisector Alliance for 8 March — although the National Housewives' Movement had stated expressly that they were not feminists,[54] that the Union should state as one of its aims that 'women should have enough time to themselves, money of their own and above all should have equal rights', and declare itself to be opposed to any kind of violence against women — shows that bridges were being built between the women involved in what we have termed struggles for women by women. Demands relating to the state taking a greater role in social reproduction (low-cost municipal laundries, provision of nurseries, for example) also constitute common ground for the two types of women's groups.

Finally, let us consider the discourse of these housewives. They participated and were encouraged to participate by an appeal to their identity as wife/housewife/mother: 'We are all women who, by doing this, are trying to help our husbands.'[55] 'Our politics is that of our husbands' wage packets.'[56]

While the aim of their struggle was clearly the defence of living standards, the motivation is generally explained in terms of solidarity ('we shouldn't close our eyes to what is happening to others') or as an extension of their role as mothers. Thus, 'young children going hungry' or those who died in the Malvinas/Falklands, as well as their own children's right to study and live with dignity, were frequently mentioned when women were asked what had led them to participate.

As Caldeira rightly points out in the Brazilian case (Chapter 2), this discourse implies a certain ambiguity: the call to participate is made in the name of the mother/housewife role, and yet the kind of participation encouraged involves going beyond the sphere used to legitimize it. This is undoubtedly one of the aspects related to forms of participation rooted in domestic roles that deserves to be researched in greater depth. For the present, a careful reading of the statements made by housewives' organizations in this period suggests 'discursive' changes. Thus, in the discourse of the National Housewives' Movement the definition of their own role is less ideologically charged with references to women's 'traditional' role than was the case of the League or even the Housewives' Front that formed part of the Peronist women's movement.[57]

The feminists
Old and new groups on the stage: As we pointed out in the first section of this chapter, since its inception at the end of the 19th century and throughout the 20th century, the history of Argentine feminism has experienced both developments and setbacks. In the period with which we are concerned here, the majority of feminist groups that had emerged at the beginning of the 1970s were dissolved after the military coup. Thus, in 1976 the Argentine Feminist Union (UFA), the Movement for Female Liberation (MLF) and the Argentine Women's Liberation Association (ALMA) ceased their activities. The Front for Women's Struggles (FLM), formed from the union of feminist groups and women from political parties in 1975, also went into recess.

One of those that continued to exist was the Argentine Women's Social Studies Centre (CESMA), formed in 1974 by a group of women acting within the Popular Leftist Front (FIP) who began to meet as a group outside the party to discuss their situation as women within it. After a major faction of the party's founding group left the FIP in 1976, CESMA continued to function with women who believed it was possible to be doubly militant. (Cano, 1982) Their aim was 'to assist in the formation of a great national feminist movement, deeply rooted in our people and which brings together the majority of Argentine women in the search for their dignity, freedom and justice'.[58] Later, in 1977, women from the National Tendency of the party and women not active in any party, formed the Association of Argentine Women (AMA) in order to exchange experiences and to read and discuss material relating to discrimination against women. Within a short space of time they joined up with other women's groups which had similar ideas, and decided to change their name to the Alfonsina Storni Women's Association (AMAS). The basic aims of the group, approved in August 1978, were to unite women to improve their social situation and to accelerate development and promote peace. To this end AMAS carried out such activities as editing a bulletin, organizing conferences and film projections. A group highly active in the field of communications and debate — the Juana Manso Association — was set up in Cordoba in 1978.[59]

The Socialist Women's Union (UMS) was created in 1979. Like the AMAS, it was linked to a political movement, being connected with the Argentine Socialist Confederation (CFA), and its President was Alicia Moreau de Justo. In its first manifesto the UMS demanded a return to the rule of law in Argentina. One sign that the women's groups linked to political parties considered that the time was ripe for entering the public arena, was the decision made by CESMA in October 1980 to organize the first Workshops on the Situation of Women. Despite all efforts on the part of the organizers, the police moved in to where the assembly was to be held. What had been planned as an open activity was once again forced to return underground and to break up into small groups. Later, in 1981, the Women's Liberation Movement (MLF) was reorganized and, under the leadership of María Elena Oddone, who had lengthy experience in the feminist movement, changed its name to the Argentine Feminist Organization (OFA). One of its aims was to try to influence political parties — when politics came back into play — to incorporate women's demands into their party political platforms.

Shortly before this, several feminists had formed the Committee for the Reform of the Exercise of Parental Authority (Patria Potestad), which launched the campaign for *patria potestad* for both parents, 'one of the many advances that Argentine women must achieve in their difficult task of becoming autonomous, free and wholly responsible'.[60]

In April 1982, the Association for Work and Study on Women (ATEM 25 noviembre) was born. This was an autonomous movement whose aim was to:

. . . contribute to the creation of a democratic society, a world in which everyone is equal, and where the differences between human beings do not constitute a justification for oppression but rather a basis for respecting the plurality of life.

It was made up of:

. . . women of different ages, levels of education and economic backgrounds, concerned and wishing to participate and to contribute our experience to building a better world.[61]

Their specific objectives included the organization of campaigns, discussion groups, the delivery of petitions to the authorities, and so on, to ensure the fulfilment of the United Nations Convention regarding the Elimination of all Forms of Discrimination Against Women. That same year, ATEM began to organize an annual day of action to commemorate 25 November, the International Day against Violence against Women. This workshop, which still takes place year after year, acts as a forum for a broad group of women to exchange thoughts and work experiences.

In August 1982 the Foundation for the Study of the Interrelationship between Women and Society (FEIMUS) launched a protest against conscription called, 'Mum, what are you going to do in peace time?' which initiated the anti-militaristic movement referred to in the early part of this chapter.

In October of that same year the First Congress on 'Women in Today's World' took place. It was organized by DIMA, a civil association of women fighting for equal rights for Argentine women, which also stated as its ultimate goal the effective implementation of the United Nations Convention.[62] Another equally successful Congress was organized in 1983.

At the end of 1982, ATEM, OFA and the Women's Meeting[63] decided to launch a movement that sought to reform the current rules governing parental authority and to replace them with rights that did not discriminate between parents. They launched a campaign to collect signatures in the streets, which lasted for approximately one year but slackened off during the 'election fervour' of 1983. Later on, once the constitutional government had been installed, the Movement Requesting Reform of the Exercise of Parental Authority led demonstrations in front of Congress requesting new legislation, which would allow parental authority to be exercised by mother and father alike.[64]

In August 1983, a Women's Place opened its doors for the first time. In the absence of any ideological agreement between its members (it comprised women representing different tendencies within the feminist movement), it defined itself as a civil association with 'feminist orientation'.[65] A Women's Place was set up to provide a space to develop activities such as round-tables, workshops, raising awareness, and study groups and exhibitions centred on women's issues. It also offered legal, sexual and psychological counselling to women. After the constitutional government took power, and as a direct result of a permanent workshop on Parliamentary Proposals, the association presented two requests to the Chambers: one requesting ratification of the Convention for the Elimination of all Forms of Discrimination Against Women, and another requesting the repeal of all dispositions that distinguish between children born in wedlock and those born out of wedlock.

In November 1983, following the initiative taken by three feminist organizations (OFA, ATEM and LIBERA), the Tribunal for Violence against Women was set up. This body aimed to 'bring to the attention of society the violence being committed against women, not only from a sexual point of view, but also socially and politically' and it organized a one day protest to demand justice in a case of sexual abuse, an issue that had recently caught the public's attention.[66]

The democratic scene: Apart from those groups that by definition were specifically feminist, both within the movement itself or in political parties, it is also necessary to highlight the role played by the appeal to women's issues during the election campaign. Different parties set out to form women's fronts and some, the Intransigent Party for example, were able to organize congresses that brought together as many as 500 delegates. Similarly, in the Justicialist (Peronist) Party both the Women's Branch and women's groups from the various sections, organized a considerable number of activities throughout the year (for instance, the congress of the Unity, Solidarity and Organization Movement (MUSO), or of the Peronist Women's Intransigent Movement). Although the political parties were careful not to define their positions as 'feminist', raising issues rooted in feminist thinking and advocated by the feminist movement was unavoidable. Women's problems and issues also emerged indirectly in the wider electoral contest. Some 'small' parties included women in their presidential nominations, putting them forward as vice-presidential candidates (for example, the Popular Leftist Front's (FIP) ticket, with Elisa Colombo as running mate, the Workers' Party with Catalina Guagnini for the same position, Irene Rodríguez on the Communist Party ticket and, finally, Silvia Díaz, vice-presidential candidate for the left-wing Socialist Movement). The appeal to women, in the form of a specific women's platform, was also clearly at the forefront of the Radical Party's electoral campaign. In addition, the leitmotiv of the campaign — 'we are life' — resurrected the issues that characterized the women's movement during the period of transition. Alfonsín's triumph at women's meetings was widely known. He spoke about divorce, and shared parental authority, male chauvinism and peace. (Feijoo and Jelin, 1983) If anything emerges from this brief description of events, it is clearly the difficulty of continuing to think of the development of the various fronts concerned with women's issues as discrete compartments. The election campaign can be seen as a time when all their paths intersected.

At the end of 1983, a small group of women began to foster the idea of celebrating International Women's Day in Argentina for the first time. The Women's Multisector Alliance 'which aimed to carry out significant actions to press the demands of Argentine women',[67] emerged from this proposal. It was formed by women from political parties and unions, feminist and women's organizations,[68] who encountered the usual difficulties of organizing and trying to avoid ideological debates while attempting to define a political position. (Casas, 1984) Finally, they agreed on some basic demands, which were to be put before Congress for approval.

1. Ratification of the United Nations Convention on the Elimination of all Forms of Discrimination Against Women.
2. Equality of all children before the law.

3. A change in the ruling on parental authority.
4. Fulfilment of the law on 'equal pay for equal work'.
5. Ratification of the Nurseries Law.
6. A change in retirement laws to benefit housewives.
7. The creation of a government department for Women.

Other demands, which were not included in the petition because the commitment of political women to their respective party platforms meant that a consensus could not be reached on these, were nevertheless presented in the public squares of both Chambers, with banners and leaflets demanding, among other things, divorce, sexual education in schools, family tribunals and legalization of abortion. (Gogna, 1984)

The meeting brought together around 3,000 women — both independent and members of organizations — who listened attentively to the details in the document drawn up by the Multisector Alliance. The document described women's situation in the critical state to which the military dictatorship had brought the country, and analysed both political and domestic discrimination. It also explained why the Women's Multisector Alliance had called on women to mobilize in defence of their rights:

> We want to be considered expressly as subjects in history, after centuries of being treated as passive objects. We demand democracy in all spheres of life: in the family, in institutions and in government.[69]

Adding to the pluralistic nature of the celebration, the Mothers of the Plaza de Mayo and the National Housewives' Movement also took part in the International Women's Day event.

On 8 April, the Women's Multisector Alliance paid homage to the Mothers; but then activity began to diminish. Some of the 36 groups making up the organization formally withdrew (as was the case of the Communist Party), others simply ceased to attend the weekly meetings. The main achievement of the Women's Multisector Alliance in 1984 was the campaign for the implementation of Law No. 20.582 on the Creation of the National Institute for Neighbourhood Nurseries, approved by Congress in November 1973. The campaign, which was largely ignored by the media, ended in October when a petition bearing 30,000 signatures was handed in at Government House.[70] This same body also organized a round-table discussion on the theme of 'Women and Work', held at Buenos Aires University and included two women unionists on the panel.

During 1984, women who had been active in other feminist organizations created the Feminist Alternative, a group that aimed to work towards 'a radically different society which does not condition women and men to live according to predetermined cultural models'.[71]

Other areas: Regarding what could be termed academic research focusing on women's issues (apart from some women researchers' individual efforts), work specifically related to women carried out since 1975 in the Centre for Population Studies (CENEP) and the Centre for Studies on State and Society (CEDES) should be emphasized. The Centre for Women's Studies (CEM), established in 1979 and concentrating its research in the field of psychology and education, and the Programme for Research and Participation for Argentine Women (PRISMA), which was created in 1983 by a group of professional women interested in theoretical reflections and research/action, complete the picture of studies carried out in this area.

Almost a decade of continuous work on women's issues has enabled this subject to gain legitimacy on an equal footing with problems traditionally considered to be 'important'. Continuing seminars, such as Women and Society in CEDES, and film series — such as those generally sponsored by the Goethe Institute — are indicative of the slow but gradual strengthening in this area.

A special reference should be made to the mass media which gradually overcame the women–kitchen syndrome and broadened the range of topics aimed at women. We have already mentioned how some women's magazines were directly involved in the military dictatorship, but an analysis has still to be made of others which — quietly and with difficulty — maintained a degree of dignity, either with special editions such as *Todo es Historia*, (August 1982) or with a permanent editorial line.

Finally, the impact on union organization of changes brought about in the position of women in the area of production should also be mentioned. Although a more detailed analysis is needed, it can be said that the number of unions with women's sections is growing.[72] In addition to traditional areas, such as tourism and social assistance, these women's sections are beginning cautiously to revise women's role in society. They can by no means be considered feminist groups but it is feasible to hypothesize that feminist discourse has had some bearing on these changes and the opening up of these institutional areas.

Some reflections: The above description of the activities of the different women's groups during the period covering the transition to democracy, and especially in the first period of institutionalization, is not meant to be exhaustive but rather indicative of the style of work and the issues that concerned women's groups. It is not exhaustive because of the difficulty, among other things, of recording with precision events that took place in the context of a movement by nature heterogeneous and inorganic. Nevertheless, we trust that our description offers an accurate picture of the topics most relevant to the different groups in existence. At this stage the groups still see themselves as self-contained and they cannot yet propose a common project that would go beyond the limits of each individual group. The need to think in terms of a movement with a greater degree of structural development has still not arisen and this is reflected in the type of activities they undertake.

Some signs, however, may be an indication of future developments in this direction. For instance, the new convergence between some demands of women belonging to feminist groups and those of women's organizations. These new relationships have already crystallized into a broader organizational form, as in the case of the Women's Multisector Alliance, but more so in the informal relations between women in the struggle for human rights, such as those that developed between members of feminist organizations in political parties and trade unions. This was a healthy convergence, bearing in mind the type of tasks facing civil society in a country like Argentina, where the population has historically been divided into numerous factions; a society in which there is a strong need for democratization within existing institutions and for creating new spaces. This will involve, among other things, not only revising the roles of both sexes but also facing up to the challenge of putting the stated principles into practice within the organizations themselves.

Another positive development accompanying the return to constitutional rule, has been the rapprochement between some activists from the feminist movement and the official body in charge of promoting women's issues: the future Women's Department. This feature is typical of the period under analysis and despite criticisms and resistance from certain sectors of the women's movement, has brought it in line with other groups forced to rethink their position regarding the potential of dialogue with the state.

If we look at the local characteristics of these feminist and women's movements, we must also include the role played by a considerable number of women whom the public considered to have made an outstanding contribution in different fields such as the arts, literature and sciences and who are just a 'sample' of what women are capable of. These women are significant in the eyes of the public and, above all, they have good channels of communication with the various forms of media (especially in Buenos Aires) which they use actively. This means that women have a voice to express publicly their own thoughts, which are often in opposition to the views generally held in society. Even within the context of a society that is embarking on a process of transition to democracy with great difficulty, and bearing in mind all the accumulated disadvantages in terms of the prevailing political culture, there nevertheless exists a favourable predisposition which has opened up channels of communication between society, the state and women's groups.

The future development of these groups cannot be linked to one single form of growth. The evolution and transformation they are likely to undergo during the period of democratic consolidation will surely depend on the chosen growth model. In extreme terms, this could range from a European-style mass women's movement, in which women take to the streets to pressurize for various demands, such as divorce or abortion, or to the formation of a small elite group, with the capacity to lobby the authorities and public opinion and to ensure that women's issues keep a high profile in the media and engage the public's interest. Obviously, between these two extremes, many other options are open, among which are ideas for creating spaces for the specific activities of all women interested in joining these struggles. This presupposes a shared willingness to work together on the part of the protagonists, who form different groups from those systematically broken up by the dictatorship. The question of restructuring society, interpersonal relationships and systems of mutual recognition is also, given a willingness to listen attentively to 'other' women, partly a question of discovering how unity can be achieved.

The exchange of experiences with other Latin American women's groups would undoubtedly be an important step towards avoiding sterile developments and wasting energy on experiences that already have proved to be largely ineffective. In any event, this exchange would mean accepting the challenge of breaking the boundaries of localism, of adopting a less provincial outlook and being prepared to learn from the experiences of women throughout the continent.

No doubt the forms taken by these new actions by women will change according to the changes in context. Women should, however, make an effort to preserve some of the spirit and relationships built up with such difficulty during the transitional period.

What the future might bring

The characteristic feature of the material presented here is, without a doubt, heterogeneity; the problems, solutions and protagonists are very varied. There are, however, some common features in all the cases we have presented. Let us consider some which will allow us to think about the future development of this history.

The originality and permanence of social movements

Seen within the Argentine context, some of these women's organizations might surprise the readers. Housewives' movements and struggles to defend human life might appear to the naive observer to have the force of novelty. But if we renew our interest in decoding 'signs' in a broader context than the local one and in a time other than 'now', we have to think about the historical dimension and continuity of these struggles in the Western world. Housewives' movements are to some extent successors to the bread riots. An historiographical perspective, more interested in processes than in events (Rowbotham, 1972) has, in the past decade, begun consistently to highlight these movements. In turn, the struggles for human life date back to one of the most important myths in Western culture: Antigone and her rebellion against the all-embracing power of the state, to find a burial place for her brother in the city where he is considered a subversive — an exact analogy, one could say, of the struggle of the Mothers of the Plaza de Mayo. From the point of view of power, Elshtain (1982) — a prominent North American political scientist — has identified the connection between the struggles for human life and Antigone's solitary battle against the Athenian state, justifying herself purely on the basis of her affective emotions.

Paradoxically, what appears to be new could in fact be the permanence of the old. Although the political context in which these struggles develop has varied significantly over time, the movements have certain features in common: they are more inorganic than centralized and they are spontaneous; it is difficult to identify specific leaders; no 'single' meaning gives a definitive form to the movement, instead it assumes different meanings for the different participants. Of particular relevance to our analysis of the role they play in the transition is the fact that they also tend to be elusive and ephemeral.

Naturally, the aspects of originality and permanence cannot be analysed without specific reference to the political system in force and to the way of understanding politics. In Argentina as a result of the parameters set by recent history — two brief intervals of democratic government in the space of 20 years — these movements would appear to have devoted themselves more to dealing with dictatorial, than with democratic governments. Quite apart from the fundamental issues at stake, which are basically the conditions in which politics develop and what is included in the political agenda, these movements and their protagonists have not learned how to deal with a democratic scenario and have little historical memory of how to do so. Perhaps this explains some of the peculiarities of their dynamics referred to in the sections dealing with the housewives' movement or the Mothers of the Plaza de Mayo. While it is true that their objectives are still far from being achieved, it is also true to say that in some periods they were the fundamental political protagonists in challenging the military dictatorship, and it was they who tabled the issues to be discussed. They have not been able to deal similarly with the political parties. To some extent the constitutional regime implies a multiplication of the spaces in which politics are carried out, including different branches of the executive, various parliamentary bodies, an independent judiciary, social movements and political parties. In these circumstances, the struggle is no longer against a single opponent, maintaining a belligerent stance without any nuances whatsoever. This is directly related to the movement's conception of how to engage in politics, a matter we shall consider later.

The housewives have come up against the same problems. They were also able to go out on to the streets and take over the Plaza de Mayo, but if the measures they propose are not implemented, how then are they to continue their resistance and carry out their programme in the context of a delicate transition, in which everyone is in permanent fear of sinking the boat?

The feminists were also unable to form themselves into an efficient lobby. They were accustomed to their discussion and self-awareness groups, to identifying the political dimension of the personal much more than the personal dimension of the political. In other words, they focused more on the political meaning of every-day behaviour than on the problem of how state and society affect their daily lives. They are now fragmented as a consequence of their ideological differences. How are they to find a feminist voice that can be heard on the national political stage, dominated, needless to say, by men?

And the women who fought for peace, against war, against conscription (they were right but basically this stems from feelings, a repudiation with emotional dimensions), how could they make their protest operational? Between their ethical repudiation and action lies a multitude of complex intervening institutional considerations that are difficult to avoid: the budget for the Armed Forces, the Chamber of Deputies' and the Senates' Defence

Commissions, careful analysis of the possible effects of any over-hasty move on the political chess-board. Also, there was the confirmation that in politics — seen in its traditional form — only male voices are to be heard, specialists in operations judged in cost–benefit terms.

This is what the Mothers of the Plaza de Mayo meant when they said that their movement went beyond the limits of what is possible, abandoning the politician's calculation of what can be done. But later they came up against the problem of how to reconcile this break with tradition with the permanent challenge of making things possible within the framework of a fragile transition. The human rights' movement remains isolated in some ways, more strongly hit than other sectors by the disenchantment of its followers — although not by its protagonists — which came about after the transition to democracy, as has been seen in other transition processes, especially in the Spanish case. (Paramio, 1982)

Although this may be a hasty conclusion, if we limit ourselves to being pragmatic it could be said that it is possible to maintain these utopias only outside the political system. The resurgence of the anarchist movement in our country (totally outside the realm of 'patterns and politicians') may be an indication that these movements raising basic issues must come from the space considered to be 'political'. In order to overcome the disenchantment, it might be necessary to restate the objectives of the new era, but what certainly is indispensable is a new adaptation of the means to the political ends. This is the substance of politics.

What is happening to 'politics'?
The interest in new forms of conducting politics in Latin America stems from two basic sources. The first is political theory which, especially in the Southern Cone countries and Brazil, observes continuation of political action even in states where it is formally proscribed; (Lechner, 1982; Vega, 1981) and the second is feminist thinking which is beginning to question the whys and wherefores of a predominantly male perspective of the public world. (Rossanda, 1982; Kirkwood, 1984) The political reality of countries with dictatorial regimes demonstrates how politics has not disappeared but has become embedded in spaces previously considered apolitical. Moreover, this reality is beginning to produce elements that enable one to make an analytical separation between politics and the 'system of political parties'. Children's nurseries, communal kitchens and women's groups thus become spheres of silent, responsive, daily politics. This politicization of the private world does then appear to be, as the Mothers and Housewives claimed, political but non-partisan, separate from the party structure. Women have found that in daily politics there is more space for their own voices, which are beginning to be heard, and that this enables them to identify themselves with 'other women'. (Rossanda, 1982)

Movements rooted in domestic roles, especially that of the Mothers, present an important innovation; the breaking-down of class barriers in the organization of basic criteria for political action. Thus, women organize themselves horizontally on the basis of relevance to their situation as women — although tainted by social class in a modern capitalist society — rather than according to ideology or the position they occupy in the social structure. Naturally, this organization, this powerful sisterhood of women, did not come about without conflict. Old and new protagonists come together in these old and new styles of conducting politics, changing the limits set by Western tradition (Arendt, 1974) to define the strict division between the public and the private domain and the fixed assignment of gender to each of these domains. But the world of politics, the great politics of democracy, is still dominated by men, and all this breakdown and relocation of issues clashes with the relative immobility of structures. Will this be the next step, to change the structures of the world of male political power?

Ethics

It is the ethical issues raised by some of these movements — above all the right to life, the right to live with dignity in terms of the distribution of wealth, women's right to control their own body and to engage in the painful construction of identity and liberation — which are the basic premises at the forefront of all their actions. These are always met with agreement, but a rhetorical agreement from society that will be violated whenever possible. Since society cannot deny the redeeming quality — if this is not too strong a term — of these movements then it will neutralize it. This can be accomplished in a variety of ways. The respect, mingled with contempt, that some protagonists evoke — 'mad women', Mothers, and so on — is extended to all women struggling to transform the conditions in which they live from the basis of their own organizations (this is not the case for those in political parties or professional and trade union associations, much less for those in charities). In some ways the Mothers inherited the admiration and respect but also the contempt and ridicule accorded to the first suffragettes, who chained themselves to the railings around the Houses of Parliament in London or who broke windows. Women's efforts to organize themselves as women are put to ridicule by a large part of society. The cause is legitimate, but the organization is ridiculous or avant-garde or divides the class struggle or is anti-male . . . This applies as much to feminists as it does to mothers and housewives. The efforts of all three groups to organize themselves from their position as women are met with the same reaction: they must wait. They are admired, but their issues will have to wait, until democracy has been consolidated, until the Gross Domestic Product is higher, until society is more modern.[73] But paradoxically, as we have shown in the previous paragraph, it is precisely the content of women's cause, and not their organic proposal, that filters through most of all.

In spite of itself, society is permeated by these demands and the changes can be appreciated at the inter-generational level. Even though some basic problems — many, in Argentina — relating to women's situation still exist, changes are noticeable from mother to daughter. There is still much to be done, but is it not true to say that our daughters are further along the road than our mothers or ourselves in terms of recognition, identity and solidarity?

Notes

1. *Patria Potestad* is the parents' (or guardians') legal jurisdiction over children. Traditionally this has been the prerogative only of the father or male head of family. (Translators)

2. Testimony of Hebe Bonafini, in *La Voz*, 28 April 1983, p. 12.

3. *El Periodista*, Year 1, No. 2, p. 41.

4. The movement of Argentine grandmothers of disappeared grandchildren was created in 1977 with the specific aim of looking for disappeared children — babies born in captivity or children taken by the forces of repression when only months old — and reuniting them with their legitimate families. In 1980 it changed its name to the Grandmothers of the Plaza de Mayo.

5. *Madres de Plaza de Mayo*, December 1984, p. 2.

6. 'The Mothers' [of the Plaza de Mayo] Page', in *El Porteño*, November, 1983.

7. Ibid.

8. The PEN project was supported by the provincial blocs in the Senate and by the UCD in the Chamber of Deputies; it was opposed by the PJ (Justicialist Party), the PI (Intransigent Party) and the DC (Christian Democrats); *El Bimestre*, Year 3, No. 13, p. 108.

9. Ibid.

10. *Mujer*, Year 2, No. 100.

11. *Alfonsina*, May 1984, p. 10.

12. Bousquet, Jean Pierre. *Las Locas de Plaza de Mayo* (El Cid Editor) 1983, p. 47.

13. *Mujeres*, Year 2, No. 100.

14. Saúl Ubaldini attributed the episode to 'groups outside the popular sector which are trying to create false contradictions between the workers and the courageous movement led by the Mothers of the Plaza de Mayo', *Paz y Justicia*, Year 1, No. 5, October 1983.

15. *Alfonsina*, May 1984, p. 10.

16. Ibid.

17. Ibid.

18. Among other statements repudiated by political leaders and human rights bodies was that of the commissioner (R) J. Colotto, in a homage to Alberto Villar (the former chief of the Federal Police), who said: 'We feel no need for revenge but neither can we allow ourselves the female luxury of weakness or of daydreaming.' *La Prensa*, 4 November 1984.

19. *La Voz*, 9 January 1984.

20. The square is strongly associated in the collective consciousness with two basic myths: that of 25 May 1810 and 17 October 1945.

21. Testimony of Nora Cortiñas in the Séptimas Jornadas, Sociology Graduate School, Buenos Aires, December 1984.

22. Hebe de Bonafini, *Humor* magazine, October 1982, p. 49.

23. *La Voz*, 16 October 1983 and 24 November 1983.

24. Some feminist theorists suggest the existence of a 'female consciousness' — a product of the sexual division of labour — that implicitly contains a language of social rights and the actual possibility of rethinking politics. (Kaplan, 1982; Elshtain, 1982; Swedlow, 1982).

25. *Alfonsina*, May 1984, p. 9.

26. *El Porteño*, October 1983, p. 16.

27. *Humor*, October 1982, p. 45.

28. *Alfonsina*, May 1984, p. 10.

29. Ibid.

30. The emergence of this political initiative linked to the social movements was closely associated with the conditions surrounding daily life and it keeps its distance from the competitive practices of party politics.

31. Bousquet, *Las Locas de Plaza de Mayo*, p. 49.

32. *El Porteño*, October 1984, p. 12.

33. 'Not only must one be honest, one must appear to be so. We do not want to give weapons to the enemy' is the explanation they subsequently gave. *Alfonsina*, May 1984, p. 10.

34. 'Our great concern is to avoid being manipulated by any political party'. *Humor*, October 1982, p. 45.

35. *El Porteño*, October 1984, p. 12.

36. *Humor*, October 1982, p. 49.

37. 'The believer in an ethic of ultimate ends feels "responsible" only for seeing to it that the flame of pure intentions is not quenched: for example, the flame of protesting against the injustice of the social order. To rekindle the flame ever anew is the purpose of his quite irrational deeds, judged in view of their possible success. They are acts that can and shall have only exemplary value'. (Weber; 1970, p. 121)

38. *Madres de Plaza de Mayo*, December 1984, p. 3.

39. The Argentine Women's Union is a national organization set up in 1947 'to unite the actions of all women of our country who want to safeguard their family's welfare, secure all their rights and watch over the future of the children and of the nation'. 'What is the UMA?', in *Aquí Nosotras*, No. 97, which generally supports the candidates of the PC (Communist Party). The Housewives' League was founded in 1956 by a woman teacher, called de Decurgez, who held the post of Education Minister in the province of Buenos Aires during two military regimes (1956 and 1967). The aim of this organization was to provide a direct bridge between producers and consumers by providing the public with information on prices and the quality of goods. The General Union of Housewives was established in 1966 and has over 20,000 affiliates.

40. *Mujer*, Year 3, No. 125.

41. *Clarín*, 19 November 1982, p. 24.

42. *La Voz*, 15 March 1983.

43. *La Nación*, 13 September 1983.

44. *Diario Popular*, 9 March 1984.

45. For example, the Housewives of Villa Diamante Commission held a social evening in March 1984 'for peace and life' attended by around 350 people, in which two films were shown on the nuclear threat. Political parties and human rights' organizations supported the event.

46. *La Voz*, 8 March 1984.

47. *Diario Popular*, 17 April 1984.

48. *La Voz*, 25 August 1984.

49. Retirement pensions for housewives were approved in 1984 by the state governments of Santiago del Estero and La Rioja. In addition, there are at least two proposals on this subject in the National Congress (one presented by Justicialist deputies and another by the Instransigent Party bloc).

50. The Decree 27.944, which extended social benefits to common law couples was annulled by the last military government. In September 1984 PAMI extended social benefits to the 'common law wives' of its members. *La Voz*, September 1984.

51. A paper presented to the round-table organized by the Intersocietal Congress in defence of the community's quality of living, at the Provincial House of Buenos Aires, 30 April 1984.

52. *Mujer*, Year 3, No. 125.

53. Interview with Ana María Pizzurno, *Mujer*, Year 3, No. 125; and the testimony of a member of the movement, who belongs to a Lomas de Zamora development association.

54. 'Feminists are against men' declared the promoter of the National Housewives' Movement, portraying an image of the Movement held by one group of women. In *Mujer*, Year 3, No. 125.

55. Ibid.

56. *Mate Amargo*, 18 November 1982.

57. The former would say: 'We are responsible for the tranquillity, security and unity of the home.' Ibid.

58. 'What is the CESMA', pamphlet.

59. Ibid.

60. Campaign Bulletin for the Reform of the Exercise of Parental Authority (*Patria Potestad*).

61. 'Who we are and how the ATEM was born' and 'Proposals on How ATEM Should Function'. (Mimeo).

62. *Boletín de Dima*, No. 1, September 1983.

63. A group of women who met with the objective of having talks on 'civic culture'. They did not define themselves as feminists and their meetings were not exclusively on women's issues.

64. At the time of writing (January 1985) the proposal for shared parental authority had the Senate's approval and was soon to be considered by the Deputies.

65. 'What it means is that we try to define the meaning of being a woman from our inner selves, with the freedom to think about ourselves and define ourselves.' (Mimeo).

66. *Clarín*, 3 November 1983.

67. Report by Oddone in *La Voz*, 8 March 1984.

68. The Women's Multisector Alliance is made up of members of the following political parties: Justicialist, Radical Civic Union, Popular Left Front, Integration and Development Movement, Socialist Confederation, Popular Conservative Party, Intransigent Party, Workers Party, Christian Democrats, Popular Socialist Party. It also includes the following groups: Foundation for the Study of the Interrelation Between Women and Society (FEIMUS), ATEM 25 November, Banking Association (Women's Department), Centre for Women's Social Studies (CESMA), Centre for Christian Studies, Women's Meeting, OFA, Association for Family Protection, Centre for Legal and Social Studies (CELS).

69. *Clarín*, 9 March 1984.

70. Tchalidy, Elena; at the round-table entitled 'Feminist Movements or Feminist Space?', University of Buenos Aires, 15 November 1984.

71. At the time of writing, according to our information the following unions have women's secretariats: Union of Argentine Teachers (UDA), Tobacco Employees Union, Insurance Light and Power Union, Association of State Employees (ATE), Union of the Nation's Civil Personnel (UPCN), Banking Association and the Association of University of Buenos Aires Personnel (APUBA).

72. 'Feminist Alternative'. (Mimeo).

73. Expecting women to wait until the Gross Domestic Product is higher is the same as telling them to wait until the country can afford their requests and proposals. (Translators)

4. Chile: Women and the Unions

Thelma Gálvez and Rosalba Todaro

The economic model in force in Chile since 1973 involves a high concentration of wealth. Based on free competition, with a highly open economy, it has resulted in the elimination of important sources of employment, especially in industry, and led to a situation of unemployment and poverty affecting wide sectors of the population.

Labour and union legislation has been restructured to make it compatible with the needs of this economic model, such changes being intended to ensure optimal conditions for expansion for the owners of capital and to prevent interferences that may serve to obstruct the workings of the free market. The state, previously a mediator in class conflicts, is thus reduced to a simple referee in labour conflicts. These conflicts are subject to the rules of the game, which assume equality between the two sides but actually ignore the unequal distribution of power. Added to this, is direct repression, which is used to assure the functioning of the whole system.

This chapter will attempt to investigate women's participation in union organizations within the situation described above. In so doing it will present the economic context and resulting changes in labour and union standards. It will provide a brief overview of the economically active female population in comparison with that of men, and of the possible alternatives for unionization according to the type of work. It goes on to analyse the attitude of the company to women's work and the behaviour of women workers in relation to their work, their colleagues and union organization. Finally, a number of points are made in relation to women's participation in the unions.

Women's work and possibilities for organizing

The general situation of economic crisis and political dictatorship under which Chile has been living for the past years is widely known. We would simply like to point to two facts in relation to paid work in Chile: first, that the official rate of unemployment has been consistently high since 1974 (25.8 per cent for men and 20.6 per cent for women in Santiago, July/September 1982) and second, the setting up of the Minimum Employment Programme (PEM) in 1975 and the Employment Programme for Heads of Households (POJH) in 1982. Both involve working in teams that carry out low-productivity activities with few material inputs. This work is paid below the minimum wage level and affords no social security rights.

In this context of crisis, structural features of the sexual division of labour persist. Firstly, the rate of female participation in the workforce is much lower than that of the male, reflecting the importance given to fulfilling women's social role as wives, mothers and reproducers of the domestic unit. In 1980, only 25.3 per cent of women over 12 years of age participated in the labour force, while men's participation rate was 63.4 per cent.[1] This meant an increase compared with the previous two decades.

More than differences over time, women's participation in the workforce differs according to where they live, that is, in the countryside or in the city. The weight assigned to women's role is possibly greater in the countryside, where there are fewer paid employment opportunities, the average level of education is lower, the possibilities of self-employment geared to the market are scarcer and the load of unpaid work, whether domestic or not, is greater. For this reason the rate of female participation in the economically active population (EAP) is lower in rural than in urban areas.[2]

We are interested in classifying the economically active female population according to their working conditions in order to have a global view of the possibilities for union organization that paid employment offers to women. One of the most important factors determining conditions of employment is the type of job held. Whether one is salaried, self-employed, in domestic service, or an unsalaried family member determines a number of aspects, including: the type and probable frequency of income, access or not to social provision, job security and stability of employment, legal protection in labour matters, hours and intensity of work, the existence or otherwise of a union agreement with the management, working in isolation or collectively, the type of participation in the market and, what particularly concerns us, the possibilities for and forms of organization connected with the work situation.

There are two ways of analysing the role classification of the sexes as regards work. One is to look at the occupations and positions in which one or other of the sexes predominates, in other words, that are typically female or male occupations. The second is to compare men and women according to the distinction between the formal and the informal sectors of the economy.[3]

The statistical report quoted in note 3 refers only to the urban EAP which, in the case of women in 1980, reached 91 per cent of the total female EAP.

The greater part of the urban EAP is found in the formal sector, although its relative size has varied over time. Data for recent decades show opposite tendencies for the 1960s and 1970s. Between 1960 and 1970 the growth in the urban EAP was concentrated in the formal sector. The proportion of women decreased slightly in the urban EAP and considerably so in the urban informal sector. Between 1970 and 1980 there was a greater increase in the informal sector than in the formal. The proportion of women in the urban EAP increased but in the informal sector women were absorbed at a lower rate than men.

The 1970–80 decade differed from the previous one. In the period following the military coup in 1973 there was a large increase in unemployment and a sharp decline in wages, which produced a more urgent need for women to find work.

Even though women were incorporated into the urban formal sector of the economy at a higher rate than men, in 1980 they still participated to a much greater extent than men in the informal sector. In 1980, 40.2 per cent of the urban female EAP was in the urban informal sector, while only 22.1 per cent of the urban male EAP was classified in this sector (Table 4.1). The definition of the informal sector includes domestic service, which almost exclusively employs women. It differs from the rest of the informal sector in that it is waged work for 'bosses' and produces for their consumption. Domestic work in private homes is negotiated in the market but its output is not. This has influenced the nature of this type of work and the evolution of the demand for it. In this respect it differs not only from the formal sector but also from those categories within the informal sector in which there are greater possibilities for self-employment. The overall volume of employment in this domestic sector decreased between 1960 and 1970 and increased much less than the rest of the informal sector between 1970 and 1980.

Table 4.1
Informal and Formal Urban Employment by Sex, 1980

	Women %	*Men %*	*Total %*
Formal Sector	59.8	77.9	72.0
Informal Sector	40.2	22.1	28.0
Total	100.0	100.0	100.0
Absolute Numbers	(969,900)	(2,003,200)	(2,973,100)
% in domestic service	19.0	0.4	6.4

Source: Paulina Espinoza. Various Tables: Statistical Report, 1984 (see note 3).

In the occupational composition of the urban EAP it can be observed that women are concentrated in certain categories: domestic service, professional and technical, personal services, office workers and commerce and similar (Table 4.2). In the first three occupations listed in Table 4.2, which are excluded by definition from the informal sector, there is a clear gender differentiation within the group 'managers and administrators', where there is a high proportion of men. In the category of 'professionals and technicians' female participation appears to be just over 50 per cent. But when this figure is disaggregated it can be seen that women are heavily concentrated in the relatively low positions.

In synthesis, women are excluded from management and ownership in economic life, but are found in administration, distribution and services and to a lesser extent in the production of goods.

Table 4.2
Urban EAP by occupation and sex, 1980

Occupation	Urban EAP Men %	Women %	Total %	% of Women
Professional & Technical	5.2	12.4	7.5	53.5
Managers & Administrators	2.7	1.0	2.2	15.2
Office Workers	12.4	17.9	14.2	41.1
Commerce & Similar	12.3	15.4	13.3	37.6
Farm, Fisheries and Cattle Day Labourers	6.0	0.7	4.3	5.6
Public Transport Drivers	7.2	0.1	4.9	0.9
Artisans & Skilled Workers	20.4	11.1	17.4	20.8
Other Artisans & Skilled Workers	5.3	0.8	3.8	6.9
Labourers & Day Workers	9.1	2.6	7.0	12.2
Personal Services	5.2	8.3	6.2	43.8
Domestic Service	0.2	19.1	6.4	98.0
Others	14.0	10.7	12.9	27.0
Total	100.0	100.0	100.0	32.6 (average)
Absolute Numbers	(2,003,229)	(969,944)	(2,973,173)	

Source: Pauline Espinoza. Various Tables; Statistics Report, 1984.

The law and unionization

The conditions of employment are a basic element in considering unionization possibilities. Of primary importance is the type of union allowed within the various categories of employment. Chilean legislation allows four types of unions:

1. Company unions, which group workers from the same workplace only.
2. Inter-company unions, which group workers from at least three different employers.
3. Unions of independent workers who do not depend on any employer.
4. Unions of temporary or casual workers (construction and dock workers) which have as their objective the provision of workplaces for their members in conditions previously agreed upon with the various employers.

Affiliation is voluntary. There may be more than one union in each company. There are also clear rules in relation to setting up a union, such as the stipulation that a certain minimum number of workers is required. Only the company unions can negotiate collectively. The rest can make agreements but these are not considered binding, although nothing prevents these agreements from being incorporated into individual contracts.

The unions of independent workers and of temporary and casual workers are to a certain extent job centres for the unemployed. The unions of independent workers (market traders, artisans, street sellers, and so on) are an attempt to organize people to deal with the problems of survival stemming from the crisis. They often derive from a common source, for example, a centre for the unemployed, a collective dining room. Given the crisis, the independent workers are at present largely underemployed or cases of disguised unemployment. The inter-company unions lack the strength of effective unions. Furthermore, currently unemployed workers cannot continue to be affiliated and therefore lose the benefits they would eventually have received.

There is a fundamental difference between the formal and the informal sector in relation to the advantages of unionization. The former is 'privileged' in the sense that it comprises the most powerful union organizations — the company unions. Only these are allowed to engage in collective bargaining and here implementation of the outcome of these negotiations is obligatory.

In 1982, 29.9 per cent of the urban EAP was classified in the informal sector (Table 4.3) which, in terms of unionization, means having access to inter-company and independent workers' unions, or more frequently, to none at all. Inter-company unions are the appropriate ones for domestic work and the rest of the informal sector can only form unions of independent workers.

Table 4.3
Formal sector, state administration, informal sector, domestic service in the urban EAP, 1982

	Men %	Women %	Total
Public Employees*	8.0	13.5	9.8
Rest of formal sector	67.2	46.4	60.3
Total formal sector	75.2	59.9	70.1
Domestic service	0.3	16.9	5.8
Rest of informal sector	24.5	23.2	24.1
Total informal sector	24.8	40.1	29.9
TOTAL	100.0	100.0	100.0
Number	(1,980,627)	(989,630)	(2,970,265)

* Data on public employees is not separated into rural and urban, so the percentages given represent the maximum possible if all state personnel was urban.
Source: Paulina Espinoza, 1984. Martínez y León, 1984.

There are, however, two types of limitation. First, those of a legal nature already outlined: in order to set up a union a large number of affiliates is required, collective bargaining is not possible because there is more than one employer, and they have no right to union permits or statutes. Second, the dispersion and lack of links between the workers makes the setting-up and normal functioning of such unions much more difficult.

The fact that company unions can exist only in the formal sector does not imply that all the formal sector has this sort of union. Apart from the liberal professions and employers, with their own organizations (professional bodies, employers associations, and so on), there is an important group of employees and workers who cannot have company unions or are expressly prohibited from collective bargaining.

In effect, those who work in companies with fewer than eight employees or workers cannot form a union. Included among these are the employees in petty commerce, who make up a high proportion of the 'commerce' occupational category.

The construction and dock workers, who belong to the formal sector, have unions of casual workers. Other temporary workers with contracts of less than six months cannot unionize in their workplace and have no alternative unions. Although we do not have relevant data, we do know that the proportion of temporary workers has increased in the last ten years. About 14 per cent of the formal sector comprises public employees (this category does not include workers and employees of state enterprises) who are not permitted to bargain collectively.

Women are concentrated in occupations in which organization is more difficult and where the benefits derived are fewer. Thus, in 1982, 40 per cent of women compared to 24.8 per cent of men in the urban EAP were employed in the informal sector. These women are divided between domestic service (16.9 per cent) and the rest of the informal sector (23.2 per cent).

With regard to the formal sector, women are also concentrated in occupations least favourable from the union point of view. Twenty-two per cent of women in the formal sector (which corresponds to 13.5 per cent of the urban female EAP) work in the state bureaucracy, which is not permitted to engage in collective bargaining.

Even though we do not have statistics on the size of the companies, we know that the majority of the salespersons and workers in personal services are employed in small enterprises (of fewer than eight people). Both occupations absorb a high proportion of the urban female EAP.

The situation of women workers in companies

There is no processed or analysed information about management or women workers' attitudes for this period. Studies carried out on labour and union relations do not take the gender differences of the workers into consideration. To explore this subject without attempting a statistically representative sample, we have turned to direct interviews with women workers who were active in the unions, analysis of a meeting of women unionists which took place in May 1983 in The Women's Studies Circle, and to discussions with people involved as union advisors and in the study of unions.

Companies' activities

We will refer to three companies that are representative cases of different types of women's work. One of these is a service industry: the Telephone Company (TEL). Originally owned by North American capital, it was nationalized during the government of Popular Unity and has kept this status ever since, so that today it is representative of state employer's management practices under the current regime. Female work is concentrated in the job of operators, which is carried out by women only and one requirement is that they must have completed secondary education. Since nationalization of the company, staff expansion has taken place only through a system of 'employment substitution' and at present a total of 1,500 operators is employed. The permanent operators have a contract of employment, normal working hours and benefits, whereas the substitutes work on average only six months of the year and have a right to social security only while they are working. Their contracts are not legal, they cannot negotiate and they are not entitled to the other benefits enjoyed by the rest of the personnel. They are not allowed to turn down a substitution job more than twice, which means that they must be permanently available for work on a casual basis at a lower cost to the company than permanent operators.

There are 19 unions in the company, including that of the operators with permanent contracts. Until about two years ago the substitutes were not unionized because, according to the company, the nature of their contracts did not entitle them to the right of unionization. Even though the company still maintains this position, substitute operators were accepted as members by the largest union in the company.

The other two companies — medium-sized, manufacturing industries — are in private ownership. They are based entirely in Santiago, whereas TEL has employees all over the country. The TEL operators are classified as white-collar workers, whereas in the other companies they are all manual workers. One company (CONF) makes women's clothing and supplies small retailers. It consists of two legal entities, one of which is the legal owner of all the machinery. One part of the workforce has permanent contracts, the remainder are rotational, with contracts of less than six months in each of the two entities, thus preventing them from unionizing. There are 80 people employed in the workshops, of which only 30 are longstanding employees with permanent contracts. Of all the workshop employees about 15 are men. Since 1979 there has been only a single union in the company, with at present, 28 members out of the 30 who have the right to join. Only women are in the union and its leaders therefore are women.

The other company (LAB), a laboratory that manufactures pills, syrups and disinfectants, employs about 70 people, of whom there are more women than men. The packaging department is entirely female: ten women workers and a woman supervisor, making labels and cardboard boxes for the medicine and closing and sealing the bottles. The work is manual and recently a production line was introduced imposing a heavier rhythm of work. There is a single union with 41 members, both men and women, with a male chairperson and a female secretary and treasurer. In the overall analysis of these cases, the first and obvious observation relates to the sexual division of labour: telephone operators, garment production workers and laboratory bottlers have no male colleagues doing the same job. In all three companies there are men doing other types of work that is considered exclusively 'masculine'. Some of the management posts could be undertaken by either men or women, as could some of the other occupations. But what is not found, at least not easily, is a workshop in which a specific type of operation is carried out at the same time by both men and women.

If we ask ourselves why these are women's jobs, the first explanation is ideological: because women have agreeable voices, know how to sew, are highly productive and are better able to put up with repetitive jobs, and so on. In this chapter we are interested in a second explanation, which for the moment is just an hypothesis: the fact of being female exposes these workers to exploitation of the type identified in these examples.

The most important indication that times are hard is the current level of wages which, by unanimous agreement, are considered to be low:

TEL: The Company has not employed permanent operators since 1973 . . . I earn 9,000 pesos as a substitute operator and if I had been given a contract when I started, I would now be earning 21,000.

CONF: There are weeks when you work yourself to death and can come away with 4,000 pesos and the next week the price per garment goes down and you earn 2,500 and they just couldn't care less about this. So, you're never sure in any one week if you're going to get a living wage.

LAB: We're so badly paid and by the time we leave at six o'clock we've been subjected to this for nine hours.

Besides the combined effect of unemployment and the free job market, which has pushed wages down, in these companies the decrease in wages has been reinforced by two mechanisms: the use of legal loopholes to issue contracts that increase the instability of the worker, and changing the system of payments.

In TEL the substitute contract assures work for only six months in a year, it discontinues benefits and avoids salary increments for length of service. In CONF, contracts for less than six consecutive months alternated between two legal entities prevent the unionization of two-thirds of the employees, thus barring them from collective bargaining and sharing in the benefits obtained by the union. Furthermore, the system of paying by piecework was changed to one of a timed minimum output. This minimum increase is in line with productivity so that there is no increase in the total income earned. This system is a disincentive to improved performance and is responsible for the present situation in which there is a light workload in the company.

Instability at work and variations in income resulting from these systems of 'permanent re-contracting' are reinforced by the continual employment of young women at a lower cost to the companies.

TEL: The Company runs annual courses. It's one way of bringing down unemployment . . . There are many new operators. They are about 18 years old, recent school leavers, so they still think that the company is the greatest . . . We have to wait until they get over that first phase . . . at least a year and a half or two more years.

CONF: Also, now they are taking on just very young ones. If they are under 18 they are paid up to 600 pesos a week as apprentices. Those over 21 years must be paid the minimum wage. The apprentices are put to work where there's a need, they don't do any sewing jobs, they are sent to clean-up. If they are free they can get sent to sweep, they are told to iron, stretch the collars, to help mark-up. I think they are really humiliated. There are young people who really have an education but since they can't find other work and want to help out at home, they work there. There are girls earning that amount who have finished 4th form in secondary school. Sometimes it makes you feel bad when they arrive and are handed a brush to go and sweep. It's so humiliating there with the bosses.

The young women's contribution to their family income is marginal and even this is much less than what is necessary to keep them. Virtually the only alternative would be unemployment or living in domestic service.

Another consequence of the policy of encouraging divisions through different types of contract is the division of the workforce into two categories, one relatively more privileged than the other. This is so emphasized in the case of TEL that substitute operators see permanent operators as the model to strive for, but at the same time as those who have everything — or almost everything — and so they see no possibility of joining forces to assert their claims.

TEL: We do the same work. But the fact that they are permanent, that is they have a permanent contract, they think it's very secure and they have rights to certain things that we don't have, because we are on a temporary contract . . . they think that we are nothing in the Company.

We did not have the opportunity to speak to one of the permanent operators to gain a different perspective, but the interviewee in the CONF, a union leader, was part of the permanently contracted group, in common with all those unionized in this sector. She referred to unsuccessful negotiations with the Inspector of Work to try to obtain permanent contracts for everyone and alluded to the keenness of those workers with no rights to unionize.

CONF: I've spoken to various people and they say they are keen to come into the union. That is, they are interested and you can see that they are very willing to co-operate, to work.

In all cases there have been innovations in relation to production methods and administration which, according to the situation, can be irritating or threatening to a greater or lesser extent. In the case of TEL, this relates to the installation of automatic equipment, which needs fewer operators. The substitute operators see this as a direct threat to their precarious work situation. In LAB the installation of a conveyor belt in the bottling section is seen not as a threat to their security of employment, but as something which intensifies their rhythm of work.

> *LAB:* On the conveyor belt you have to concentrate a lot. They say it's modern but it's exploitation.

In CONF the reform of the payments system introduced a couple of years previously adversely affected the workers' incomes and provoked dissatisfaction: 'people work without enthusiasm, they don't hurry': they are discouraged and have to defend their incomes because the new system reduced the price paid per item, while productivity rose.

To this list of economic measures that create instability, insecurity and division among the workers can be added others, more directly repressive, such as: informing, harassment of union leaders, warnings to new workers.

> *CONF:* Whenever we have a meeting, the next day when we get in early, I don't know if someone telephoned this fellow in the night, but when we get there he knows everything we discussed at the meeting.

> *CONF:* At the time I started to work here, there was a woman boss who was terrified of the union, so she made trouble for anyone who joined.

> *TEL:* When we are given the operators training course in the company, we are told that we shouldn't join the union. I think in part it's because they're afraid and they've already kicked out about two or three substitute operators who are in the union.

> *TEL:* I'm on maternity leave and it's 95 per cent likely that when it finishes I'm out.

We believe that the company is able to use most of these methods because the workforce is female. To attempt to prove this hypothesis it is necessary to examine the views and behaviour of the women workers as related by the leaders whom we interviewed.

The women workers' motivation
Women workers share with men the same economic need, which affects them equally. But for men, earning a living is natural and unavoidable, while for women its importance varies according to their family situation and is influenced by their own estimation of the extent of their domestic and reproductive role.

> *CONF:* The majority are . . . all women, women with children and almost all separated. Of course they have to work to keep themselves and some of them really have nothing. Sometimes they come in on a Monday asking for

money for their bus fare because they haven't got enough.

CONF: There are women who really would prefer to be at home but what their husbands earn now isn't enough. Others say their husbands give them money, they help them out but they say: it isn't like earning your own money, when you can buy what you like and no one is watching what you spend and all that sort of thing.

TEL: Really you come into the company always thinking that you'll look for another job that's more stable, because this business of working one month on another month off causes a number of problems.

LAB: They take the job for economic reasons because their husbands' salary isn't enough but they think: I could be with my child but I have to be here.

This again confirms that paid work is not seen by the women as an obligation. It is an option that goes with their 'real' obligation: unpaid work in their own home. For those young women from homes which they do not feel bound to support, the option might be for the future: 'I'll work and contribute while my fate is decided.'

The market does not make things any easier for them. Once the woman, for whatever reasons, decides to join the labour force she finds that even with the same level of formal education, there are less opportunities of employment for her than for men. This is the result of the sexual division of labour, which assumes and leads to her self-segregation by looking for 'women's work'. Her self-esteem is weakened and she is more likely to accept inferior conditions in her job because of this narrow range of possibilities and the fact that she has opted for a less obvious alternative than housework.

In their workplace women are faced with company actions against which they need to defend themselves. For example: low wages, threats of new contracts, contracts that differentiate between them, instability of work and variations in the income received, technological and administrative innovations that prejudice them, and authoritarian and repressive work practices.

Although recognizing that women can also find some advantages in paid work, we want to stress their negative views, because it is these that facilitate the high degree of exploitation they suffer. One of the most important is having a fragmented view of the whole workforce in their section or company. Objective divisions, such as different conditions and labour rights resulting from different types of contracts, differences in wages, unequal allocation of jobs, the existence of informers, all serve to create divisions. These have a more wide-reaching effect and obscure the company's responsibility in creating these situations. An individualistic ideology is reproduced in which family interests seem to conflict with those of society but this is not seen to be the origin of the conflict. It is interesting to note that the interviewees mention the family as a symbol of union and common interests. In the company, the individual worker or group of women would appear opposed to the interests of the whole workforce. There is no feeling of belonging or of shared oppression but rather of competition.

TEL: There's like a vicious circle in the company. The supervisor has her group . . . who are all friends. It's not bosses and workers there but . . . friendship. It's very difficult to go in fighting for things together because we are the black sheep.

I think that has always been the problem — working with so many women. Because where I worked before there were 14 of us and I was the only woman. It was much nicer because I was the spoilt one in the group.

CONF: To earn a bit more people fight over work. Then sometimes they won't even speak to each other because of work: 'You're really miserly', and, 'You want all the work for yourself' and . . . so the arguments go on.

There's someone who allocates the work. She's like the section's assistant but she also has her friends. Everyone there has their special friends in the workshop. They aren't united but divided into groups. If this group joins with that group, those five people will join with the other group, then one person begins rivalry against another. I sometimes say to them: you're more than a family because you're together all day, from half-past-eight in the morning till seven in the evening, you arrive home to do little more than eat and sleep.

LAB: Things have to be put to the union tactfully. It's very united, we're very united. If something happens to someone, we're all involved seeing how we can help. We work as a family.

People don't talk much in meetings because things said get spread about afterwards.

The division between the workers makes it difficult to visualize the primary cause of the conflicts and makes union work discouraging. With greater or lesser participation, the conflicts and negotiations reported are presented to the management by the leaders alone. On this point, it is interesting to note the hypothesis that women participate with greater enthusiasm in matters that depend on their individual decisions and less on the process of fighting or negotiating, which seems more foreign to them. Examples of this are the interest and discussions that are aroused in LAB by the decision on the annual works outing, the discussions in CONF on the sharing out of work, the interest aroused by the Christmas parcels given out by the union, the celebration day for the substitute operator by the union in TEL. To deliberate on everything considered to be one's own business seems to increase participation. To unite against the company to fight for some benefit is much more difficult and remote and generates divisions.

TEL: There was a battle in there between the substitutes, the permanent workers and the supervisors. They practically won't look at us now. Because first of all we're substitutes and considered troublemakers. I don't know how to explain, according to them we have no rights to anything and we're asking for things to which we are not really entitled.

Paid work competes with the necessary unpaid work in the home for the time, concern and energy of women. Because the first is a source of conflict between women, and of exploitation — perceived as such to a greater or lesser extent — the reaction it provokes is one of rejection. It also leads to the idealization of household responsibilities that are abandoned in favour of paid work. This also explains why there is an apparent lack of interest in improving working conditions in the company and it makes it difficult to formulate demands and participate in the process of negotiations. But union or work life is lively when it offers the more agreeable aspects of daily life: conversation, friendship, social activities, outings, parties. Paid work offers the opportunity to socialize with colleagues and share the experiences of their other work, that of the home, which is a source of solidarity and not of conflict.

CONF: They leave in a hurry because they all have children. If their children are older there's the husband. There are husbands and husbands . . . there are some that at least understand that the woman goes out to work and others that don't. So they have to get home to cook. Also some say: 'I'll go to the meeting for a little while before my husband gets home.' They have to leave in a rush. So that is the problem for women.

LAB: Some say: 'Sometimes I can't even talk to my husband because I have to make the meal. If I stayed at home we would have more contact.'

TEL: On the first day of the National Consultation they were a bit tense, they didn't have the nerve to say anything. Once they were together, in the same hotel and all that, they seemed to become more united. When they arrived, we asked if they had any problem. They said no, but when they were about to go then they all opened up.

CONF: They are not very interested in things to do with negotiations, they prefer . . . what's on offer. To get people to come to the meetings, I have to prepare refreshments. They don't go to meetings just for the sake of it . . . Mostly they like the sort of thing in the union where they talk about their problems, if they have a problem they say so to discuss it with one another, so they can share their experiences.

Summary: why women's work?

To be a woman, to carry out or be responsible for the housework in its widest sense, bring in an extra income for the household or for oneself, to have limited employment opportunities, to look for satisfaction and reward in unpaid work, all these phrases can be applied to us. These things are so well-known they are often trivialized, but they are also realities used against the exclusively work interests of the female workers. How is it possible that since 1974 they have been able to contract substitute staff in TEL with virtually no rights, without established working hours, at the total disposition of the company, working and earning at half rate? How is it possible that to this day many women have remained working under these conditions? Why is there a family economy to which they only 'contribute', even when in reality it is women who sustain it? Because ideologically they are able to. Because bringing young women in to the labour force costs less than their maintenance. Because there are fewer work alternatives than exist for the male population. Because their double role as workers in the company and at home gives them expectations about their other work and individual compensation for the collective suffering. Because the competition or contradiction between the two jobs also presents itself as an ideological contradiction which divides and weakens them in face of the company. The dilemma is: should they concern themselves only with their husbands and children, or should they commit themselves to the class struggle. For as yet there is still no integrating ideology — although signs of one are beginning to appear — which simultaneously criticizes and questions both roles.

These are answers that can be supplied to almost all questions. How can a permanent erosion of wages in CONF be sustained? How is it possible to make a worker do cleaning jobs that are considered humiliating? Why are working conditions at LAB not perceived as excessively bad, even though the women leave work totally exhausted?

As in other situations, the employers' attitude in the public sector is no different from that in the private sector. The interests of the workers are equally affected by one as by the other, and the same is true of exclusively women's work. In addition to the political struggle that workers have ahead of them to regain their rights, women also have a political and cultural struggle to stop being second class workers.

Aspects of women's participation in unions

Within the Chilean union movement's formal structure there are various inter-union groupings at a national level. Among these is the National Union Coordinator (CNS). Created in 1978, it brings together confederations, federations and unions of left-wing and Christian-democrat tendencies that oppose the government.

The National Union Coordinator has a Women's Department which was created in 1979, basically, it comprises workers' wives and has political representation. Its function is to try to motivate women's involvement in the struggle for democracy. When it was set up, no explicit consideration was given to the specific problem of women in general or women workers in particular. The Department held three national meetings, the first two were open mass meetings, and the third, held in 1981, was behind closed doors and of little importance. Women from all sectors of the political opposition, and feminists, attended the meetings in 1979 and 1980. For many women this forum was unsatisfactory as it appeared to be a way of incorporating women into political work without taking gender problems into account. In addition, the resolutions, and even the conference reports were filtered through the power structure of the CNS. From then on, women's groups that took into account the specific situation of women began to emerge and grow and the Women's Department stopped being a mere space for the general interests of the different women's groups which had participated.

Through interviews with the leaders and by reading documents of the national organizations we tried to formulate an idea of:

1. The extent to which the specific problems of women are taken into account.

2. The existence of gender awareness and how it is or is not related to class consciousness.

3. The degree of participation and interest of women from the grass-roots, the topics of greatest interest, obstacles to women's participation and methods to overcome these obstacles.

We have organized this section according to a series of assertions discussed below.

Class contradictions tend to obscure gender awareness.

Until now the predominant union ideology has subordinated gender problems to class problems and created a false dilemma concerning priorities. It would appear that this is beginning to change in some sectors of the left, but it is a slow process and not without setbacks.

From what we could observe in meetings with women involved with the Women's Department of the CNS and the traditional left, these meetings being exclusively for women (including feminists), the theme of oppression does arise, although not under that name. Complaints such as: 'Men are very well-off, they don't help at home, they are chauvinists and don't want women to participate in organizations . . .' are expressed, but these are at the level of confidences and do not impinge on the activities they propose to engage in within the organizations. They appear as individual problems that do not require collective action, except to improve training for women in questions of labour in order that they feel motivated to increase their participation. At the meetings in which male leaders participate, these types of complaint are not even mentioned.

Documents are now available, however, that include paragraphs such as the following:

Our demands rest on the principles of the right to work without any discrimination whatsoever, total guarantees of work, rights to child and maternity protection, to social security, to rest and culture and to equal wages, and against traditions and opinions about our inferiority which are firmly rooted in men and which work against an improvement in the situation of women in general and rural women in particular.

. . . the seasonal harvest workers . . . are without doubt the most ignored and anonymous women workers, exploited by the boss and *often by their own class*.[4]

In any case, the themes generally appear in outline only (often in an ambiguous and even contradictory manner) in documents in which it is obvious that paragraphs such as those just cited are the products of arduous negotiations between some women and the leadership.

Women workers' specific problems are barely considered or perceived as the common problems of all workers. For example:

The need for, crèches and nurseries, maternity rights,[5] pre- and post-natal leave, rights to work breaks for breast-feeding.
That paid work has not reduced women's domestic workload.
That domestic responsibilities limit the possibilities of participation.
That women's reproductive responsibilities are tasks carried out for society as a whole but not recognized as such.
The existence of limitations and self-limitations imposed on women in their attempts to obtain more training and to occupy higher posts in the hierarchy.
The needs of the system to use low-skilled and undervalued labour to perform inferior tasks for which women continue to be seen as secondary labour, temporary, and so on, even though a large proportion are heads of households.

These specific problems of women workers seem rarely to be considered in union struggles. For example, the resolutions of the First Conference of Women Workers carried out by the Women's Department of the National Union Coordinator in May 1985 covers 54 points, eleven of which mention women: one makes a specific demand for maternity rights, pre- and post-natal leave, baby rooms, nurseries and the right to time off for breast-feeding. Another refers to the rights of temporary workers; and another protests about the lack of women's presence in the National Workers Congress, which has no female leaders. The remainder mention women in order to call on them to mobilize for national sovereignty, to work for the national stoppage so that non-organized women join the workers' struggle. The remaining 43 points are general topics relating to the workers and people of Chile living under a repressive regime.

Women's union participation is limited equally by physical (time, working hours) and ideological obstacles (rejection of 'politics', fear of participating in public, and so on).

We women leave at six o'clock worn out . . . The majority get home to make lunch for the following day, to do the washing, look after the child.
Women have a lot of responsibility. That's to say all of us women have too many responsibilities. The man hands over the money and he doesn't care if it's enough or not. Men are too comfortable. (LAB)

Female union leaders see the obstacles to women's participation in the unions as stemming from their role as wife–mother–housewife, obstacles these union leaders themselves share. They emphasize the need to count on the collaboration and understanding of the husband and/or paid or family domestic help.

> Union work must be shared between the couple, in this sense the woman needs to be supported by her husband . . . or as a last resort, have a domestic worker. (TEL)

> I think that at that moment [a difficult negotiation] it helped a lot not to have a husband because otherwise I wouldn't have been able to do the things I did at the time. It would be two in the morning and I had to stay because the others all had to get home.
> (María Angélica, in a women's union meeting)

To hold posts as leaders and/or participate actively, women need exceptional domestic conditions. Seemingly a woman can get to be a leader when her living conditions are similar to men's with regard to responsibilities outside work.

As yet, methods at work neither take these obstacles into account nor try to overcome them.

Although the women leaders interviewed sometimes attribute the problems to limitations in women themselves, they all put forward the need for different methods of work.

Personal development (LAB), socials (CONF), fashion shows, teas ('I ask myself how I'm going to get them to come, you start thinking and you don't have a clue.' (TEL))

The women union leaders use their intuition about different needs that must be reflected in the methods; sometimes it seems a spurious way of attracting the women. But there appears to be an implicit recognition that women's private and working lives are closely related. Furthermore, it is also clear that at meetings women want to discuss personal conflicts between work mates. But they have not taken the leap and recognized that the problems in their private lives and those concerning work and union are not separate. For the time being women union leaders see unions as one more service for women: a meeting place provided by a union, with a family outlook, in order to encourage women who are 'afraid of politics'.

The companies devise manoeuvres that lead to low participation, by provoking divisions between the women, to labour instability and intimidation.

We have given examples and evidence above of the form in which this occurs in those companies in which union leaders whom we interviwed were employed.

The type of contract given to substitute operators in TEL, the impossibility for those with contracts of under six months to unionize in CONF; the payment system together with the allocation of work in CONF; contracting of badly paid young women with no experience into extremely bad working conditions; the use of informants; the role of women managers, which goes further than grading the women's work; warnings about the union — all these different forms of manipulation are used by the companies.

In order to be clearer about the differences, this evidence, which seems to be general and of which examples abound, would need to be compared with those methods used to divide male workers, or workers of both sexes.

There is, however, one aspect in company–worker relations that, by definition, is different. This is the effect of women, on relations with men (supervisors or other leaders), in negotiations.

> Man to man dialogue is harder . . . Being a woman gives you the capacity to create conditions to talk . . . not flirt . . . I try to put it into my colleagues heads that they shouldn't use sex as a weapon. Not to take advantage of being women in those terms. (María Angélica)

Women's 'weak and delicate nature', that wins them some considerations, is a double-edged weapon. At critical moments in negotiations the use of violent intimidation, usually verbal, upsets women to the point of tears and, by exposing their supposed weakness, they are left in a bad negotiating position.

Within the union there is also a sexual division of labour and of masculine and feminine roles.

Women continue to be the ones who serve the coffee, act as secretaries, and so forth.

> I'm the chairperson but I make the coffee, serve it, wash-up, of course you do everything . . . you're a woman . . . I write the letters, type them, sign them . . . (Adriana, at a meeting of women unionists)

Similarly, in the federations and confederations, it is women who are concentrated in the Welfare Departments, which are considered to be typically female activities. But over and above the activities themselves there is an apparent general 'female' attitude. This is maternal behaviour, 'self-sacrificing' with regard to her colleagues and organization.

> The other leaders are married, so I usually let them decide on the time, place and when it will end because they have to account to someone and I don't. (Adriana)

> Women are always looking for an ideal, but it is not for our own benefit but for the rest. Because you feel a bit like everyone's mother you look after everyone else's well-being. (María Angélica)

The underestimation to which women are subjected forces women leaders to try to emphasize the differences regarding women as a whole.

This gives rise to a certain separation between the leaders and members:

> We women are divided in two, those who are in the struggle and those who just let themselves be carried along in a more comfortable way. (Adriana)

> Women are a bit empty in reality. One tries every possible way to get women involved. But they are more concerned with their children's illnesses, a fight they had with their husbands, they give each other advice . . . You talk to them about politics and it frightens them away. (LAB)

However, the women leaders fluctuate between an understanding and solidarity with the other women and the need to differentiate themselves in order to win a greater acceptance in the predominantly masculine union environment.

To be considered an exception, without these 'problems' usually associated with women, is attractive and makes some of their work easier. To identify with the oppressed group is disagreeable. To accept that a situation of subordination exists is equivalent to accepting that it is incurably so without differentiating between what is culturally acquired and what corresponds to women's nature.

With regard to the differences between men and women leaders and the feelings of the women leaders about men, one interviewee said: 'I have seen differences but not in my case . . .' (LAB)

She comments on the problems that she has because of lack of knowledge, lack of culture, insecurity and fear of being ridiculed for not knowing. She also says: 'When there are more men your small contribution is more difficult.' But she immediately adds: 'Oh in general, of about thirty only five know . . . and you can't find the way to put it across, it's not embarrassment, but how to say it . . .' And she ends by saying: '. . . but differences, no . . . The only thing is lack of training.'

Notes

1. National Institute of Statistics (INE). National Census of Employment. October–December 1980.

2. It should be borne in mind that in agricultural employment there is a gross omission of statistics on women's work.

3. The following data come from the project 'Modes of Insertion of Women Workers in the Informal Sector. Basis for Action' by Ximena Diaz, Eugenia Hola; Statistical Report by María Paulina Espinoza, April 1984. Santiago, Centre for Women's Studies. In this report the urban informal sector was quantified according to sex, using the PREALC definition of the informal sector. This includes, 'all the occupational categories of workers: self-employed, unpaid family members and domestic service, and excludes professional and technical occupational groups,

managers, administrators, categories of bureaucrats at management level, office workers and related, and members of the armed forces'. We have also used, 'The Involution of the Development Process and the Social Structure' by Javier Martínez and Arturo León, Discussion Paper, No. 53. Centro de Estudios del Desarrollo, November 1984.

4. *The Present Condition and Labour Situation of Rural Women.* Women's Departments of the Confederations, Worker–Peasant Unit, Nehuén-El Surco, May 1985. (Our emphasis.)

5. Maternity rights (*Fuero Maternal*) means rights in the broader sense including absence to look after sick children. (Translators)

5. Bartolina Sisa: The Peasant Women's Organization in Bolivia

Rosario León

The literature on social movements in Bolivia makes almost no reference to the participation of women. This attitude is in contradiction to the very clear presence of women in the popular movement: women have not only been present in the struggles but in recent years they have organized themselves independently — although not in isolation — from the predominantly male organizations. (Sostres and Ardaya, 1984; Muñoz, 1983; Calderon and Dandler, 1985)

An important example of women's presence on the socio-political stage is that of rural women and their main organization, the Bartolina Sisa Federation of Peasant Women.[1] This organization has, perhaps, established and consolidated its own identity to a greater degree than any other women's organization in Bolivia. Its formal status in relation to other popular organizations is still under discussion, but it has considerable ability to negotiate with them. In addition, the Federation has ties with other popular, women's organizations, such as the Housewives of the Mines, Housewives of the Popular Neighbourhoods and others, in as much as their demands combine their concerns as women and as workers.

It is not by chance that peasant women have managed to set up a union organization of the sector that carries weight in the public sphere. The continuity and unity between these women's domestic and productive roles have bridged the apparent gap between the private sphere of the family and the public sphere of politics, and have established the specificity of the female situation within the peasant movement. Their socio-political activity is based on their social condition as women, which is defined by their role as consumers, administrators of peasant production, as the principal traders in rural markets, as mothers, wives and daughters of peasants. In carrying out these roles they experience the contradictions of the market system in a number of different ways. Nevertheless, in so far as they do not enjoy several of the 'benefits' that are the rights of citizenship, they are at the opposite extreme from urban culture. Illiteracy and, in many cases, speaking only their own indigenous language, limit their capacity to negotiate with a Westernized society that stigmatizes their cultural differences and very low standard of living. The participation of peasant women in an organized way within the peasant and popular movement, therefore, through the demands they make, integrates the class, nationality, gender and ethnic contradictions to which they are subjected.

Taking these different aspects into account, this chapter will centre on an analysis of the formation and development of a peasant women's organization within the peasant movement between 1979-84, a period that saw a deepening of the economic crisis in Bolivia.[2]

Organizing the Bartolina Sisa federation of peasant women

The Banzer period in Bolivia (1971-78) was characterized by the underground struggles of peasant leaders. Social pressure from civil society, the Church and from outside the country, weakened the dictatorship, whose image and legitimation in rural areas had clearly deteriorated with the 1974 massacres at Tolata and Epizana in Cochabamba and the torture and persecution of peasant leaders. Throughout this period, as a result of the public activities of some peasant women within organizations 'for women', such as the mothers' clubs (Munoz, 1983), or political organizations such as the Katarista Movement (L. Mejia de Morales, 1984), there emerged a female leadership that actively encouraged peasant women to organize independently. Following a long period of retreat and the repression of popular and peasant organizations, the democratic opening in national political life that came with the elections of 1978, presented a challenge to the popular masses and their organizations. They could now exercise their citizenship in a conscious and critical fashion on the basis of their own political demands. (Calderon and Dandler, 1984)

The reorganization of the peasant movement came as a result of the triumph of the Sole Trade Union Confederation of Bolivian Rural Workers (CSUTCB) over other organizations and other leaders imposed on rural workers during the decade of repressive regimes. It was therefore necessary for this Confederation to consolidate itself as a legitimate peasant organization within the popular movement and the Bolivian Workers Centre (COB). To achieve this it was necessary to increase social and political participation in the countryside at the grass-roots level.

The influence of the political activism of women such as Domitila Chungara and of the organization among housewives in the mining communities, were also decisive in women raising their voices to confront the dictatorship.

Over and above their role in forming a leadership, some organizations that brought women together in the countryside (such as the mothers' clubs and the Oruro Departmental Association of Peasant Women (ADEMCO)) played an important role in making peasant women's problems a social issue. In fact, these constituted the first fora, outside the peasant communities, where women shared their problems and developed an initial perspective on their situation with regard to the public sphere. (Munoz, 1983) These organizations did not propose the unionization of peasant women, but they did seem to have an important function in providing a link between women at the grass-roots level and the female leadership that grew out of the Katarista movement. During the repression, these organizations became the alternative channels of communication for the resistance, which also used more traditional ways, such as meetings between women and men at rural markets.

All these factors made it possible to plan a Congress of Peasant Women with the aim of bringing together the various dispersed forces. The most active women held various preparatory meetings before the Congress, which were sponsored by the Katarista Movement and other institutions involved in social action. Lucila Mejía de Morales, who later became one of the main leaders of the Federation of Peasant Women, spoke about one of these meetings:

> At a seminar held in Cochabamba, organized by CIPCA [the Centre for Research and Promotion of the Peasantry] we met *compañera* Irma García. I was a representative of INADES [Institute of Research and Action for Development], but as they didn't pay me or anything, they didn't consider me to be an employee but a representative, that's why I said at the time: 'I represent the peasant women of La Paz'. Since then, they've taken that title from me.
>
> At that meeting we talked about the organization of the peasant leaders union, about everything. It was then I heard the name of *compañero* Geñaro for the first time. It seems that it was Irma's idea. After the seminar we all returned to carry out our duties. I, for example, was delegated to the Human Rights Assembly. Then I made contact with the *compañera* Paulina Matias and we have co-ordinated a bit; there wasn't a lot we could do; Irma was also involved.
>
> (Mejía de Morales, 1985)

The electoral experience of 1978 made a considerable contribution to the development of peasant women's political awareness, as they had to confront a resurgence of the old patronage and 'clientelistic' practices of the political parties with the peasant leadership. The women's rejection of such practices reinforced the idea of an independent peasant women's organization, not only in the plans of the women leaders but also in the Confederation (CSUTCB). Without a doubt the male leadership of the CSUTCB saw the organization of peasant women as a way of exerting political control in face of the manipulative intentions of the political parties. Since 1978, they had to contend with a new political actor in the countryside: 'The men let themselves be bought. We women will not allow them to buy off our leaders.' (L. Mejía de Morales, in conversation with the author.)

The experience of participation and awareness

The Túpac Katari Revolutionary Movement (MRTK), the political cradle from which some peasant women leaders emerged, participated in the 1978 elections as part of the political front called Democratic and Popular Unity (UDP). The participation of the MRTK in the front formed by left-wing parties was constantly called into question by peasant militants, especially because of the marked disparity in peasant representation compared to that of the other parties in the front. (Muñoz, 1983)

Women militants of some left-wing parties disseminated UDP propaganda and organized the grass-roots women's groups. Their intervention caused some problems with women in the peasant communities, as there was an evident distance between the party agents and their *compañeras* at the grass-roots. It became apparent that the organization of peasant women into unions could act as an efficient political filter, independent of the political parties and even from its principal advocate, the Katarista Movement.

In 1979 the process of organizing peasant women was put to the test, revealing a certain degree of maturity in the process. Peasant women's massive participation in the road blockades in November that year showed the capacity of the leaders to summon the women into action.

The road blockade was carried out as a response to the economic measures of the provisional government of Lidia Gueiler, which were adopted following the military coup of Natush Busch. (Muñoz, 1983) These economic measures led to a notable deterioration in the peasant economy, causing massive numbers of peasant women to join the collective actions called for by the Katarista Movement from November onwards.

The economic crisis had a very particular effect on the role of women. As housewives they were faced by shortages and dwindling purchasing power for even basic consumption items. Faced by the critical situation with respect to basic supplies, which forced women to seek alternative survival strategies that involved an intensification of their 'domestic' time, women learned to collectively express their problems and worries from their basis in the domestic sphere.

In their role as workers, peasant women in the Andean region are responsible for marketing their output; rural markets are predominantly women's domain. During this period peasant women were faced with a drastic prices policy. As the prices of peasant output were frozen and the cost of rural transport more than doubled, there was an alarming decline in peasant income.

Peasant women's experience of participation in different organizations and in collective events helped to increase the value attributed to their economic, social and political functions. Events prior to the democratic opening, as well as women's participation in the road blockades in 1979, were decisive moments in the development of a gender identity, of belonging to a common universe, which was defined by the discrimination they suffered as women.

> In Banzer's time, women were not passive, they were participating in blockades, in strikes, in protest marches and also in the hunger strike. I was there for six days. We want to be valued as women, as people. Also this democracy, which didn't come about just like that, even now that we have democracy we still can't live in peace. We have to continue to make our voices heard. Just because we are peasant women doesn't mean that we have no value, we should be valued. And we also have to teach our little ones, we must begin to organize from there. These are the demands of peasant women.
>
> (L. Mejía de Morales, 1984, interview with Fernanda Sostres)

It was only following the participation of women in the road blockade in the *altiplano* in 1979, that the peasant unions explicitly recognized the need for organizing peasant women into unions.

> The idea of a Confederation and the advantages of having women participate in the struggle in an organized way have been thought about since the road blockades in 1979, when women's participation was so crucial. At the start, it was thought it should be an organization for women only, because men, in the unions as well as at the community level, don't let women participate. After going to a meeting they didn't tell people at home what had been discussed or even explain how meetings are organized . . .
> (Lidia Anti, in *Mejía de Morales y Otras*, 1985)

Years before, however, Geñaro Flores, the principal leader of the CSUTCB, had already distinguished himself as the originator of this idea. In January 1979, Flores led the meetings where peasant women reorganized the ad hoc committee which had been created in previous years. On this occasion Lucila Mejía de Morales was elected as President, Irma García as Secretary and María Mejía as committee member. These leaders convened the First Congress of Peasant Women, which was planned for the 13–14 of November 1979, but had to be postponed because of the military coup led by General Natush Busch.

It was not until January 1980 that the First Congress of Peasant Women took place, the high point in the process of organizing. (Muñoz, 1983) The congress concluded by setting up the Bartolina Sisa Union Federation of Peasant Women.

The establishment of this Federation was an important landmark as much for the peasant movement as for the popular movement. It was the first national level union organization for women in this sector and provided peasant women with their own forum where they could voice their class, ethnic and gender demands.

The process involved in organizing peasant women that culminated in establishing the Federation allows us to reflect on the development and consolidation of their political awareness. The formation of the Federation marks a dividing line between two periods of struggle.

The ethnic dimension of women's consciousness

Women's participation in the countryside, especially at the leadership level, was strongly influenced by an ideology with an ethnic content. In this respect the Katarista movement played a decisive role in the formation of a political consciousness among the Aymaran women of the *altiplano*.

At first, the massive participation by peasant women in the social struggles was prompted by the deteriorating economic situation suffered by rural families as a result of economic policies that went against popular interests, and of the political repression that affected men in particular. But then the Katarista movement contributed to the development of an historical and political awareness by reclaiming from the past a sense of ethnic identity and collective historical consciousness. During the ongoing struggle this was projected as a future utopia. (Rivera, 1985)

At precisely those moments of greatest repression the Katarista movement called on the peasant women and appealed for them to become organized and participate in the movement, perhaps for tactical reasons. It was in this context within the Katarista movement itself that such fearless women figures as Bartolina Sisa, the partner of Túpac Katari in the anti-colonial struggles of the eighteenth century, were resurrected from the past. As the battle flag of peasant women, she is an historical reference point and symbol of belonging to a common socio-cultural universe that includes Aymara peasant women.

> The women's organization was born almost at the same time. This was done so that women and men could take up the fight together, taking into account that women have been marginalized in their work. But we also considered it advantageous to incorporate women into the liberation struggle of our peasant *compañeros*. Of course the banner is Túpac Katari for the men and Bartolina Sisa for the women.
> (Geñaro Flores, 1984; interview with Fernanda Sostres)

The development of an ethnic cultural discourse on the part of the Aymara peasantry, and its internalization by peasant leaders, contributed to a more explicit identification of the forms of discrimination and of oppositional social contexts:

> We peasant women are made to look small, they call us 'dirty Indians'. On the buses those women painted like clowns make us give up our seats. In public offices we count for nothing and are told to come back the next day.
> (Quoted in Muñoz, 1983)

As various authors have mentioned, there is no doubt that the ethnic consciousness that developed in the *altiplano* gained strength within the community organizations that predominate in the area. The system of ethnic solidarity and complementarity that exists among these communities, strengthens their strategies for economic reproduction. (Albó, 1981; Rivera, 1985)

In the first phase of women's participation and of the federation, the Katarista movement promoted the unionization of women. The ethnic discourse was very notable at the Congress and the participation of Aymara women predominated over that of peasant women from the rest of the country. On the basis of this experience, shared by about 1,800 peasant women from seven departments of the country, ethnic manifestations acquired a more culturally pluralistic tinge.

> . . . At that time we still didn't know how to manage a congress. Besides we didn't know each other. We didn't know how the women from the eastern region live, those from the altiplano were in a majority. Maybe that's why

they said: 'it should be someone *de pollera*', although the other *compañeras* were wearing dresses.[3] As I was *de pollera*, they elected me unanimously . . . (Mejía de Morales, 1985)

. . . They want the indigenous race to disappear, they want the working class to disappear but because we are all the same, *compañeras*, we will not allow this genocide. (Fragment of the speech by L. Mejía de Morales at the First Congress)

Thus, the period before 1980 was characterized by the influence of ethnic principles and by the development of an historical consciousness as members of an exploited class. Its practice was clearly influenced by the leaders of the Katarista movement and, from 1979 onwards, by the CSUTCB. Until the First Congress the peasant women's plan for action did not vary significantly from that of the CSUTCB, apart from the formulation of some more explicitly female demands:

. . . As it was our first time, the men from the CSUTCB helped us to organize it. In the various commissions one of the men would reflect on the issues and then we would join in the debate. Since they managed everything, we just followed their lead . . .
(Mejía de Morales, 1985)

The First Congress of Peasant Women
An analysis of the conclusions of the First Congress shows that the diverse demands put forward — on the political, social educational, economic and union levels — corresponded to the demands of the CSUTCB. On the whole, gender demands were not well-formulated and perhaps suffered from the imposition of topics. Under the heading of 'birth control', the following demands were made:

We request that the government bans the import of foodstuffs containing chemical substances which cause sterility among the peasant classes.
We demand that the Supreme Government abstains from authorizing foreign Rhodesian immigrants to come and take over Bolivian agricultural land.
We reject and energetically protest against any form of birth control since this is against Bolivia's peasant women.
(Summary of the conclusions of the First Congress of the Bartolina Sisa Federation)

During the First Congress, therefore, what emerged as most central was the peasant women's identification with the main platform of the CSUTCB, which was centred on the 'male' Katarista movement and the crucial dimensions of ethnic identity and class.
As far as the actual practical experience is concerned, we quote one of the leaders:

It could be said that the Congress was in part positive and in part negative. Positive in that women are getting themselves organized in all their communities. I say this because many women come to the Peasant Federation to ask about how they should organize in their sectors. Before the Congress women wouldn't put a foot in the Federation; now it is mainly the women who are in the offices finding out how to get their organizations off the ground. Negative, because there was no preparation, as it was a Congress organized from the top down. Inevitably, there were many communities that did not know that they should take part. From the north of Potosí, for example, they just came to listen; from Sucre the same. They were very timid. The women who participated most were from the altiplano as they had some experience of unions and organizations. Those from Santa Cruz didn't have much experience but they spoke all the same.
(Mejía de Morales, 1985).

Organized peasant women and machismo
Increased awareness of the role of peasant women seems to have begun with the organization of the Federation of Peasant Women. Their organized participation raised a number of issues within the family, in particular their relationship with their husbands. The latter, in turn, began to express frequent criticisms.

According to the evidence provided by the peasant women, conflicts between spouses were frequent during the democratic period, a time when male militants enjoyed full freedom and did not require the clandestine work of the peasant women.

So, little by little, we are opening our eyes because we are breaking away from our husbands' chain. It is very difficult for a married woman to leave the house because they say: 'What are women going to do, they only know how to sit and wet themselves, so what are they going to do?' They don't value us, because of machismo, all that male chauvinism. Just when peasant women want to assert themselves, the men say, 'She won't pay any attention to me, she's going to do what she pleases, that's no good for us.' That's what our comrades say . . . The more politically active ones say, 'You don't want to get into that union, that's political. When the repression comes, they'll catch all of you!'
(L. Mejía de Morales, 1985; interview with Fernanda Sostres)

The peasant women's activities in the Federation, the fact of having their own organization and a collective identity, which they established during the First Congress, led peasant women to begin to express their rights and political possibilities more explicitly. Gender demands began to appear once they had discovered their right to a public life and to engage in public actions. The women continued to identify with the popular movement but gave themselves greater operational autonomy. This process became more evident after the Second Congress of Peasant Women in the process of defending a union organization that was no longer under the tutelage of a male organization, as we shall see later.

But the emergence of a somewhat more feminist discourse did not come about simply because they refused to continue to be marginalized and were not prepared to accept gender discrimination in certain spheres. They were also influenced by the messages from organizations and people with different political and ideological perspectives and especially the female leadership exposition of and adherence to a more 'collective female' discourse.

Two tendencies become apparent from reading the women's testimonies and analysing the development of the Federation. First, the development of a feminist discourse as the ethnic discourse disappears. Second, the growing politicization, that legitimized independent union practice, as in defence of their gender differences peasant women begin to relate and increasingly link up with other women's grass-roots organizations (the Housewives' Committees in Mining Communities, Popular Neighbourhoods Housewives' Committees).

Legitimation of the peasant women's union movement

A Federation rather than a Confederation
The Federation of Peasant Women is a national organization, but does not have the status of a Confederation. The CSUTCB attributes this to its lack of an organic structure at canton, provincial and departmental level. In fact, the Federation's structure developed in the opposite way to that of the Confederation. First the national body was created and only later did it develop at the departmental, provincial and canton level.

As an institution that brings together the country's peasantry, the Federation is faced with many economic, cultural and political contrasts, not only in regional terms but also in relation to the social differentiation within the peasantry. The early influence of altiplano and Aymara women in the peasant union movement is giving way to a more national dimension, with the incorporation of peasants from other regions, each with their own special features.

Besides this specific feature, the Federation has other traits linked to the fact that it is a women's organization. The terms of its political convention are different: the CSUTCB brings together rural workers, while the Federation draws women together whether they are housewives and/or workers. This double dimension to participation determines its forms, rhythm and intensity and therefore its way of conducting politics. Peasant women are adapting the union form of organization and participation to other aspects of their daily lives, such as networks to distribute basic supplies, kinship networks and local solidarity networks. Because the traditional forms of association of peasant women are a part of their daily lives and of their domestic and local spheres, they go unnoticed; they are 'invisible' and play an underground role in times of social and political repression.

The Federation attempts to reclaim the daily world of peasant women and adapt itself to female time. Perhaps for this reason it is difficult to meet the requirements of 'male' forms of participation in which time is dominated by the requirements of the public sphere, while the women's sphere has a dual dimension — the public and the private. (Jelin, 1984)

The Federation's first stage: organization and legitimacy

The first six months after the formation of the Federation of Peasant Women were devoted to creating grass-roots structures in the communities. The leaders travelled to the interior of the country and organized women's unions in the places they visited.

In this period, when there were signs of the *coup d'etat* that was to come in July (1980), an agreement was signed between miners and peasants, as part of the popular defence strategy. This agreement was ratified by the Federation of Peasant Women and Housewives of the Colquiri Mine. It was the women — peasants and miners — more than the men, who put into practice this important pact of solidarity. They learned together and were enriched by each other's experiences when it was up to them to resist the military coup on 17 July 1980.

> The 17th of July arrived. Men, women and children, miners and peasants — we all resisted until August 3rd. We women were determined to defeat the coup's leaders . . . But the planes, bombs and machine-guns could do more. Each day we buried the dead, two, three, five, like that. We were shaken on hearing about the massacre at Caracoles, we also heard about the dead in the cities. The COB was silent, so was the CSUTCB, but we carried on resisting until they also silenced the miners' radios. We women kept our spirits up until the end. Then faced with the impossible, we weakened. So we said: 'We must get organized all over the country, prepare and train ourselves, so that the next coup won't find us with our hands filled only with courage.' (Mejía de Morales, 1985)

In the period following the *coup d'etat* in July 1980, the popular organization turned to underground activities. Women returned to their communities and put themselves at the service of the peasant struggle. There was, however, a big difference from the time of the dictatorship in the 1970s. Now, peasant women had their own organization and had made connections with women's organizations in the mining areas. The CSUTCB belonged to the COB and this allowed a more favourable system of alliances than in the Banzer period.

At this time (1980) peasant women's own specific demands took second place and, once again, alternative women's organizations began to appear. Their objective was to maintain contact between women while at the same time serving as 'bridging' organizations for the peasant movement. From such bases the various resistance activities against the dictatorship were planned. As alternative forms of bringing people together and organizing, courses in handicrafts or on forming co-operatives were set up in the countryside. The number of meetings increased, and contributed to the continuity and strength of the peasant organizations and, therefore, to the weakening of the dictatorship.

In the 1981–82 period, peasant women participated in hunger strikes, marches and other forms of collective action, demanding the return of exiles, a political amnesty and that the military hand over the government to civilian rule. At this juncture the peasant movement as a whole played a key role in the resistance against the military regime. Peasant organizations were at the forefront of the political struggle and it was very striking that the top peasant leader, Geñaro Flores, became the leader of the COB in the final months of the dictatorship (1982). For the first time in the political history of the COB, a peasant held a post in the hierarchy of the national workers' organization. This event drew to the attention of other popular sectors the importance of peasant participation in social struggles and thus strengthened and reaffirmed the peasant movement.

The second stage of the Federation and the democratic process (1982)
The government of Democratic and Popular Unity came to power on 10 October 1982 leading the way to a new democratic juncture in Bolivia. Regaining democracy after two years of repression had a high social cost for the popular classes and the peasantry. Peasant women's role in the struggle for democracy had been vital for the survival of the peasant movement as a whole. The tactics that were linked to women's roles were once again politicized, and constituted the most effective channels for resistance. Once again, the domestic erupted into the public arena.

The Federation restarted its specific activities with a vigilant attitude toward the UDP Government and its role in the new democratic process. The political and ideological consensus, which existed in the Federation in the previous period, began to erode. The cohesive capacity of peasant women, demonstrated during the resistance, began to weaken and gave way to a process of political definition and growing differences between the women peasant leaders in La Paz. The questioning of forms of participation and leadership gave rise to divisions among the union members. Added to this, the Federation's presence in the democratic political arena brought it to the attention of different social and political organizations. The political establishment and a number of other ideological groups attempted to make alliances with or even to absorb the peasant women's movement.

From then on, the Federation's structure was transformed. Intermediary institutions were set up in the form of departmental federations, which acted as a link between the grass-roots and the leadership. The new structure of the Federation brought about new forms of union leadership and power. These provided spaces where different currents of political thought could be aired by peasant women, thus laying the ground for internal confrontations, which were very evident by the Second Congress of Peasant Women in 1983.

The Second Congress of Peasant Women
The Second Congress of Peasant Women was held in November 1983, in an

atmosphere of factionalism and strong tensions caused by the national economic crisis. The topics covered in the Second Congress differed little from those in the First Congress. But the positions taken in the proposals put forward showed a new political perspective.

The speech by Lucila Mejía de Morales, who was still the General Secretary, was clearly indicative of the new structure of the Federation and of the character of the new demands. The content of her speech expressed a wider social context and was enriched by her experiences in different countries and by the experience of different political moments in Bolivia:

> In this Congress we must speak about our reality, our problems. But our problems are no longer just hunger and fair prices. Now we must also talk about the liberation of peasant women. I remember our sisters in Nicaragua. They are also illiterate like us but they have taken up arms. If in the previous forty years they were unable to solve their problems, now, in three years they have already begun to resolve them. We want to be at that same stage now. (Mejía de Morales, 1985)

It is not the conclusions from the Second Congress that stand out, but the events that occurred before and during the Congress. These reflected the political currents within the Federation and showed how the contradictions between women in the Federation were taken on board and resolved.

At the Congress two tendencies fought to take over the leadership of the Federation. The controversy appeared to be over the terms of reference and future plans of the Federation. Leaders from La Paz were more closely linked (subordinated?) to the male (chauvinist?) current of the Confederation, which wanted to reincorporate women into the head peasant organization, CSUTCB, maintaining that the main struggle should be inside the Confederation. They criticized the search for autonomy and the influence of Domitila Chungara (the women miners' leader) over Lucila Mejía de Morales:

> Lucila thinks that being autonomous means not consulting with the headquarters and only associating with women, even if they're not peasants. (Lidia Anti, in Mejía de Morales, 1985)

In turn, Lucila Mejía de Morales defended the political autonomy of the Federation and indicated that these peasant women were members of a party unrelated to the women's union movement, the Nationalist Revolutionary Movement of the Left (MNRI). And, very importantly 'they were not married' and therefore did not know what it was like to be a wife, involved in conflicts with a husband, or having to make the sacrifices that are part of the role of mother, which make rural women workers much more aware.

Lucila Mejía de Morales was re-elected as General Secretary, thereby consolidating a position similar to that of union self-management and autonomy. She denies belonging to a political party, but she takes a left-wing ideological position and is in solidarity with women's struggles in other popular sectors, calling for the recognition of female demands but always linked to the 'liberation' struggle.

The re-election of Lucila Mejía de Morales by a large majority of peasant women from the interior of the country would seem to be a criticism of the one-dimensional, ethnic discourse of Katarism and of the discriminatory position of the CSUTCB. It also means a step towards the legitimation of peasant women's autonomous participation, with their own demands, within the popular movement. But this position is not explicitly stated in the conclusions of the Second Congress, which do not express the specificities of peasant women's struggles or how to carry these out. It would appear that women find it easier to express themselves in practice and in activities rather than in the formal language of declarations and conclusions of congresses.

Bartolina women and the creation of a female identity

The Bartolinas and the CSUTCB
The Second Congress of the CSUTCB, held in November 1983, revealed yet again the discriminatory treatment of peasant women.

> In this Congress we women have participated at the kitchen level and in the commissions. In practice doña Lucila and I have been in charge of the food. We cooked for only the first four days; in the last two we have given the comrades a sort of allowance so that they could go out and buy something to eat.
> (Lidia Anti's version in Mejía de Morales, 1985)

Women's participation is very limited, and controlled in the CSUTCB. Women are responsible for 'Female Membership'. This portfolio is subject to the party political position of those who hold it. At the same time, because it is held by four women, it is a symbolic expression of an attempt at 'controlled participation'.

The Confederation's vision on the role of peasant women is one of active participation in support of the Confederation, especially during periods of repression. Thanks to the social networks that women create in their domestic life, peasant women are able to establish effective channels of communication and resistance and thereby protect the lives of their leaders and the movement's continuity. But when it comes to questions of power and leadership, peasant women are not fully incorporated. This attitude is demonstrated by the top leader of the CSUTCB himself, Geñaro Flores:

> . . . In fact we are making the organization of the women comrades more viable: we could frustrate their struggles, their organizations but we are thinking that women could run the economic side of the Confederation. For instance we are intending to organize *pirwas*, peasant shops. As far as we are concerned, women could practically take over the control of all the *pirwas* in

all peasant communities throughout the country. The *pirwas* control products such as rice, sugar, all items of basic necessity.
(Geñaro Flores, 1984: interview with Fernanda Sostres).

Many peasant women were firmly opposed to the plan to unite the men's and women's peasant movements around the Confederation:

> . . . Men always win, in those joint meetings we are afraid to speak out. But when we women meet alone, we have a good discussion, we are not afraid of throwing out ideas. We understand each other more quickly, without so many words and we also speak about women's things which we couldn't discuss in front of men. But in meetings of men and women together we stay silent. Now we know what we would lose if they join us together again with the men. This is why we are going to struggle so that we don't lose what we have gained.
> (Florentina Alegre, in Mejía de Morales, 1985).

The Bartolinas and other women's institutions

The system of alliances with other women's organizations established by the Federation of Peasant Women is selective, and determined by certain forms of identification of objectives and by the class situation.

On the one hand, they do not recognize organizations that spring up in the countryside and seek different objectives. Thus they do not recognize and, indeed, repudiate the work of the mothers' clubs, which they think would demobilize peasant woman. They firmly reject the clubs, unaware that these were part of the organizations that originally created the Federation itself, as well as their important role in times of repression. They also criticize the anti-union role of the Departmental Association of Oruro Women (ADEMCO), although they hold talks with women who participate in this organization, to link them to the Federation.

On the other hand, the demands expressed by the Federation are also part of women's demands in other sectors, such as those of domestic workers and housewives in the outlying poor neighbourhoods. They also unite with women from the mines in other, more political ways.

> Very often people are confused because women from the poor neighbour-hoods and peasant women are very different. But we are aware that we have the same blood, that we are the granddaughters and great-granddaughters of peasant women who migrated to the city and have to live in poor neighbourhoods on the outskirts — we are their daughters. So that is why I embrace all our women in sisterhood.
> . . . we follow their example because our blood cries out that the time has arrived for women to organize, to end this marginalization we have endured for years, for centuries.
> Our peasant sisters are not alone. I want to tell them, they are no longer alone, as when they were thrown out of their own Federation, or when they

went on hunger strike. At the time we were still not aware, but now we are in solidarity with them and if at any moment they need our support, we are here. The Housewives of the Popular Neighbourhoods are ready to carry on the struggle and we hope they carry on, because they are an example for us to follow just like the women miners, who are also daughters of peasant women. Peasant blood is everywhere, tell me where it cannot be found. (Dominga Velasquez, Executive Secretary of the Federation of Housewives from Popular Neighbourhoods)

Conclusions

We know we have the right. Sometimes husband and wife would fight. Something in our customs was beginning to change for women's own good. In my province we have organized really well. Now we know who we are, where we are and what we want.
(Mejía de Morales, 1985)

Peasant women who participate in the peasant movement nowadays are daughters of the women involved in the 1952 Revolution. The discriminatory political practices and forms of exploiting women that existed then, are still vivid in the minds of unionized peasant women. For this reason they reject the type of political activism and participation of that period:

We produce, we feed you all, you live off us and yet you don't recognize that we are equal, that we have rights, that we are people. For this reason, there is no way the Federation of Peasant Women is going to seek co-ordination with you. Besides, how many of you are there? Who do you represent? Does being the widow of a patriotic general make one representative?

If you want to work with us, give your solidarity to peasant women and come to work in the countryside. We are not going to reject you but we don't want to come and look for you, to knock on your doors like before, not any more. We are not the peasant women of 1952 but of the 1980s.
(Mejía de Morales, 1985).

To summarize, we have outlined the process involved in one of the peasant women's organizations, which has still not been consolidated. It began spontaneously as peasant women joined the peasant movement, participating in peasant struggles without questioning. Although linked to the fight to regain democracy and civil liberties, this initiative was also linked to the demand for a space that was female and domestic and which began to be politicized through the practice of participation. Following a period of military repression, women acquired a greater awareness of their crucial role within the popular movement, but at the same time recognized their continued subordinate position. This apprenticeship in collective practice culminated in them setting up a more autonomous body — the Federation. Starting by organizing thesmelves, women moved on to a process of self-appraisal of their female specificity, protesting against the supposed differences that emanate from a definition of 'women's condition' imposed by a male chauvinist view of society. This awareness contributed to the formation of a new ideology more in keeping with the new protagonists who emerge in the historical process of struggle and development of the popular movement.

Notes

1. In this text the terms peasant women and rural women are used to translate *campesiña* or *mujeres campesiñas* and refer to the women who are part of Bolivia's peasantry of poor rural workers, smallholders and farmers of indigenous community land. (Translators)

2. There are only two published studies on the unionization of peasant women. Muñoz (1984), provides an important overview of the formation of the Bartolina Sisa Federation of Peasant Women. The other is a work on the Federation based on testimonies and compiled by Javier Medina (Mejía de Morales, 1985). In preparing the present work we have also had access to the texts of two interviews with women peasant leaders of the Federation and the Sole Union Confederation of Rural Workers (CSUTCB) carried out by Fernanda Sostres who is a researcher with FLACSO (Latin American Faculty of Social Sciences), Bolivia. I would like to thank Javier Medina and Fernanda Sostres for their kindness in lending me this material and for giving me permission to quote them in this work. The responsibility for interpreting them is entirely mine.

3. *De pollera* refers in this context to indigenous Bolivian women from the altiplano who wear the traditional dress consisting of very full skirts. (Translators)

6. Indigenous Women and Community Resistance: History and Memory

Andean Oral History Workshop (THOA)
compiled by Silvia Rivera Cusicanqui

Markasan Warminakataki:
Mamanakataki, Tawaqunakataki,
Jisk'a Imilla Wawanakataki

To the women of our community: women, young women and girls.

This work provides evidence of the participation by Aymara and Quechua women in the indigenous Indian insurrections. In the reflections presented here the women explain their history and thoughts.

These thoughts and messages have been written down by the Andean Oral History Workshop (THOA) so that women everywhere may learn about Andean women. We, in THOA, consider this text to have been written by all the women who participated* and our aim is that one day they will be able to write their own history, which is the history of the Aymara and Quechua world.

La Paz, May 1985

Introduction

This work is part of a wider study on Andean Rebellions 1910–50 in which, using the methodology of oral history, we sought to investigate the motivations, aspirations, structure and historical development of the mobilizations referred to as the rebellions. Until now, these have been presented as irrational, violent outbursts, the sole objective of which was revenge for an intolerable situation involving oppression and humiliation.

The research work undertaken by the THOA team has contributed to the discovery that behind these brief, violent episodes, there was a growing ideology, a specific programme of demands and a wide leadership network which, through legal struggles and, on occasions, open confrontations, sought to defend the indigenous Andean community — *ayllu* — from being usurped by

---

* For a list of participants see p. 208.

the ruling *criollo* class and incorporated into their large estates.[1] Even though this movement has left innumerable documents and other written traces, it would have been impossible to examine their significance and objectives without the inside view provided by the survivors and witnesses of that period, such as those who maintain the long oral tradition of the *ayllus*, and indigenous communities in which we carried out the research.

Initially, in compiling the testimonies and documents, we did not aim to include the theme of women's participation, perhaps because of the urgent need to record the personal histories of the principal leaders — the community chiefs empowered to act on behalf of the community, and scribes — of the movement organized to defend the *ayllus* by legal measures. In this almost totally masculine universe, women were relegated to a secondary place, both in those aspects with which we were concerned and in the history we were researching. Part of the present work is based on the material gathered in that first phase of the investigation, where the most salient feature is the 'absence' of women. Later we collected some testimonies that were intended to illustrate specific questions referring to the ways in which women participate in community struggles and relating to women's historical recollections. We set ourselves the task of explaining why there was an apparent absence and non-visibility of women in history, as well as examining the extent of their silence and invisible presence.

This work is of a preliminary and hypothetical nature. We have, therefore, chosen to present it in the form of a collection of testimonies and reflections that allows us to indicate a series of themes and ideas, rather than attempting to prove a preconceived thesis. Moreover, we want to preserve the freshness and variety of the women's voices and the richness of the oral language in the testimonies. That is why we have respected the original language of the interviewees (*aymara* or *q'ishwa*) and translated its meaning as faithfully as possible.[2]

Community struggles: the context

For the indigenous Andean communities, Bolivia's achievement of independence as a republic led to no substantial changes in the colonial relationship between the state and the oligarchy of Spanish origin and the oppressed majority native population. Furthermore, from the second half of the nineteenth century, the conditions were created for new seizures by private landowners of land which the Andean *ayllus* had managed to hold on to by means of a fierce struggle to defend them from the colonial *encomenderos*[3] and large landowners.

The main legal instrument of this expansion of large estates was the 1874 Settlement Law, which came into force after the 1881 General Review. This law declared the indigenous communities 'extinguished' and abolished all forms of communal authority and self-government, with the objective of breaking up communal territory into individual transferable ownership. The indigenous communities responded in a variety of ways. In areas such as the north of Potosí, where the larger *ayllus* remained strong, the review bodies responsible for measuring and dividing the land were unable to even enter the communal territories and, at the beginning of this century, they were forced to stop the whole operation. (Platt, 1982) After the first stage of dividing the plots and selling communal lands began in the Andean highlands, a wide network of Indians with legal power to represent the indigenous population (*apoderados*) was organized. Many of them also held the position of *jilaqatas*, the traditional indigenous authority. This leadership network was the basis for the armed indigenous mobilization that erupted in the heat of the civil war in 1899, under the command of Pablo Zárate Willka. After the defeat of this rebellion, the indigenous communities continued their legal battle and strengthened their own network of communal authorities, who were then called *caciques- apoderados*.[4] At the peak of this new stage in the struggle, Santos Marka T'ula had become the *apoderado* of 400 communities throughout the country, while maintaining his role as the head *cacique* of the *ayllus* in his own *marka*, Qallapa. (THOA, 1984) As in the previous phase, the struggle of the *caciques- apoderados* was based on the legitimacy conferred by law on title-deeds for the composition and sale of land obtained by the *ayllus* in colonial times.

This legal mechanism of the Indian *apoderados* allowed the indigenous communities to uphold and legalize their own system of authority before the republican courts. At the same time, by making use of alliances with certain *criollo* sectors, the struggle of indigenous communities achieved the passing of a law in 1883. This law provided for the exclusion of those community territories consolidated during the colonial era from the process of subdivision and granting of individual land titles that was being carried out in many regions. (THOA, 1984)

Nevertheless, violence and fraud were used frequently in the expansion of the *latifundio* to usurp indigenous community lands, which continued to increase in value due to their location near the railway lines and roads built by the conservative and liberal governments.

In this period there were instances when, having exhausted all legal channels, open rebellion was the last resort in the communities' self defence. The Pablo Zárate Willka rebellion in 1899 has already been mentioned. Taking advantage of the civil conflict between conservatives and liberals, Pablo Zárate Willka organized an Indian army and launched his own programme to defend the *ayllu* lands and communal self-government. Similarly, rebellions such as those at Pacajes in 1914, Caquiaviri in 1918, Jesús de Machaca in 1921, Chayanta in 1927 and Pucarani in 1934, were the violent culmination of the indigenous communities' long process of resistance and organization in defence of their land, their own forms of organization and ways of life, which *latifundismo* threatened to eradicate.[5]

The prospect of becoming tenants on the estates was more threatening to community families than the loss of their lands and the exploitation of their labour. It meant an end to their autonomy and the dismantling of their symbolic world and collective identity. The indigenous communities' resistance was one of the most heroic and tenacious events in contemporary social struggles.

Suffering on the estates: a first approximation to a women's view

How did women see these confrontations and how did they participate in defending their community? The following testimonies illustrate what the expansion of *latifundia* meant for the indigenous communities, as well as the transition from the relative autonomy of the communities to subjugation on the estates.

Doña Marta Colque, widow of Aruquipa, spent her childhood and youth in the community of Punku Uyu (Warina), which she left to marry a *colono* on the P'axchan Molino estate.[6] This was not her own decision but that of her family who 'gave her away in marriage'.

> My husband took me there. Without knowing each other we got married. That's how I was taken, that's the truth. I was brought up by my aunt and uncle and my grandparents. They were encouraged to drink a lot of alcohol and then they took me away. My aunt and uncle gave me away. So I was taken to P'axchan Molino which was a huge estate.[7]

In Doña Marta's recollections, community life was not a great burden; work was carried out in a festive atmosphere and was linked to the permanence and reinforcement of community ties.

> In the community we worked as much as was necessary for ourselves. We tended the land between us, family by family. We would eat together in the fields, cooking in huge pots. It had always been like that. During the carnivals and the Espiritu religious festival, which is our holiday, we cooked and ate together. We all went to a green field with our pots and we would eat and drink there.

This same work — cooking and taking food to family members at work — became an ordeal on the large estates. The obligation of the tenants' families to work in the fields and pastures of the estates, required an enormous increase in physical effort, which reduced their capacity to provide for themselves.

> On the estate it was different, there was too much work.

> We had almost no clothes. We only worked for the landowner, not for ourselves. On Saturdays and Sundays we would wash our clothes, but there was never enough time, that's what it was like. At five in the morning we had to go and collect the manure. I had to carry three meals on my back with my baby on top and the other in my arms. I was so loaded I almost fell in the water. It was a long way across the enormous plain and we had to go all the

way around. There were seven or eight different places for grazing and this is where we got the manure from. It was the same when we had to do the threshing, we would go out at dawn, field by field. We also had to carry our meals to where the grain was piled up. It was the same when we were spreading the manure and ploughing the fields; we had to finish a furrow by five o'clock with one of us sowing the seeds and another ploughing. That's what it was like.

Working for the estate also meant using up goods and resources that were intended for the family's own subsistence. Doña Marta brought a considerable dowry into her marriage, but it was consumed during the time she and her husband spent as *colonos*. The excessive workload prevented her from properly fulfilling one of the vital tasks of Aymara women: making the family's clothes, instead she was forced to buy in the market:

> I had 75 good sheep, not to mention the average ones. That's what I brought to my marriage. I knew how to sell a mule to buy a calf, or get two calves for a bull. He had nothing. I knew how to weave him a poncho. He too knew how to sew, with a bit of flannel or cotton we made shirts, trousers, jackets and I would buy his hat. That's what it was like then. But I had to buy clothes because they were ruined by work on the estate. It was a big estate, we only had time on Saturdays and Sundays and we had nothing to weave with. The *jilaqatas* would guard us flicking the end of their whips, the head foreman looking on from the seat of his horse.

But Doña Marta seemed to attribute all her suffering to the fatality of destiny and not to the injustice of the system. In the final instance she blamed her husband's laziness for the impoverishment they suffered on the estate. After he died she returned to her own community where she was to 'know real food'.

> These children lost their father when they were very small. I had to bring them up on my own because he died just after I gave birth to one of my daughters. I was left with nothing — no clothes, nothing to eat. Their father was lazy. I said: 'Well, how am I going to bring them up?' I began to weave from dawn to dusk. Then I returned to my community, where I had to dig the soil with my own hands. But I've produced everything: barley has grown, as big as wheat, I've tasted *chuno*.[8] It's only been since my husband died that I've had real food. That's how I've lived.

Women and men in the resistance

The prospect of subordination on the estates meant that the indigenous communities strongly resisted any such eventuality, not only because it meant excessive and forced work, but also because it brought with it intolerable humiliations to the dignity of community families. The network of *caciques–*

apoderados in the highlands and valleys undertook to fight the take-overs through legal channels, which involved the leaders of the movement in long pilgrimages through the republic's courts and archives. In 1914, Martin Vasquez, leader of Pacajes made a trip to Lima with his lawyers, searching for the colonial title-deeds that would prove that the communal possession of land in the region was legitimate. His successor to the post of *apoderado*, Santos Marka T'ula, made similar trips to a number of archives both within the republic and beyond, looking for justice, which was always elusive, and exclusive to *criollo* society.

> They say that Santos Marka T'ula had to travel a lot. He left his wife and children for months, years. My father says that he didn't know how to go home. The community rewarded Santos Marka T'ula. They would catch up with him on the road and give him food. On other occasions the police took him prisoner with his hands in chains.
> (Testimony of Manuel T'ula, nephew of Santos Marka T'ula, THOA, 1984:22)

During the long absences of Santos Marka T'ula his wife took charge of domestic and agricultural production. She also accompanied him to the city or went to his aid when he was imprisoned. His daughter, Doña Celestina, remembered the situations the family experienced. She also indicates the lack of understanding among the *colonos* on the neighbouring estate concerning the *cacique* struggle, and the humiliations suffered at their hands because of this.

> I had to go with my mother. She would say: 'I'll go to your father' and she would be off to the prison to see him, taking him food. She would take the cloth dolls, *k'usillos* and horses my father made and sell them. The relatives of the *caciques* were generally hated. The people from Ch'uwa even took our land and it stayed in the hands of the estate. They despised me saying: '*Cacique*, little *cacique*' and they would come on to our fields to plough them. When I tried to defend the land we had worked I was pushed about, they even pulled my hair.

Members of the indigenous communities did not always understand or share the situation of wives and daughters of the leaders of the *cacique* struggle. The prolonged absences of husbands and fathers led to their isolation, endless work and suffering. Even today, the family of Santos Marka T'ula and those of other highland *caciques* are among the poorest in their communities.

The Chaco war (1932–35) was also a critical moment for indigenous community women. With the departure of husbands, fathers or sons to the battle front, many community women were forced to take over working the land to support their families. Forced recruitment confronted them with the violence and oppression of the system. Although in many cases the women were resigned to this new situation, the war helped to overcome their isolation and provided the opportunity for more direct political participation. These aspects will be considered later. For the moment, we turn to some testimonies that illustrate the most common problems experienced by the Andean highland communities' women.

Marta Colque, widow of Aruquipa (Punku-uyu and P'axchan Mulinu) continues her story talking about the army's recruitment methods:

> During the Chaco war, many soldiers arrived at our estate of Punku-uyu and they went with the local officials to find the community authorities. They began to recruit, choosing men at random. How did this work? They would say: 'You, you're coming, and you.' They would choose some and not others. My husband didn't go, but two of his brothers went. He was the second brother. Their wives were jealous and would say to him: 'You haven't gone, only my husband went. There were three brothers. The youngest returned from the war, but the eldest still hasn't come back yet.'

In this testimony, the misfortune of recruitment is linked to 'luck'. Recruitment is not perceived as an aggression against the indigenous community but rather a fate that befalls some and not others.

We know, however, that recruitment in the majority of the Andean communities was characterized by organized violence. Landowners managed to persuade the state to assign them quotas, which they filled by choosing the most rebellious tenants or those least willing to submit to the masters' demands. Similarly, the mining companies negotiated an exemption from the requirement of joining the army for most of their workers.[9] Thus, the indigenous communities were the state's basic reserve to fuel the army's campaigns. Forced recruitment in the communities was carried out with a huge show of strength, intimidation and violence. Cresencia Quispe, widow of Huaracacho, of the Uyu-uyu community (Italaque) remembers these events:

> The soldiers had come running to Janq'u Qarqa, to Pikutqala. At the time my husand was taking bread to Muju, and in his absence they burst in. But they only found us women there. Then in the fields they threatened to shoot me, saying: 'You're hiding your husband, make him come out.' I replied: 'My husband isn't here. He went to Muju with the bread. Don't worry he's as able as you, he isn't afraid. As soon as he gets back he'll go and join up.' Then he said that if I didn't speak up he would shoot. He aimed at me and wanted to kill me. I was sitting in the kitchen doorway, I gave a yell and ran away and hid among the broad-bean crops. There was a house further up where I asked for refuge. The owner was there and I said to him: 'Friend, a soldier wants to kill me, he says I have to make my husband come out.' He replied: 'Hide inside the house.' And I hid in his kitchen while he watched the soldiers. He said: 'Better not to come out, they won't be able to shoot you easily.' And so I remained hiding in that dark room. Then he said the soldiers had gone to my mother-in-law's and I could come out. Later she told me that they had also tried to shoot her, saying she was hiding her son. That's what happened in those days.

During the three years of the conflict (1932–35) uncertainty about the fate of community members on the war front was aggravated by the difficulties women faced in obtaining news of their husbands, brothers or sons. In trying to communicate with the Indian recruits in the Chaco they became aware of the social oppression and cultural segregation to which they were condemned by the class society in which they lived. An Aymara woman from the highlands explains.[10]

> We used to say to the *q'aras*: 'Please write this letter to send to Paraguay, with this parcel.' We had to plead with them. But did they want to? We would go bearing potatoes, eggs, cheese but not even that helped. In those days our sons didn't know how to read and we suffered a lot in order to send them letters. All the men were away, the patrols caught all those who went into hiding. That's why the *q'aras* made a lot of fun of us. Now the situation has changed, what will they be saying?

These degrading situations, added to the numerous state taxes levied on the indigenous communities, and the land invasions by estate owners, became unbearable pressures leading to open resistance in many regions. The indigenous communities mobilized at intervals throughout the war and in 1934 there was a massive rebellion, which began in the zone of Pukarani.

Doña Matilde Gutierrez Suxo, originally from what used to be the community of Anat'uyani, witnessed the rebellion of Pukarani in which her father died.

> I don't know why there were so many fights in the period when it was an estate. They say there was an uprising. It was during the Chaco war, when I was very young. The people rebelled a lot, that's why the soldiers came from Pukarani. They even came from Tiwanaku to Anat'uyani. Oh Lord! There were many soldiers, they came on foot, in cars. They went into Pukarani intending to destroy, then they came to our estate, looking for someone called Pereira, who had been killed by the rebels. They came to look for his remains. That's how my father died: the soldiers killed him at the top of Q'atawi hill.

This ex-community member lived through these events as a young girl but she still has traumatic memories of them. Not only did they bring about the loss of her relatives but also her forced migration to the city — the last resort when faced with the prospect of being subjected to servile work on the estate.

> It's hard work on the estate, they made us work like slaves. That's why, when I was very young, we came to the city with my adopted parents. It was too hard, that's why others work on the estate now and all the people that were there left to come to the city.

The rebellion described by Doña Matilde took place at the beginning of 1934 and extended throughout the areas of Jesús de Machaca, Waki, Tiwanaku, Pukarani and Yunka in La Paz. It coincided with an uprising on a similar scale in the Department of Chuquisaca. In Pukarani, community members and tenant farmers seized a number of estates and killed Alberto Ascarrunz, a judge, and Carlos Pereira, a landowner (to whom Doña Matilde referred in her testimony). The government response was drastic: dozens of *caciques* and leaders were imprisoned, and rebels were massacred by the air force and a special force of 800 armed police recruited primarily to put down the rebellion.[11]

Nevertheless, Doña Matilde gives us a passive picture, perhaps because she was young at the time. She remained in hiding during the rebellion and does not remember women participating, except later, in the exodus to the city after the movement was defeated.

The common response of women in the testimonies we analysed seems to be one of resignation to fate. This was possibly because, although women did not fully participate in decisions and actions, their subordination to fathers and husbands meant that they had to suffer the consequences.

For example, when Doña Marta Colque, widow of Aruquipa, talked about her experiences during the Chaco war, she underlined her position as a passive witness to the events, saying: 'I just know how to listen, I don't know how to participate in anything, I don't know how to get involved in men's things.'

Doña Clementina Limachi, daughter of Benedicto Limachi, an important *cacique* of Tiwanaku linked to the network of Indian *apoderados* led by Marka T'ula, is more scathing in her views on women's limited abilities to take part in community resistance.

Q. *When the* caciques *rebelled did women also participate?*
A. No, no they didn't participate, it was only my father who joined in the uprising, the women stayed at home.
Q. *And what did the women do, just watch on indifferently?*
A. They didn't understand, women have little intelligence, that's what they're like.

This dialogue shows what appears to be characteristic of indigenous community women's view of themselves: extreme modesty that borders on self-deprecation.

The question arises at this point as to whether their silent stance conceals a sort of resistance that is neither mentioned nor given social recognition. Given that these practices have not left their mark on history, how can we examine their meaning and forms of expression?

We have looked at a set of testimonies that depict the indigenous community woman as someone who suffers passively the oppression and the problems and defeat of the community struggle. In what circumstances did this passivity transform itself into active and conscious participation? Finally, in which specific contexts did women develop a practice and produce an ideology of resistance?

In answering these questions we will first focus on the daily practices of women in their lives in the communities, as these are the basis of their view of the world and society. We believe this will be a more faithful approach to those situations in which indigenous community women project their activities on to the political sphere, where there is open resistance and where they consciously defend their social and cultural world. Given that these practices are generally immersed in silence, examining women's daily lives will allow us to detect their resistance in apparently trivial and modest events. Though these are given little value they reveal the specificity of women's presence in the history of community resistance.

The daily struggle for life

Family activity in the Andean communities revolves around agricultural and domestic work. Agricultural tasks are generally subject to a sexual division of labour, with men basically in charge of the crops and women and children of the animals. Women also participate in agricultural work, carrying out complementary tasks such as transporting manure, selecting seeds and sowing. Ploughing — with a hand, or animal-drawn plough — is normally done by men. In many regions, women's participation in agriculture is also frequently considered to transcend the economic realm to acquire symbolic meanings. For example, in the ritual of the 'New Land' the Qata *ayllu* (Charazani) during the ceremonial sowing, the man walks in front with the plough in his hand while the woman follows planting the seeds. The meaning is explicit: the reproductive capacity of the earth will be strengthened because it is woman who carries out this task of sowing. (cf. Bastien 1978)

In contrast, domestic activity is almost exclusively women's responsibility. Community women's main tasks include food preparation, child care, the allocation of output between present consumption, food reserves and reproduction needs, making clothes, tending the animals, and many other tasks related to the reproduction of family life and organization of family provisioning.

Unlike urban or proletarian women, however, indigenous community women cannot clearly separate the sphere of production from that of reproduction. Their domestic activities are intimately linked to agricultural production, to preparing the future conditions for production (for instance, selection of seeds for the following agricultural cycle) and to the reproduction of the labour force (food and clothing). In the difficult climatic conditions of the Andean region, a bad harvest could totally disrupt production, except for the accumulation of a reserve of non-perishable or dried products, or the marketing or exchange of small quantities of surplus animal or prepared products, for example, in which women's work is the predominant factor.

Other related activities, whose importance varies according to the season or region, include domestic manufacture — which in the case of textiles is basically a female activity — bartering between different ecological zones, and participation in the market. These complete the range of family activities throughout the annual cycle within a system that aims to minimize the risks and ensure the long-term subsistence and reproduction of the domestic unit.

Jaqichana: 'to be people'

The complementary role of these economic activities finds its expression in the symbol of the couple in the Andean inhabitants' vision of the world and values system. The Aymara verb *jaqichana* means to 'get married' and literally that 'one becomes a person'. In other words, nobody (neither man nor woman) acquires the full status of an adult person until society joins them and their partner together, thus completing the unit of the social person (*jaqi*).

The importance of the Andean couple is also projected into their symbolic universe and wider social structure. There is a clear dualism in the organization of the *ayllus*, with complementary and hierarchical halves (top/bottom, right/left). This seems to derive from the supposed symmetry between the two halves of the human body or the inseparable relation between complementary parts of the countryside (for example, hill and plain), which are associated with the masculine and feminine. In this respect ideology operates as a mechanism to even out inequalities. Counterposed against the (real) hierarchy of the couple, in which the male has social authority, is the ideal of equality, expressed in symbolism and ritual practices that reinforce the complementary man–woman relationship. (cf. Platt, 1976) '*Taqikunas panipuniw akapachanxa*' (In this world everything is a pair) is an Aymara proverb expressing the projection of this image of the couple into the real world.

In Andean societies the social practice and ideological concept concerning the couple also differs from the characteristic role assigned to women by patriarchal societies — that is, considering them closer to 'nature', while men are located in the cultural domain (Ortner, 1974); in some Andean areas, however, important evidence suggests variation in this concept. The couple is regarded as a wholly cultural and social entity and it is unmarried men or women who are closer to the 'wild' space of nature.[12]

Nevertheless, there are many instances and situations in which women tend to have a mediating function between nature and culture, due, perhaps, to the characteristics of the sexual division of labour. Thus, in many Andean communities women's daily activity is on the 'margins' of society. They are at the mercy of thunder and lightning in the highlands used for grazing, and to the wearing effect of water due to washing clothes in the river. In contrast, men's activities are situated in the centre of the community, ploughing fields that have been cultivated and civilized for generations or occupying those spaces in which authority and political power are exercised.

Andean women weavers

Spinning and weaving are two of the basic activities in which women in the communities specialize. They involve a high level of aesthetic and technical skills and knowledge, which are transmitted from mother to daughter and constitute some of the most important expressions of the communities' cultural identity. Each Andean *ayllu* or *marka* has its own textile designs and traditions, jealously guarded by the women in their tireless activity as weavers, in which they combine traditional practices with a degree of individual invention and creativity.

In a detailed study of this subject carried out among the Aymara communities of Isluga (north of Chile), Verónica Cereceda shows that female ideology, and its interpretation relating to the textile designs of saddle bags and sacks, carries a wide range of meanings, sometimes at a very abstract level. At the same time, they reinforce those values associated with the mother–child complementarity, the reproduction of life and 'making food go around'. (Cereceda, 1979)

For this reason, textile work is an important sphere in which to examine women's specific contribution to the production of cultural meanings and particular forms of resistance, the more so when these meanings are constantly attacked and called into question by colonial aggression.

Andean women ritualists

Women's role in Andean society also includes specializing in ritual activities. Besides participating in various agricultural rites as part of the complementary *jaqi* unit or couple, they also perform ritual activities independently, which, in many cases, are linked to their 'mediating' role with groups external to the community. A researcher has described the rites conducted by women in Charazani, where women cast away bad luck by throwing it into the rivers that border the community, and calls these women 'border ritualists', in that they protect the borders of the communal lands. (Bastien, 1978)

There are also *yatiri* women who are called upon to cure a variety of physical and spiritual illnesses by means of signs of the supernatural such as lightning. Unlike the male *yatiri*, who use concepts and expertise that are inaccessible to ordinary men in the community, the female *yatiri* synthesizes and projects in a more coherent way female ritual activity that is linked to daily life. Compared to most men, Andean women retain a range of magical beliefs and experiences; they use and have a deeper understanding of natural medicine and are more aware of the supernatural world. Hence, *yatiri* women provide a prime subject for examining the specific nature of women's perspective in the production of ideological content concerning cultural reproduction and resistance.

Political projection of the daily struggle for life

In the previous section we have shown Andean women enacting a series of social, productive, domestic and ritual activities that, in our judgement, form the basis for women's active and conscious participation in the resistance of indigenous communities. We now turn to some testimonies that illustrate this transition and reveal the characteristics and specificity of women's presence in history.

The defence of life

The value women place on the struggle for life is manifested in numerous daily strategies for the survival and care of the family. When faced with oppression by the dominant society, these efforts to survive can be transformed into the active defence of their people, who are threatened with social and cultural extinction.

The Chaco war — a pre-eminently destructive event — offers a great wealth of evidence on the resistance of indigenous women in the communities. In those difficult times, when the army needed indigenous people as 'cannon fodder' for the firing line, and used brutal methods to force the community members into recruitment, there were moments of uncertainty and internal dissent within the movement linking *caciques apoderados* in the Andean communities. We know, for example, that one section of the movement saw the need to go to war as yet one more 'service' rendered to the *criollo* state, in exchange for which they expected a commitment from the state to respect the communal ownership of their territories. Another section — under the leadership of Santos Marka T'ula — rejected the war, thus expressing their deep distrust of the state, after more than 20 years of frustration in their legal battle to defend their communities. One of Marka T'ula's companions recalled his words:

> He said: 'Let the war end, don't let them exterminate our people'. Because the Spanish, the *q'aras*, came to get us peasants, but they themselves didn't go to fight. He also said that whether we went to the barracks or not, they rounded us up to exterminate us.
> (Testimony of Celestino Vasquez, Ilata community member, THOA, 1984:41)

Marka T'ula's 'pacifism' was very much motivated by the outcry of women — the wives, sisters and mothers of recruits forcibly despatched to the Chaco.

Aymara women's unanimous rejection of the Chaco war was felt not only in the indigenous communities but also on the estates. Because of the oppressive vigilance of the landowners and foremen on the estates, however, individual resistance strategies prevailed, such as hiding relatives and helping them to flee. Isabel Duenas from Janq'u Amaya explains:

> They took several away; they caught Siprico, Almukitu, Tiburcio . . . My mother said: 'There are a lot of soldiers about in the fields, where are you going to hide?' There was a narrow yard, for the pigs that my mother raised. My brother got in there with difficulty, then we covered him with stones to hide him. So they didn't get him.

In the communities, on the other hand, the war was rejected in a more open and collective manner. Women joined together in rituals intended to reverse the destructive effects of the conflict and to protect their loved ones from extermination. As Catalina Kuyabre, a community member from Iskuma relates:

We cried a lot. On Wednesdays and Thursdays we went to the hills and burned incense as an offering, praying for our sons to be returned to us. We prayed to our Father: 'Make them come back, return them to us good Lord, you who are our defender'. We bought incense and lit candles. And so some came back and others were just killed.

In the community of Ilata, the birth place of Santos Marka T'ula, a *yatiri* woman who supported him in his struggle conducted the women's collective, propitiatory rituals for the return of their husbands and sons from the war:

An elderly woman knew how to make offerings with papers, it was she who brought our sons back from the Chaco. In front of the chapel she would jump up and down saying: 'Spirits of our young ones, come, come back, return'. This came true because after that they began to return.

In the regions more closely linked to the *cacique–apoderado* movement, women's participation went further than individual strategies and collective rituals. Around 1935, a large demonstration of indigenous community women got as far as the seat of government — perhaps for the first time in the republic's history — to demand the return of their relatives and an end to the conflict:

So the women came together to protest. They demanded: 'No more war, stop the war, no more extermination of our people.' They say that Santos Marka T'ula came into the city with a hundred and twenty women protesting in this way.

In La Paz, indigenous community women presented a document to the government authorities in which they demanded the return of community members from the Chaco. Their petition also defended communal land rights, arguing that Indian blood spilled in the Chaco, while defending the territory of an abstract 'nation' was more than sufficient guarantee in exchange for state protection of the legitimacy of their possession of the *ayllus* and community lands. For this reason, they also demanded the annulment of all sales and appropriations.

Another protest by the orphan women of the war. 'Gentlemen Mayors and *Caciques* of the Altiplano regions: if you will, read my testaments and the ordinances left by the King, let our sons, husbands and nephews return from the Chaco, where for three years they have been slaughtered. We annul and completely reject all the treaties and protocols of October 15, 1879, February 10, 1887, (. . .) 23, 1894 and other sales of territories and communities by the government of Mariano Melgarejo, and all sales and deceitful transactions. In the name of our husbands, sons and nephews who contributed their lives and spilled their blood in the Chaco. La Paz, May 11 1935.' (Signed by 120 women)[13]

There are two dimensions to women's mobilizations in 1935. On the one hand, it was male leaders who brought the women together and went with them to the city to protest. They also drew up the document in which the language and views of the *caciques*, regarding the legitimacy of *ayllu* rights, is clearly perceptible. On the other hand, however, the protest was organized around women's feelings: their anguish and suffering for their loved ones gave force to the mobilization and rendered the *cacique* petitions more effective.

In this whole process there is an evident link between the masculine and feminine vision, but not in the sense of subordination or the usual manipulative attitude of men toward women. In all the documents prior to the war, the arguments put forward by the *caciques* were based on the title-deeds and the sale of lands that were given to the *ayllus* by the colonial authorities. In other words, in the final instance, the state confirmed and guaranteed the possession of communal land. In the particular document, however, it is the bloodshed in the Chaco that furnishes the most irrevocable guarantee: it provides a glimmer of hope for a *de facto* annulment (without state confirmation) of the usurpation and 'tricks' suffered up till then. This viewpoint, which borders on the utopian, was to provoke a growing radicalization of the organization of *caciques-apoderados* after the war.

These testimonies on community women's participation during the Chaco war all share a common characteristic. The defence and protection of life constitute a conviction and a source of ethical values, bringing women together in a series of cultural and social resistance activities. These activities have the common trait of political participation through concrete ties of family and affection. Through these, women confront and criticize oppression, develop concepts of injustice and put their seal on male politics. Their stance is not governed by momentous ideological or pragmatic definitions and is often concealed in silent actions and codified in ritual language.

Complementarity within the couple, and women's role as mediators

Andean women also participate actively in many instances of collective resistance, complementing male action. Their presence reproduces the internal hierarchy of the man/woman relation, without breaching *jaqi* unity or the social person. Paulina Flores, originally from Qaraqullu (Oruro), recalls one of her grandmother's tales about the rebellion of Zárate Willka (1899):

Q. When there were confrontations with the soldiers did the women help the men or did they just stand by and watch?
A. No, they watched while the men fought the soldiers but then when the men had no strength left and could no longer defend themselves, women helped with stones, sticks and other things, and stood up to the soldiers. That's what my grandmother told me.

Taking a stand when men weaken: perhaps this practice reproduces women's role in the *tinku* or ritual fights, where the confrontation between men and women of two *ayllus* or contending halves is carried out according to precise norms that regulate the balanced but hierarchical participation of both sexes in the ritual battle.

In other situations, the participation of men and women in collective and violent mobilizations reproduces, and at the same time inverts, the complementarity of their tasks in agricultural production. Eduarda Ibáñez Chura, a community member from Pukarani, remembers her grandmother's tale about the civil war in 1899, when men used weaving implements as weapons to fight the soldiers and hid among flocks herded by women and children.

My grandmother told me how in Alonso and Pando's time there were many confrontations over here, over there. They said that Juan Lero had started an uprising. The soldiers came on horseback from that side. The community, men and women alike, rose up as one. The men tied needles and bones from the loom on to sticks and hid among the llamas to attack the soldiers. Men went in front armed with slings, and the women, youths and children collected stones behind. That's how they fought the soldiers, so my grandmother said.

Complementarity between men and women is also evident in adverse circumstances, but here, the aim is to reduce the consequences of defeat. If defeat is imminent, the women will humble themselves and beg the masters' forgiveness, with the intention of at least saving their partners' lives and regrouping the community. Isabel Dueñas tells about the confrontation between a foreman and *colonos* on an estate, which led to a massacre with intervention by the army. In circumstances such as these women play a mediating role between the landowner and the *colonos*.

He beat us; they must have beaten up many men; then he said they escaped by throwing the *liwk'ana* at the foreman. That's how the confrontation began, and then they refused to harvest the potatoes. I suppose the landowner heard about it then and brought in the soldiers from Warina. There were many of them and they were armed, they killed two men who were only armed with sticks and stones, which couldn't do any harm. The others had to escape and the soldiers searched for them everywhere. This went on for one or two weeks. Then the principal *jilaqata*'s wife called the women together saying: 'Come, the landowner is going to forgive us, we shall go and make peace with him.' The women agreed and they went together, just the women went to apologize. Only then did the men come back and were reunited.

These testimonies show that women's participation in situations of violent confrontation conforms to the model of the complementary and hierarchical man/woman unit and reproduces those aspects of daily life in which this model is apparent. Likewise, the event illustrates how women's mediating role is used as a self-defence mechanism when the physical inequality of the Indian combatants is no match for the landowner's show of strength. In this case mediation at least safeguards the physical integrity of the families and prevents the community's dispersion.

The reproduction of culture

There are numerous examples of how women engage in the continuous activity of reproducing their own cultural values and how they are reluctant to accept changes that would mean the loss of their culture. We shall illustrate only one case here, a particularly eloquent example of an *aymara* woman's resistance to the cultural impositions of the oppressing society. By stubbornly conserving her own indigenous clothing she defended her community's identity and their concept of what is appropriate and beautiful. Isabel Dueñas continues:

> In those days we dressed in dark colours decorated with flowers, black *awayos*. When we wore coloured clothes they would call after us: 'Green bottom, red bottom!'. We always wore dark blue. But we had to put on coloured clothes because the landowner scolded us: 'How long are you going to continue going around in black, when will you change?!' The foremen would go from house to house and whip those wearing dark blue skirts and destroy the tubs used for dying. But we carried on wearing our clothes. That landowner is dead now. The foreman would beat us up and say furiously: 'Damn you, don't you have ears?' We would escape to some corners or the river and change our clothes: the dark skirt that we had on underneath we put on top and the other underneath it.

The tenacity of this act of defiance, carried out in silent but meaningful gestures, illustrates that women were very conscious of the symbolism of their clothing and weaving. We consider that this sensitivity is due not only to the fact that women are the producers of the family's clothing but also because in the woven textiles, as in a silent text, they generate a language full of complex meanings that enables them to express the specific identity of the community.

It is for this reason that the landowner's imposition regarding clothing, besides provoking gibes and humiliation, is intolerable to the women and is resisted with a stubbornness that contrasts with the submissive attitude adopted after the defeat of a rebellion. The conflict about their dress affects them in their most intimate sphere: it threatens their concept and ordering of the world, their valuation of behaviour and social norms, in sum: their contribution through a language of their own to the civilizing function of culture.

Rituals

As we have seen in other sections, Andean women actively participate in various aspects of the community's ritual life, whether in family or communal rites. Women have a prominent role in those agrarian rites aimed at warding-off evils, such as drought or frost, or those to dispel 'bad luck', as in the case of Charazani.

One dimension of these rituals relates to the theme of cultural reproduction referred to in the previous section. Doña Catalina Kuyabre, from Escoma, attributes the current agricultural crisis affecting the Andean communities to the relaxation of ritual customs and the deterioration of the traditional functions of the communal authorities.

> Offerings must always be made to the earth. The authorities no longer remember about this. Offerings have to be made to the hills, to Q'apa, Jik'i, Ch'illuni, homage has to be paid to all those places. Nowadays they don't carry out these ceremonies, that's why these places are crying out with hunger. That's why we don't know what's happening. Not even the rain is like it used to be, or the harvest. Today, having authority means carrying two saddle-bags, wearing a beautiful coloured poncho and a scarf around the shoulder and a new *ch'ullu* and hat on top and strutting about loftily, holding the staff of authority and with a whip crossed over the chest. Before the Escoma episode, 24 communities would meet up: 12 from Jilat'a and 12 from Machasku; the women would drink a toast sitting on the ground and we would get a hundred *taris* together. Now all this has been lost. Now they just drink and the authorities behave like young people in love.

Thus, the decline of ancestral customs is seen as degrading the meaning of social life and threatening the community's capacity to regulate its relation with nature, on which it depends for nourishment.

Another instance of female ritual practice relates to the subject of mediation. In the community of Ilata, a *yatiri* woman performed ceremonies aimed at purifying the community documents and title-deeds that Santos Marka T'ula carried with him on his pilgrimages through the country's courts.

> It was an old woman who officiated at the offerings to the documents. They came to make the offerings because otherwise illness might have befallen them. They arrived at our house from all the communities: Ilata, Aransaya and Urinsaya, Champi, Junt'u and Ch'uwa bringing sheep. A lot of llama and sheep's bones were collected and offered up at the Willkani lagoon. In those days it was a place to make offerings, a big lagoon with green water, now it's used for sowing. The communities arrived with a pair of cows for the sacrifice. Papers were piled up and the offering was burnt. After the sacrifice, my father disappeared for years. I was just a young girl at the time. (Testimony of Celestina Warku, daughter of Santos Marka T'ula, THOA, 1984: 30–31)

This testimony suggests that the legal struggle taken up by the *cacique-apoderados* brought with it the risk of contamination from the adverse world of the dominant society. Ceremonial offerings were made to the documents and title-deeds that the *caciques* handled in order to ward off the potential malignancy of their links with the *criollo* world; at the same time, the rites aimed to protect community power in its path through the courts and the state.

The relation between men and women is very clear here. While in the city, the man runs innumerable physical and moral risks and hovers dangerously on the brink of losing his cultural identity, the woman (the *yatiri*) officiates as the ritual mediator to exorcize adverse forces, re-establishing the *caciques'* link with the sacred and inalienable places of their ancestors.

Finally, there is a third dimension to the rituals of Andean women: the *yatiri*, or ritual specialist, uses her skills to develop the production and reproduction of an ideology of resistance, rooted in the long memory — mythical memory, it could be called — which gives form and meaning to her presence in history.

We shall illustrate this dimension as well as the other aspects analysed up to this point with the testimony of a *yatiri*, thus culminating our presentation with a voice in which passive resistance and silence have already given way to the active development of what I. Silverblatt called a 'female culture of resistance'. (Quoted in Larson: 1983)

An Andean *yatiri*: Doña Matilde Colque from Jach'a Qullu

'I didn't know how to see with coca.'

I've known how to read in coca for about four years but before that I was seriously ill after giving birth. In vain the doctors examined me but they couldn't cure me. I sweated heavily, my blood pressure went up and I became unconscious.

Then my brother came over and my husband said to him: 'Your sister is giving herself up to attacks.'

He replied: 'Why should my sister give herself up to attacks? That can't be it, it must be something the lightning did to her.' When I was very young, about two years old, lightning struck our house once at midday. It threw me from one side to the other, as if I were a rag-doll and made all three of us lose consciousness — my brother, my mother and me. We were in the kitchen when it happened. A long time later my father and the neighbours came in and they took us into another room. They say you shouldn't look at people in this state because you can die from it; that's how my mother-in-law died. Later, I was on my feet again, just like that. My brother knows how to see with coca; my mother always knew how to read with coca and my brother as well. That's why they were struck by lightning. He wanted me to learn about these things but I didn't want to at first, because they say that's why my mother died. She wasn't cured properly, her stomach was swollen as if with pregnancy. Remembering this, I didn't want to see with coca, only my brother knew. He didn't always tell the truth about how he came to know.

'I've always wanted to cure, ever since I was a young girl.'

A woman who lived over yonder came and asked me: 'Can you read in coca?'
'Yes, I can see', I replied.
I was being cured at that time.
'Look at it then', she said. She brought a little bit of yellowish coca and some

money. She wanted to know about a robbery.

I said to her: 'It's the little one who hid the money.' Inside me, I begged God that this was true and it really had been him. The little boy had hidden one thousand one hundred pesos and they reappeared. So then I gave thanks: 'Lord, how was I able to . . .' They punished him severely and my name was mentioned: 'Why did you hide grandmother's money?'

Afterwards the woman told other people that I could see with coca. I've cured many people, it must be over a hundred. One was a baby who was unconscious, he was dying. '*Señora*, do you know how to cure attacks?'

'Yes I know', I replied. Later, holding some earth and a bell I called out: 'Come now, come spirit!' I took a spoonful of earth and made him swallow it. He was cured of the attacks after that. I still know how to do all this. Since I was a young girl I've always wanted to cure. People sometimes ask me: 'Where will there be deaths?'

'Someone could die in Velasco or in Jach'ini.' What I say comes true, what I think happens. For example, they asked me if Banzer was going to die. I said: 'Banzer is going to die.' And the same with Jota. I said that he was going to die later, when he was far away and that is what happened.[14] Once I was really astonished, I saw a lot of people with candles and chickens. It was happening somewhere like Macchu Picchu. From the hill I called: 'Come!' That's how I called them all. And suddenly the sun came out . . .

'Everything my grandmother said is coming true.'

Our grandparents lived in straw huts, the way they used to live before. There were no cars or airplanes then, they had to go by donkey. It took us three days to get to Llallagua and back. The money was pure white silver then, now it's just paper. My grandmother told us these things, she lived for many years. When she was still alive I used to ask her about things. She felt everyone was her family. My brother used to say to her: 'Huh, for you the cat and dog are your family, you should marry them!' That's why she used to say: 'Oh, the children of today, the things they say! But a time of much suffering will come, even if you don't believe it, a time for crying will come. But the Indian will always rise up. There is a law in Chile made by a Mapuche . . .'

I didn't really understand. My grandmother spoke about this Mapuche, a legitimate Indian: 'Some time from now you'll know, what he says will be written on a hundredweight stone and this knowledge will be brought by a man in rags. This law cannot be laid down by the *q'aras*, only by the Indian.'

That's the way my grandmother told it, that's how the elders spoke. Then she said to me: 'Neither you nor I will see what is to come, it will be your children who see it, who live through it.' That's what she said and everything is happening, just as she said it would. Everything my grandmother spoke of is coming true, nothing has been left out.

When I was a child my father said: 'It doesn't want to rain daughter, let's go up to the hill.' At midnight he took us and about ten children to the hill to make an offering with incense; we knew what to ask: 'Father give us a soaking, we are asking you for a soaking.' And that was it! Clouds began to gather. Offering incense makes it rain. Do you think the *q'aras* can make it rain? I don't think so. They used to make many sacrifices before, now nothing. When we were sowing potatoes we also used to make offerings with incense and *q'owa*. Now it doesn't work: it doesn't produce potatoes or anything else. In the old times it was different, it was better.

'The Spaniards were sent from far away by the devil himself and they murdered the Incas.'

After, when the landowners came, nothing was the same anymore. When I was a girl we didn't know any *q'aras*, we hadn't seen that type of clothing. I wore clothes made from sheep's wool, a little skirt and *ojot'itas*, that's all. Then a teacher arrived, I thought he must be a *q'ara* who was against us. I said to my father: 'Dad, a *q'ara* is coming, he's going to kill us!' and I ran off screaming.

'No', he said, 'it must be the one who buys our sheep.' My father used to tell us something else about those people: 'These *q'aras* are Spaniards, they don't come from this land. They were sent from far away by the devil himself and they murdered the Incas.'

I kept on asking him questions: 'Why have they given names to all of us? And why did you let them?'

'I've already told you, the *q'aras* are the Spaniards,' he said. I didn't understand very well then. It was only later that the landowners began to expand, over by La Paz, by Sucre, there were many of them. You should have seen how they treated our people! They were whipped with a knotted lash, they were hit until they finished roasting the grain, and pregnant women were thrown out when they couldn't work: 'Damn you, that's it *ponguito*.' The landowners only knew how to shout.

I haven't known many landowners, it was my father who used to tell me about them. He said that to this day the Spaniards keep coming and killing, and that when they arrived they finished off all the men. Before then there were no Incas with beards. According to my father, the Incas considered bearded people to be their enemies, they cursed them and wouldn't even speak to them.

'So how come we don't have beards?' I asked.

He told me that women don't have beards and our people don't have facial hair.

Thinking about this I realized that — it must be true that women can rise up. It must be true — because if it hadn't been for the women resisting in the past, our children would only have been sons of Spaniards. I came to realize this.

'Men and women must always rise up together to accomplish anything.'[15]

When a woman gets married she is told by her mother-in-law what mine said to me:

'Now that you are going to marry my son you have to knit pretty designs and weave ponchos, belts, bands, different kinds of bags, slings, sacks. The man gives the woman clothing if she weaves well . . . when the man runs out of sacks, the woman has to make more. Between themselves man and woman have to help each other. But the woman works more: she has to cook the food, wash the clothes, carry the babies, graze the sheep, weave ponchos, sacks, *lliqllas* for the babies, women must do all this. Perhaps you don't work very hard, but here in the countryside men have to take the cows out, take all sorts of things into town, sow potatoes and grains . . . phew! A woman has to do a bit of everything. She has to help her man a lot if she loves him. Do you think he can manage on his own? If we cut a wing off a bird, will it be able to fly? With only one wing it can't. Man–woman are always willing to do anything, but the woman does more.'

'It would be good if women joined together, there would be enough of us then.'

Some men's women certainly know how to speak out. One of them said: 'Go there, find out what that law is about, where those men are going, let me know.'
    'So come with me.'
    My husband went to the meeting where they spoke of many things. What could they have been talking about? But my husband didn't tell me everything they had said, just a few things and when I asked him what happened, he said: 'This and that.'
    But I knew they had said a lot more. So I followed him to hear what they were talking about and find out everything. Some men go on their own and then they tell us very little. I want to know a lot more. But if they don't want me to speak, I say: 'If a woman knows, then she can express her opinion and discuss with the rest. We women could learn to speak together, just among ourselves and it would be good, there would be enough of us then, I and other women could participate better with women that have a mind like yours. If there were ten with a good brain we could do a lot: many women could meet together with everything that we are told and what we learn.'

'It was true that there are documents about the Indians.'

Even after getting married the landowners still treated us in the same way, like all the others, even though we were a couple. They wanted to control us and made us suffer in every way. There was one time when they carried out a census of the cattle and all our belongings. So my husband, who has a head on his shoulders, went to find out more. I sent him off at night, with the toasted grain I had just made. Two of them went to find the way and they realized that it was true, there were documents about the Indians, where it says that we don't have to pay for land or for anything. These documents were drawn up by Titiriku and Marasa.[16] My husband brought them back and went to tell the community. By talking to this one and that one a co-operative was formed, but I really suffered for it afterwards. There was someone called Meliton Gallardo, who they say was a big *apoderado*, he was like a brother. He also went and returned a month later, confirming that it was true, we didn't have to pay anything.

'They took my husband away with his hands tied.'

There were two men. Anacleto Nina and Cristobal Nina from Kurawara de Karangas. They arrived here and the police arrested them. Then a lot of police came to Wanuni, oh Lord! They came with their guns at the ready saying: 'Open the door, now! Don't close it!'

'What do you want', I asked.

'Now you are all going to rot in jail, savage Indians!'

I kept quiet, my baby was very small. But you should have seen how they treated my husband! They took him away with his hands tied behind his back. So I followed them to Wanuni, I left about midnight and got there at half-past nine. I went to the court to ask after my husband: 'What has my husband done for you to lock him up like this?' I asked.

'Well hell, since you are traipsing about at all hours, you must know what your husband has been up to. Hand over those papers right now!' they said.

'I'm not giving you anything!'

'Then you are going to die too.'

'If my husband is going to die, I must die first.'

'Who taught you that?'

'Nobody taught me, it came from my heart, that's all.'

'Well, if that's what you think then you can both die together.'

'You are a *q'ara* and you are insulting a poor woman.'

Then he said: 'Damn, this insolent woman!'

And they took me straight off to jail. I was kept locked up in there for three months because I argued with them.

'There were many of us walking that road.'

It's folly, and has been right from the outset. There were many of us walking that road: many authorities, mayors, even a school governor, many. Together with those from the valley, from Espiritu and the communities north of Potosi, there were a lot of us. These authorities had come to the prison to enquire and they, too, were locked up. They had held a meeting at night and a snooper followed them . . . Then the soldiers arrived and they had to hide. Many of us were prepared to die, there are always about five killed. Of all those in the same situation, some are still alive and we continue forward. The rich did all this to us, saying: 'This has always been the law, this is the law!' But a time will come when at least one of my bones will appear. They can kill us: I shall die for being an Indian, I shall die because that's what the law says. But a time will come when they will search for my bones, they will have to search forever. The things I know! I'll need a couple more meetings to tell you everything.

'They should be burnt, they're not Christians!'

One of them had a horrible death, he was shot with three bullets. His son arrived on the day we were being taken off to jail. We continued the struggle

and they kept pursuing us with no let-up, no one cared about us. Then I decided
to learn about the gospel, thinking I might find my salvation there. My husband
only knows how to plead with the thunder, and so I decided to go on my own.

'Why are you going to join the evangelical church?' he asked me.

'Because you drink too much and besides, they are still after us, so I'm going
to join.' And that's how I went. But they said to me:

'Damn it, they're *Chullpas*, they're *Tawantinsuyas*, they should be burnt.
How can they be Christians, they're *Chullpas*, people of darkness,[17] they're
Tawantinsuyos, *Kullasuyas*, *Antisuyas*, *Chinchasuyas*', they insulted me like this.
They even took our grazing land. For me there is no justice anywhere now.

'It's in the hills that God hears us best.'

I left the evangelicals because of what they said to me. Even the brothers called
me *Kullasuyu*, *Antisuyu*, *Kuntisuyo* . . . they just went about talking. They
rejected me but God hasn't abandoned me. Again I went to make an offering
with incense at night, pleading: 'God our Father, listen to me Father.'

Now I go to the hills. For me, He is my whole health. I'm still alive for the
moment, although my house has been destroyed, my sheep slaughtered. I've
suffered like this because I'm an Indian. But I don't suffer for myself alone, I
suffer for all of us. I have many brothers and sisters and I suffer for them, not
just myself. What do they know about the things I do here? They just manage,
there are so many lies they can't do anything else. But I say God doesn't lie, so I
will take the same path he took.

But I speak of the Incas, just about the Indians. Of course God is always God
even if I don't know him. Nobody knows him, not the priest nor anyone else.
But God is hearing us now, if we speak to Him He hears. But it's in the hills that
God hears us best. I plead for the sick, for those who are seriously ill, I plead for
them and make sacrifices. I cast *q'owa* to the four corners[18] with a sling, and
people get better. God helps me and is with me when I make these offerings and
pray for the people to get better. I make sacrifices with the image of the sun and
with all that's necessary and then the people just get well.

'Those places belonged to the people of darkness.'

I've been over to Sucre where there were *Chullpas*, there were little houses, clay
pots and jars . . . Then I said to my sister Ricarda: 'I'm going to sit on that bare
headland.'

'Don't let's go there sister, there are lots of snakes, don't sit there', she said.

Then I said: 'I'm always going to come to this place at dusk', and I went back
there. There were no snakes or anything like that so I just sat there.

'Oh sister, don't sit there, it's true that the snakes can bite you, that's where
they sleep', she said to me.

But I hadn't seen snakes or anything else. So I said: 'Here lies the Inca
achachila and the Inca *awilita*, the burial site of *achachila* and *awilita*, I will pray
for them.'

Although she didn't want to, my sister also sat down and started to watch.
'What are you looking at sister?'
'The snakes are coming.'
The snakes aren't going to come! Besides, what could they do to me? Later I asked my neighbours about what my sister Ricarda had said.
'Yes, that's right, it's true there are many snakes there.'
'Why? Where do they come from then?'
'They say they come from the *Chullpas* . . .'
Those places belonged to the people of darkness. There are many around Sucre. There are figures engraved upon the rocks of the hills, there's a bell of gold, a woman weaving on one of the hills. I always have to go and see them, no matter what. They say that on the rocks you can see the woman weaving *salt'as* on the loom. There are many things to see there but it's so far away.

'Why do some *ayllus* fight with one another?'

During Carnival they had the *tinku*, they still have them now. On Carnival Sunday, phew! They put on hats, it was the Spaniards who brought the hats but now it's the Indian who wears them. And now Indians from the same group fight among themselves and trample on each other wearing these hats, saying: 'I'm *tatala* damn it, I'm *tatala*. *Waj, waj, Sikuya, Chullpa* . . .'[19] That's how they fight, really viciously, and women too: 'Boy, come here — just come over here . . .'
The women get right into the fight, and hit each other alongside the men. Phew! *Tinku* fighting is really vicious. It has always been like this, it's how they've always fought. It was even worse before, some even killed each other. But I say:
'Are we in the time of *Atawallpa*? Why is it that in the countryside some *ayllus* kick each other about? None of our *ayllus* are *Atawallpa* or anything like it.' That's what I say.

'The Inca has always seen with coca.'

And the Incas, were they like this? In the museum I've seen that the Incas had golden slings and staffs of gold. Today there still are Incas, they are the *warayoq* and also the *aysiri*. Why can't the *q'aras* be *aysiris*? It's always the Inca who sees with coca and who *akullika*, and in this way he makes people healthy again. That's why with our medicine everyone is cured and healthy here. Why can't the *q'aras* learn these things? Because here everything belongs to us. Are they the owners? Look, they can come to my house and I can go away and leave all my things; and then I can suddenly return and find that they have done away with everything. They must give the things back to me then. To the Indian, the Spaniard is only a tenant, as it were. And we have to hit him, complain about him and tell him to leave, because we are the owners and we are going to return.

'Many of our grandparents died with Alonso and Pando.'

There was a man called Lero, Juan Lero. They said he was much sought after. His house was up there. Many books were buried there in heaps and we went to dig them up. We found a lot of books with stained writing. What could they be? They were sewn with leather. I was only little then.

My father spoke about the books: 'That's why Alonso and Pando fought.'

My dad was a boy in those days. Oh Lord! Many of our grandparents died with Alonso and Pando and they were buried there.

'Why are so many souls buried there?' I asked.

Then my father said: 'Those are the ones who got killed because of Alonso and Pando.' That's why they were buried there.

'The *caciques* were in charge of the books of grievances.'

The authorities were the Mayors, the *cacique*, the *mallku*. In those times it was the *caciques* who took the letters. They say that before then they had to do a *postillonaje* to La Paz. There was land to be had there and this *postillonaje* was a way of getting the land. The ones who complied with this service were rewarded with land, and those who didn't got nothing. That's how my brother got his land when I was a young girl. He had to go about in this stupid way. They had to be taken from one post to another. The *caciques*, *mallkus*, mayors, *jilaqatas* and others took the letters but the *caciques* were in charge. The *caciques* were also in charge of the title-deeds. All this traipsing around with deeds in the hope that we Indians saw justice done. The *caciques* were in charge of the books of grievances.[20] That's what my father told me.

'I'm a legitimate Indian, owner of the land.'

It was just my father who looked after me in those days, he was on his own without my mother. During the war of the Chaco, they took him away.

'Where is your father, where is he?' they asked me.

'My father is dead', I replied.

'Damn you, you bloody *imilla*. You say your father is dead but he's here!' Saying this, the soldiers went into the house and took him away. I began to cry loudly.

They used to round them up like llamas and take them away at gunpoint. Many people died like that. It was Toribio Miranda who put a stop to all this, saying: 'I'm an Indian, Indians shouldn't go to the Chaco or anywhere else.' So Toribio Miranda presented papers to the court. He was called a *cacique*. The *caciques* who went around before were Toribio Miranda, Santos Marka T'ula and Chuquimisillu; they all died. Carlos Kunturi also died. Between them they had to give testimony many times.

'Are you going to obey the law?'

'No sir, I'm not going to obey that law because I'm a legitimate Indian, the owner of this land.'

'Landowner, like hell! you're a communist . . .'

They put the evidence down on paper, swearing by God and making a cross with a rod. It was an Inca rod, just as *tata* Santo Domingo was an Inca. For three days they testified.

'As they become educated the young men become alienated.'

All the *caciques* also went to see about schools. We got a private school. There were no state schools then; now there are, but in those days we had to pay. I used to ask my father about this:

'Dad, let me go to school.'

'No, *imilla* if I let you go, you won't know how to weave or knit, you'll just be a nuisance, writing letters to men.' So I didn't go to school. To this day when I think about my father I say: 'If only he'd let me go to school . . .' I realize that's why only boys learn and girls don't. But what also happens is that as they advance in their studies, the young men become alienated and enter the world of the *q'aras*. Boys from my village have studied and become doctors, lawyers, teachers. Now they don't understand us any longer. It's as if they were calling us 'Indian! Indian!' That doesn't seem right to me. The *q'aras* are causing us to lose what is truly ours: people don't even want to work the land now. But the Indian was put here to work the earth, the Indian is owner of the earth. People before knew a lot more, I know less. All that knowledge is coming to an end now, the *q'aras* want it all to disappear. What can we do? They are powerful. Our people who study just want to become like them. The *q'aras* are leading us astray, I don't understand this. I think a lot about it and I plead with our *Achachilas*: what are we going to do? What's to become of us? I'm close to death now but I carry on working quietly and following my destiny as an Indian.

'I've become another from so much wandering.'

I've always known the way, I've kept going despite all the suffering, and right now I'm going to continue along my way. I've become another from so much wandering. God watches over me while I'm on my way. The star of the Inca and the house of the Inca are protecting me while I walk, and I know I shall die walking. But I shan't die because my soul will continue living when it leaves my body.

Conclusions

We have spoken of a female silence in history. A researcher of *aymara–quichwa* toponyms and anthroponyms attributes this silence to the social position of Andean women, which dates from pre-hispanic times.

> The use of the surname Sisa reflects back to the real status of the Aymara–Quechua woman in the pre-colonial period. Only men were given the 'name of the *ayllu*' and later on the indigenous surname. The names of Aymara animals only express masculine qualities. There is thus a female 'silence', a

lack of female expression in the Aymara *ayllu*. Woman is silent as Pacha Mama is silent. (Aguiló, 1983)

We consider Aguiló's statement to be derogatory. We still know too little about the kinship and the inheritance systems in the pre-colonial Andes to be certain that there even was an *'ayllu* name' transmitted from one generation to another. In the Pacajes region it has been shown that the inheritance system differed considerably from the patrilineal succession of surnames imposed by the Spanish. (Rivera, 1985; Platt, 1976) Moreover, the history of anti-colonial resistance makes several facts evident. Firstly, colonial oppression condemned the whole of Andean society to a state of degradation and 'collective anonymity' (Bouysse-Cassagne, 1976) by dismantling internal social hierarchies to make way for the common condition of Indian or colonized peoples. In this light the 'silence' of Andean women cannot be considered a product of an unchanging structural condition. We should rather examine its significance within the concrete historical conditions of colonial oppression.

Furthermore, we know that many of the Andean rebellions produced very little explicit 'discourse'; that is to say, their collective expression and attitudes — often filled with symbolic meaning — are more eloquent than any public declaration or manifestos could ever be, impoverished as these always are by translation into a language and code of thinking that are foreign. This lack of cultural communication, characteristic of colonial oppression, permits us to place the silence–word relation in a different perspective. Communication was possible, for example, when the oppressed adopted the way of life and thinking — and ultimately also the word — of the oppressor. In these conditions, is stubborn silence not a form of resistance?

In the light of these reflections we would suggest that the 'silence' of Andean women in the context of inter-cultural relations, is a deliberate form of anonymity, which contrasts with their verbal eloquence within the *ayllu* or family. This anonymity complements the male activity of relating to the *q'ara* world by means of the word (files, documents, petitions) which places the man in a vulnerable and intermediate space. Female silence could therefore be said to constitute a cultural self-defence mechanism: to protect the man from the dangers of his links with the *q'ara* world and to reproduce the cultural and moral values of their own origins.

The resistance of indigenous community women is linked to their daily life. Although in critical moments of the community struggle women actively participated alongside men, even being incorporated into the Indian armies, this must be seen as an extension of their constant and daily activity of cultural resistance. For this reason, when women's participation becomes visible it is as a complement to their male partners, a projection of the activities and perceptions of their private life into the public sphere (see Jelin, 1984: 13–14). This also reinforces the Andean notion of male–female complementarity, which forms an integral part of their world vision.

The ideology of the indigenous community woman develops from her concrete situation: her family ties and immediate social relations, her productive and reproductive activities. Specifically female values stand out in this ideology: the defence of life, the conservation and equal distribution of the means of subsistence, and a notion of 'justice' stemming from the cyclical model of nature. These values modify and help shape the specific demands of the male, which are based on the legitimacy of autochthonous power and the memory of colonial and pre-hispanic state relations. This explains the radicalism that women occasionally were able to bring to bear on the community resistance struggle, investing it with moral and emotional imperatives, which allowed no conciliation whatsoever.

The Andean woman is the privileged repository of cultural resistance. In her weaving activities as well as in her specialized ritualistic role, the woman actively produces symbols and interpretations that form an important part of the collective identity of the Andean communities. Textile work is also the space where the Andean woman exercises, and is best able to transmit her aesthetic, social and philosophical concepts, which are a source of enrichment and a contribution to the development and dynamism of Andean culture.

Likewise, rituals express an ideological activity that synthesizes the collective memory and reproduces the mythical memory of the indigenous communities. The *yatiri* woman is one of the most faithful and creative bearers of the myth as a category of historical thought. She shares with other community women the gift of a great narrative ability and a wide repertory of oral traditions.

Finally, many questions remain about the contemporary historical fate of these features of community women's history and memory from the pre-1952 revolution period. Changes that have occurred since then lead us to think that many of the conditions in which these forms of women's participation were practised have completely disappeared. Today, women in the Andean communities are organized in unions, they demand autonomous and direct participation in the political life, in organizations representing workers, and they attach less importance to traditionally female roles and activities. How is this conflict formulated and resolved by organizations such as the Bartolina Sisa Federation, which aims to defend the specific rights of rural women as well as the symbols of traditional cultural identity? How are the memory and ideology of indigenous community women affected by the universalization of market relations, the widespread imposition of Spanish and the migration to the cities? What sort of inter-generational problems are caused by such brusque changes, and how do these affect the possibility of self-assertion and the historical continuity of the Andean communities?

Questions such as these lie beyond the chronological framework of my study. But I would like to testify that it is these present dilemmas that have constantly directed this explanation into the past of the indigenous community struggle.

Compiler's epilogue

'Writing history means citing stories' (Walter Benjamin)

Writing the history of 'peoples without a history', on the basis of oral tradition, is something that has less to do with science than with experience. It is also subversive with respect to 'power'. This is because, in the case of historiography, it explodes the positivist taboo according to which data from the past serve only to fill the fiction of an empty and homogeneous time span, and in its most naive version, to give substance to the lineality of a history, which confirms people's rationalist and theologically-based presumptions. According to these presumptions, history is either the history of the class struggle or the history of salvation, where pain, failure, exclusion, defeat and silence are robbed of their uniqueness and singularity, and are dissolved or used to unite the social and sacred epic in an ideal continuity, in a 'meaningfulness' that leads inexorably, to the Classless Society or to the Kingdom of Heaven (the two faces of Janus), in other words the rectilinear concept of time.

History on the basis of oral tradition, on the other hand, breaks with the ideology of progression, of continuity; of the idea of the historical drama or, if preferred, of the tragi-comedy of the Absolute Spirit. It is inspired, rather, by an old Andean tradition, specifically female, which conceives of history as a woven cloth; it consists in recognizing the warp and weft, the texture, the forms of relationships, in knowing the back from the front, the value and significance of the detailed pattern, and so on. In other words, we are trying to read in the book of life that which has never been recorded in written form; we are attempting to capture the image brought to mind and revealed in the moment of the interview before it is lost again to silence.

Indian materialism does not aspire to a homogeneous and continuous exposition of history: it does not believe in lineality, but rather seeks to bring the past up to date in images, in an iconic condensation where past and present become a coherent whole. The past persists in the collective unconscious as in a dream (for the defeated, more often as a nightmare). The writing of history, then, opens the dream to the vigilance of the present, giving verbal expression to that still unconscious knowledge sleeping in the twilight of exclusion and aphasia. Remembering and awakening are thus one and the same thing. 'My eyes were opened' is a leitmotif accompanying the ceremony where mythology is dissolved in the space of a history that now begins to become one's own. Like the dawn, identity emerges mysteriously from the night of the past through memory, by means of images. It is precisely here, I believe, where lies the strongest epistemological rupture with the discourse of bourgeois and proletarian historiography: not a progression but the present, not concepts but images, not discourse but narration, not science but experience. Indian materialism challenges the epic elements of history, since the memory of the defeated, which is the memory of the body trampled by 'Logos', must first come to terms with unredeemed pain, humiliation, scorn, the surge of all suffering buried in the soul, or the blows of life, as Vallejo would have said.

Hence this memory can be nothing other than reminiscence about what is near, of the detail: daily life.

Woman, and most of all indigenous woman, is the subject who articulates all that is infra-political:[21] the dominion of the reproduction of life, defence of LIFE, the axis of change towards a new civilization in 'peripheral societies'. Without this articulation no change worthy to be called civilization will occur, because the struggle for production (in the sense of enlightening progressivism and of entropic expenditure of energy), is already lost to us, and its final logic — the threat of total annihilation — cannot therefore be achieved.

The indigenous/*katarista* movement has to submerge itself in the still-glowing embers of its own past, in order to find a common language and a passionate common feeling, to be able to overcome the present factionalism and consolidate an alternative proposal for civilization. In this return to imbibe from their own sources, the rediscovery of women is decisive. Woman is the clearest paradigm of oppression. For this reason the indigenous struggle and that of women are complementary; in fact, they are one and the same struggle. Following the long feminist search, which in its most ultra-vanguard groups has ended by proposing the doubtful chimera of the Land of the Amazons — radical lesbianism — it is healthy to return to the Aymara understanding of the couple, of complementarity: *Taqikunas, panipuniw akapachanxa* — in this world everything is a pair. This concept lies beyond Western dualism and to think of the Andean way as a synthesis would be a benefit, a step ahead for all humanity. It seems to me that, furthermore, this could be the only cure against the self-confidence of Western history. If there is a totality, this can be concealed only in the fragment, the dual fragment that is humankind:[22] man and woman. Only in this manner can there be justice since humankind is neither the son of God, nor below the angels, nor the measure of everything, but simply another link in the incommensurable discourse of nature, a blink between the flowers and the stars.

It is for this reason also, that this work constitutes a montage: the reunion and joining of that which has been dispersed into a new unity, always provisional, and respectful of heterogeneity. The quotations and the fragments are thus threads which, little by little, we collectively weave into the seamless fabric of a new sense of existence on earth.

Notes

1. See glossary (p. xii) for the translation of *ayllu* and other Quechua and Aymara words. The *criollos* were usually of Spanish origin. The first *criollos* began to settle in Bolivia during the colonial period, when they administered the colonial state. (Translators)

2. The transcription and translation of Aymara into Spanish was carried out by members of the Workshop. Primo Nina and Casandra Torrico collaborated in the translation and transcript of Q'ishwa (Quechua) into Spanish. For technical reasons the Aymara and Q'ishwa text has not been included in the Spanish or the present edition.

3. The *encomenderos* were those who held land granted as a concession in colonial times and these were in a powerful position *vis-à-vis* the local indigenous community. The land grant also gave them rights over the local Indian population, who had to provide free labour services or to pay taxes to the landowner. The right to labour services continued in the post-colonial period and the estate population was regarded as the property of the landowner, an integral part of the estate for purposes of sale, although sales were rare. (The *encomendero* for his part was supposed to look after the interests of the Indians in his territory and convert them to Christianity.) Extension of the boundaries of an estate (legally or otherwise) therefore increased the landowner's command over labour as well as lands. In practice, there was little difference between landowners whose holdings derived from a colonial concession or grant and others — they all drew forcibly on Indian labour. (Translators)

4. *Caciques–apoderados.* *Cacique* is the Indian name for the local Indian chief. Those who were empowered to act as proxy for the community in legal initiatives relating to the community's traditional land rights were therefore referred to as *cacique–apoderados.* (Translators)

5. *Latifundismo* refers to the private ownership of *latifundia*, large landed estates, common in South America. (Translators)

6. *Colono*: a type of tenant farmer tied to the estate in a work–rent relationship, whereby the *colonos* and their family had to provide labour services on the estate owner's land and house in exchange for the precarious tenure of a plot of land.

7. P'ajchan Molino was in effect one of the most extensive estates in the province of Omasuyos, covering more than 2,000 hectares.

8. *Chuno* are dehydrated potatoes produced by soaking potatoes for several days in very cold water and then drying them in the sun. (Translators)

9. Information provided by Carola Echalar from her study 'Formation of the mining work force in La Paz, 1900–1952', doctoral thesis in preparation, Columbia University.

10. This testimony was taken at the First Meeting of Elderly Peasant Women, sponsored by the Bartolina Sisa National Federation of Peasant Women, La Paz, 26–27 May 1984. We were unable to identify the name of the woman from the tape-recording.

11. Data given to the Workshop by René Arze, from his unpublished work: 'War and Social Conflict'.

12. Verbal report to the Workshop on data collected in north of Potosi by Olivia Harris.

13. Documents collected in a leaflet entitled, 'Of interest to the Indians', Imprenta Libertad, THOA Archive.

14. This refers to the ex-president Juan José Torres, who was assassinated in Buenos Aires while living in exile (1976).

15. The original text refers to *hombre–mujer*, meaning man–woman, which emphasizes the notion of unity or an entity comprising complementary parts. (Translators).

16. This refers to Gregorio Titiriku and Feliciano Marasa, *caciques–apoderados* who participated in the legal struggle led by Santos Marka T'ula.

17. Members of the Andean communities also tend to use the term *chullpa* (see glossary) to refer to an original mythical time in which darkness reigned. In this testimony *chullpa* time and *inka* time are frequently mixed and refer to the sacred places of the forefathers, which are charged with ambiguous powers that instil

respect and fear. These places, and all the symbolism associated with them, hold a central place in the rites and ceremonies carried out by the *yatiris*.

18. In Q'ishwa, *Tawantinman:* toward the four places that make up a complete unit. It could be a direct reference to the *Tawantinsuyu* or indeed a more general appeal to the organic and cosmic quaternity, in which the sacred number four (*tawa*) is combined with the idea of unity, harmony and 'completeness' (*intin*).

19. *Tatala* is an Aymara term that is often used as equivalent to 'Indian' with disrespectful connotations, denoting savagery. *Chullpa* and *Sikuya* are two major *ayllus* in the north of Potosi.

20. In effect, the *caciques* of the period carried with them large bundles of documents that contained the communal title-deeds, demands and petitions put to the authorities and a number of files concerning the legal defence of their lands. (cf. THOA, 1984; Ticona, 1985)

21. Silvia Rivera Cusicanqui 'Lo infrapolitico en Quimera' (1985).

22. The original Spanish text referred to *el Hombre*, which translates as mankind. Bearing in mind the subject matter, however, 'humankind' is a more appropriate word or concept.

7. Citizenship and Identity: Final Reflections

Elizabeth Jelin

An important distinction has been introduced into the mode of thinking about women's participation in social movements and their role as protagonists (or not): the difference between women's participation, women's movements and movements for (or by) women. This distinction points to the fact that, as a response to their class situation, ethnic identity or because they belong to social groups or categories, women participate and have participated in struggles and social movements since the dawning of history.

From time to time, the history of popular movements registers the presence of exceptional women, of heroines, whose participation has determined the path these struggles have taken, but the great majority of women, especially those participating at the grass-roots level, remain invisible and silent. To this type of participation — subordinate and minority, given the sexual division of labour and differences of power — must be added those organizations developed by women themselves for various ends and significance. In popular sectors in Latin America the better-known of these organizations are those promoted by the Church and charities, all of which are, therefore, promoted and directed from the outside.

One important historical innovation in Latin America, which has spread to significant sectors of the population during the 1980s, is the search for autonomy within class/gender organizations. There has been a development of women's movements from popular sectors seeking to take control of their own destiny, whether within the women's organizations promoted by the Church or political parties, or in those in which women are subordinate and in a minority (such as the unions). These movements are novel in the form of their organization, development and participation as well as their ideological and symbolic content.

The cases we have studied aim to show how the various types and planes of actions converge in social reality, thus obviating the analytical need to differentiate between women's participation, women's organizations and feminist movements. We sought those spaces in which women are more universal subjects, rather than those that emphasize the segmentation of positions and roles. In other words, the challenge was largely to find the rationale and significance of women's action rather than to classify their actions according to types of organization or stated objectives.

In this sense, rather than studying feminism as a movement distinct from other forms of women's collective action, we are interested in recovering its role in two senses. The first is the sense of 'critical consciousness': a nucleus that elaborates the content and significance of demands and needs, an essential element of popular movements, until such time as the women of the popular sectors are themselves able to recognize and appropriate these claims, either through their own elaboration or by learning alongside militant women. The second sense is that of an axis serving to generalize demands for action, which if left to the multiplicity of specific and concrete situations might not come to be reflected as a new social protagonist present in the sphere of global society.[1]

Women's social position: public and private distinctions

It is now commonplace to refer to distinctions between private, public and socially defined gender roles (man in the public arena, woman in the private sphere) which limit the forms of women's public actions. The division of labour is not symmetrical and equal. In effect, participation in the public sphere of social production in contemporary societies implies access to an income, of great importance in terms of personal autonomy and the control of resources and alternatives for action and, above all, access to the sphere of power and social control. Power and control are established in the public sphere and although these are not totally independent of the domestic sphere, the latter is becoming increasingly subordinated to events in public life. Furthermore, it is in the public sphere that solidarity links are established with others sharing similar social positions, that awareness of common interests is acquired, and that networks of communication and information are set up. (Elshtain, 1981)

The distinction between what is private and what is public has come about as a result of a combination of historical and social factors. (Donzelot, 1979) Even in areas as apparently 'private' as sexuality there is an undeniable social pressure to conform.

the majority of we women do not have free control of our bodies. As with slaves, others make the decisions for us about our needs and our fantasies. These decisions are generally expressed in terms of 'control' of our reproductive potential. This 'control' is apparent in the areas of health, family, medicine, social security. Political decisions which focused more on the process of social reproduction or reproduction of the labour force and of increasing or decreasing the demographic potential of countries and the region, than on the people who are the protagonists of these processes and their needs, suffering, happiness, frustrations. (Feijoo, 1984, p. 23)

Recognition of this historical background to privacy and subjectivity has still not been assimilated by the very subjects, women, nor has it been clearly incorporated into their collective actions, at least not in Latin America. Nevertheless, the dialectic of women's collective action in terms of their 'traditional' role, provides the potential to discover and incorporate such recognition into such current and visible issues, as sexuality, or women's reactions to the crisis in state services, and the recognition of how it affects and determines the quantity and the onus of domestic work over and above the traditional aspects of 'duty' and 'labour of love'.

There is no clear-cut distinction between the sexes with regard to degree of power. Excluded from power in the public domain, women still have the domestic domain. This domestic role of women implies specific forms of social relations:

> Oppression has not only meant a lack of rights and subjectivity but also a filling up with other rights and identities . . . capable of forming a complicated network of relationships . . . (Rossanda, 1985)

Housework is not only socially unrecognized, servile, isolated and heavy work, but also something else:

> It produces use values, in exchange for which it receives greater or lesser degrees of power in the interpersonal field of the family and the couple. Women are experts in this type of power, based on the idea of love, affection, seduction. The institutional value of all this is worth nothing, but its social value, its value in terms of life, is enormous. (Rossanda, 1985)

The strength of this identification with the domestic sphere is immense, as is the association of this world with that of the female world. The product is a two-gendered world, both biologically and politically.

> Women have enormous social power based on the immediacy of affections but they adapt badly to institutionalized politics based on the masculine logic of power. Capable of political passion, they only act in moments of extreme tension. Their long history of oppression has converted them into brilliant conservatives or ardent anarchists, never into administrators of civil peace. (Rossanda, 1985)

The organization of the family and the sexual division of labour hinders women's public participation because of their domestic responsibilities and the ideological burden of being female. It would seem, therefore, that women more frequently participate in protest movements at critical moments than in long-term, formal, institutionalized organizations that imply taking on responsibilities, dedicating time and effort to the organization and also — why not say it? — the opposition of men.

Consequently, women can either enter the public domain by adopting masculine codes, behaving like men — demanding equality — or they can set out to transform this domain by incorporating the knowledge and experience of their own sex, an historically difficult task.

The private sphere in the public domain: urban movements

The private domain is that of the family and affections. In this sphere lies the strength of the woman/mother, it is her speciality and it is here that the ambiguity of her oppression becomes apparent. It is, therefore, decisive first to recover the public and political dimension of the domestic role and also the social forces that 'create' this private sphere. Thereafter, it is important to recover the symbolic context of this widening of the private domestic role into the public world. Let us go in stages.

As organizers of family consumption, women necessarily enter into contact with institutions in the distribution sector and with the state as provider of services. There is, in effect, an obvious public dimension to women's role as housewife because they constantly relate to those offering goods and services and to other consumers. In addition, a large part of basic consumer services are offered or regulated in a collective manner by the state (education, health, housing, transport, sanitation services, price control, and so on) and the absence or deficiency of these is also felt and shared collectively. This is why the organization and defence of living conditions is a real and potential sphere of participation for women of the popular sectors at various levels: neighbourhood, community, urban, national. Moreover, at times of defeat, when popular conquests are retracted in the face of authoritarian regimes that question the level of participation and the very material conditions of existence and survival of subordinate social sectors, organizations such as these are among the few viable social movements able to answer back.

Neighbourhood movements are the typical venue for women's public participation in Latin American countries. Since the decade of the 1950s, rapid urbanization and the process of internal migration has led to a rapid increase in the urban population (especially in the largest cities). The growth of cities was not accompanied by a concurrent expansion of urban public services, to which must be added the diseconomies of scale when the size of the urban population multiplied into millions. Deficiencies in urban areas are well-known and have already been carefully studied: the lack of provision of public housing, and speculative and land monopolization that rendered housing inaccessible, have led to the proliferation of squatters on empty lots and the creation of illegal settlements (shanty towns, varying in name according to the country). The provision of urban services (electricity, running water, drainage, paved roads, security, schools, health centres, recreation areas, nurseries, and so on, and, of course, collective public transport) has been and is extremely inadequate in these settlements; but these are also deficient in 'legal' popular neighbourhoods.

Living conditions, and the means to carry on with the daily task of maintaining and reproducing the working population, are acutely deficient. These services can sometimes be bought on the market — which converts into shortages each individual family's strategy to increase their income level and decide on how to allocate their income. Most of the time, however, and in all cases for those services that cannot be individualized, these deficiencies can be corrected only through collective mechanisms, generally state agencies.

Consequently, collective action deriving from this situation is twofold: it makes demands on the state to provide services at the same time as generating collective action aimed at meeting some of the neighbourhoods' needs through local organization, with local autonomy. The bodies that assume these demands and possibilities for collective action are in the organic form of neighbourhood councils, development societies, neighbours' associations, and so on. There is a great variety of activities and organizations, depending on the relationship beween demands and state policies and on the existing tradition of association in each community.

Numerous studies and projects of promotion and action on women's situation in the popular classes emphasize the involvement of women in the neighbourhood sphere and in demands for services. Their action and analyses are centred on women's responsibility for the reproduction and maintenance of members of their domestic unit. (CEPAL, 1984) This role necessarily implies women going out into the known public world of the neighbourhood, thus kindling hope for a greater participation by women in collective action to press for demands, since this can be done without contradicting — in fact rather seeming to reinforce — women's traditional role as housewife/mother.

Numerous questions are raised by this type of participation: who are the women who participate? who benefits from these movements? More specifically, it is relevant to ask whether the conditions under which women leave their traditional role rooted in daily life to enter the public domain, constitute a significant departure with regard to social changes in women's subordination, helping to form gender identities that put in doubt the current system of domination.

Women pioneers creating a neighbourhood
The history of a neighbourhood of Lima serves as a point of departure for the analysis of women's participation in the creation of the city. In the case of the neighbourhood of San Martin de Porres, women migrated to Lima in the 1950s. The changes in their life cycles, tied to the history of the occupation of urban land, are crucial aspects in establishing their new identities as migrants in the city. Marriage, family, the occupation of an empty lot and building a place to live, become the pivot of their lives. Throughout the process of getting somewhere to live, women develop networks of solidarity and mutual help, as much on the basis of coming from the same province of origin as on the basis of relationships formed through daily life in the neighbourhood.

The family is fundamental: not only does it help women to put down roots and to 'belong', it also becomes a unit of social reproduction and management, given the limited labour market in the city. Those who do not have a family must create one and those who do must contribute to the family economy.

Marriage or cohabitation opens a new stage in the process of insertion into and consolidation of settlement. Women, responsible for daily reproduction, invest the first years of living as a couple in building their domestic space, while men go into the job market to earn the basic income. Relations of mutual help and spiritual kinship develop between women neighbours, protecting them from the new environment and providing solidarity with child-care. In this period, although their reproductive and domestic role is reaffirmed, women are also in almost permanent confrontation with various governmental bodies in order to consolidate their land claim.

The participation of migrant women settlers in the social movement is closely linked to the cycle of family life and the project of building the family which, in the final instance, is the axis of urban settlement. For this reason, their presence in local mobilizations to obtain services for the neighbourhood is basically fortuitous and unstructured. Their participation is instigated by the need to have certain guarantees from the state in order to consolidate their land and domestic and family unity, but it does not necessarily include an orientation toward social change nor does it have a defined political objective.

Nevertheless, confrontations with other institutions, and learning about democratic forms of participation, even when carried out from the domestic sphere to obtain very basic objectives, begin to predispose men as much as women into accepting other social practices in women. The case study showed the passage from the situation of the *waqcha*, migrant women on their own in the city 20 years ago, to the present self-image of pioneers who recall with pride the path of their struggles. This is a process of creating subjects.

Women's active presence in the family, a unit of social reproduction but not strictly domestic, opens new spaces for popular female participation and transforms the initial idea that situated women within the confines of the family.

More recently, the economic crisis and its repercussions in popular sectors — in so far as unemployment grows and the purchasing power of salaries decreases — has led to a new situation. In many cases women are forced to carry the full weight of the family economy or to contribute in a systematic fashion. This reality has compelled them to go out and find paid work. But as they have few qualifications the alternatives open to them are basically casual and domestic work. Hence, another of women's needs is further training to obtain qualifications that will enable them to earn a larger income in order to maintain their families.

The mothers' clubs, local venues bringing women together that initially developed as forms of institutionalizing the self-help between women, clearly influenced by government assistance agencies or Christian groups, are now beginning to take on a protagonistic role. Collective kitchens are strategies emerging from this context that propose a new form of female organization. They are characterized by bringing women together in a public activity replacing the private and almost intimate activity of the kitchen in the domestic sphere. Collective kitchens are the new scenario for women's political work. Sustained by the acceptance of differences in the socialization of males and females in the patriarchal system, they are proposed as a necessity in view of female responsibility for social reproduction under conditions of marginalization and domination and nurtured by the history of female participation to consolidate the family. A new space is opened to women of the popular sectors enabling them to partake in social confrontation, decision-making and supervision as social and political subjects.

The development of such specifically female organizations as popular kitchens is significant, because it encapsulates in a single space actions aimed at bolstering incomes, women's domestic chores and activities of a communal and social nature. In this way, new areas of social organization emerge, which group women around a basic problem, such as food, transferring a fundamentally private and domestic chore to the public and collective domain, encouraging the socialization of individual tasks and, in many cases, the socialization of individual problems which are recognized as social problems. This trend implies learning about forms of organization and the exercise of horizontal and democratic relations between members, as well as interacting with other institutions, and it begins to constitute a new scene of social action for women of the popular strata to press for their demands.

The widening of women's sphere of action and traditional roles, as much in the sexual division of labour as in the public and private arena, is coming about through necessity in popular daily practice and as a response to the needs of survival. This implies that they are not put forward as demands nor can they be considered the achievements of a process of becoming aware of a situation of subordination. Their potential for change is, however, significant.

'Women's talk/political things'

Women's participation in the world of the neighbourhood, originally linked to satisfying the reproductive needs of the family, can have complex, subversive implications for the traditional order and ways of organizing. Teresa Caldeira's work on women in the neighbourhoods of São Paulo aims to highlight the symbolic and cultural content developing as a result of this participation.

Caldeira distinguishes various forms and types of women's participation in neighbourhood affairs. First, there are women who, without belonging to any movement or institution, are concerned about their living conditions and organize petitions and address the corresponding public institutions. They do not want to organize anyone nor necessarily secure things for the whole neighbourhood, they are often satisfied with obtaining improvements in their own street. They are typical housewives, married with children, without paid work outside the home, whose political activism is clearly an extension of their domestic role, accepting clientelism and subordination.

The activism of these women coexists, with varying degrees of harmony, with that of women who participate in local movements or institutions and who speak in the name of the people and voice their demands in a discourse focused on the interests of the neighbourhood as a whole. The meaning of this participation for the women is clearly different from the justification they give for their actions. Women appeal to their condition as mothers to justify leaving the home. This implies a widening of their role as mothers: to make demands and participate are seen as a responsible mother's duty, because in a hostile city, such as São Paulo, it is necessary to face public authorities and press for the collective goods and services required for reproduction.

The meaning of their activism is to be found elsewhere — in the distinction the women make between 'women's talk' and 'political things' when referring to topics they like or dislike talking about. It also indicates a space in which women include themselves, and another from which they exclude themselves. Within this context, women emphasize those forms of participation close to the sphere of 'women's talk' as positive and do not conceive of their activism as political. Politics is something distant, a space in which they do not know how to act, while local movements and Christian Base Communities are spaces known to them.

They clearly distinguish between what they do and what they categorize as 'political', that is, between the immediate interests of the neighbourhood 'of the people' and something distant and strange that takes place in another sphere 'between them out there'. The struggle for power involves a struggle for personal interests and is 'theirs'; 'ours' involves struggling for collective interests, for needs.

This contrast has a further characteristic, which is associated with gender differences. A new identity is created in contrast with two already known experiences: that of the traditional housewife and that of the man in politics. Although it is justified in terms of their role as responsible mothers and housewives, the new experience means that the private sphere is also beginning to be transformed. Women are absent more, they leave domestic chores undone. They participate because of the value they attribute to 'knowing', the possibility of losing their fear and learning to speak in public, all of which increases their self-esteem. In contrast, alone at home, women do not learn.

Participation also has a non-instrumental significance. The content of what they are going to is less important than the actual going out and meeting people to do it. This explains in part the transforming effect of sexual segregation, which can lead to small changes in women's role. It seems difficult to leave the house and legitimize participation, it seems difficult to enter into the world of the job market identified as masculine, it seems difficult to find their place in a pre-established world — hence the attempt to find a form of public activism that is separate from the sphere considered as strongly masculine and competitive, where individual interests are delineated and on which images of corruption and filth weigh heavily.

Housewives and the political juncture

During those periods when the process of democratization of a country is at stake, all actions and movements take on a political colour, a meaning which has to be deciphered from the code of their contribution to building democracy. Such is the case of housewives in Argentina in the past years. The case studied by Felipe and Gogna was a movement that surpassed the limits of the neighbourhood or locality. Do extensions of space and widening of significance necessarily coexist?

The protests of housewives began during the final years of the dictatorship (1981–82) in the greater Buenos Aires area. The growing deterioration of the standard of living and the impact caused by the Falklands/Malvinas war led a group of middle-class women to 'confront the dictatorship' in their own way by preparing leaflets that urged people to 'cast their fear aside', getting women neighbours interested in their proposals, speaking to shopkeepers, linking up with neighbourhood associations and facing the authority's threats. At first the mobilization grew, but later shrank, overshadowed by the electoral process and the concentration of public attention on the theme of institutional democratization. Once the new government was installed the housewives re-initiated their activities, which continue with ups and downs although their presence is not very visible in the mass media and public awareness.

There are new features in this movement, linked to the moment of political transition in which it emerged. First, different types of women merge in the movement, some have political experience with a history of neighbourhood action, and others are without previous experience in social and political movements. This heterogeneous group of women distances itself as much from politics as it does from connotations of welfare. This trait is shared with other women's movements.

A second feature arises from the type of relations established with other social movements, especially those related to human rights and those pressing for women's rights. Although it is a movement for demands which does not go beyond the framework of sporadic protests, in the specific period under analysis the housewives manifested an opening-up to subjects that were non-traditional in their sector. Faced with the visible presence of other democratic and renovating social movements, the housewives developed an activity which, on the one hand recognized their specific sphere of action in defence of women's role in reproduction and as consumers, and on the other, showed signs of participation in wider matters: solidarity with human rights' movements, participation in activities linked to women's issues. In a seemingly contradictory fashion, through their discourse appealing to the identity of wife/mother/housewife, women are considered active protagonists pressing for their rights: 'that women may have the necessary time and their own money and above all, equality of rights'.

Public politicized domesticity: scope and limitations
What is achieved by this participation stemming from women's domestic role? What is the balance? There are some irrefutable points concerning the effects of these collective actions. First, it forces political and social recognition of the public face of reproduction. This removes from women part of the load and responsibility (with its measure of guilt) for the conditions in which the family is maintained. Second, women learn about participation and solidarity, which is necessary to create a gender identity, although the degree of progress in creating female 'spaces' varies from case to case, as does awareness of this fact on the part of women themselves. Third, as the forms of association generated by these practices are inserted into pre-existing systems of social relations based on traditional clientelistic channels, the tensions provoked in this way open-up a great potential for change in this type of social relation.

Conversely, it must be pointed out that this type of participation does not automatically lead to the recognition of women's rights. Like the process of building a new gender identity and the establishment of women as new social actors, it is the result of a series of factors, particularly the relations established between the women's neighbourhood movements and other social and political, popular, democratic and feminist movements.

Over and above those achievements linked to the immediate socio-economic situation (that is, the justification for action: the crisis, poverty) is the shattering of the passive image of women and the transformation of this passivity into combativeness that is moving towards the redefinition of the collective practices of women. The cases studied demonstrate the socialization of the ultimate symbol of private domestic activity — food, external activities that transform the sense of domestic time; changing the orientation of women's time from being geared to the needs of others, to time for themselves. In other words, politicization as a result of the inertia of the political juncture.

In search of equality: incorporation or institutional change?

Women's subordination and discrimination can be interpreted as the banners of the struggle for justice and equality, seeking to extend to the discriminated or subordinate group rights already enjoyed by other social categories. The classic concept of citizenship is a perfect reflection of this problem, in terms of the historic processes of forming the nation state and building democracy.

Women's struggles for the recognition of their citizenship have been long and tenacious. First, the suffragettes' victory and the extension of voting rights; then, changes in civil rights — the recognition of woman as an economic and social subject; finally, equality in the field of family rights. The fulfilment of the United Nations Convention on the elimination of all forms of discrimination is a goal still to be achieved.

Equality, however, is not only a legal struggle. The field of social practices is especially complex: legal equality does not guarantee equality in reality and the inertia of 'male' social organizations is very strong. But in some of these fields, particularly labour, the theme of equality is permeated by women's specific situation which is linked to the sexual division of labour and maternity.

Perhaps unions are the sphere in which some of these questions are posed in paradigm: an institution fighting to extend workers' rights but also a classically male institution. How do women establish their place as workers with rights? How can they fight for recognition of their right to equal working conditions without discrimination? Their demands relate to pay, labour relations, access to the labour market but also access to workers' organizations. Historically, women's access to these organizations has been limited because of competition in the labour market and the possible 'subversion' of women's family role. (Baxandall, 1976)[2]

Consequently, women workers have a double struggle: as workers and as women. In no other place is the convergence of class and gender as visible as in the process of organizing women workers. Should they integrate into male workers' organizations or should they organize themselves separately? The first option benefits the class struggle but retains gender subordination. The second benefits the gender aspect but causes class 'divisions'.

These are the historical dilemmas of the labour movement that have emerged repeatedly under varying circumstances. How is this subject tackled now that women's issues have gained legitimacy and space in the social debate? It is also a period of political repression of the labour movement (Chile) or of incipient and weak openings (Brazil, Uruguay, Argentina). What influence does this have? How is it affected by a context of economic recession or limited expansion?

It is not surprising to find that women's participation in union organizations is limited in countries with varying degrees of development. (Baxandall, 1976; Chang and Ducci, 1977; Hartman Strom, 1983; Gitahy et al, 1982) Studying women's practices in relation to union organization provides an insight into the ways in which women are incorporated into male organizations: are they participants with equal rights and duties, or do they bring a different perspective — interests, practices, ideas, symbols — presenting a 'female approach' into the sphere of formal organizations?[3]

Their struggles are timid, their presence minimal. Let us take a look at some specific cases.

The Brazilian case

In Brazil, in contrast to other countries in the region, during the 1970s women were incorporated in large numbers into assembly industries. (Gitahy et al, 1982; Abramo, 1985) In São Paulo especially, large contingents of women were integrated into metal–mechanic industries, while simultaneously there was a decrease in their importance in other more traditional branches, such as textiles, clothing and food. (Humphrey, 1983) Parallel to this process was an increase in women's unionization in the first half of the decade.

While for some this increase is simply a reflection of the general increase in the number of women in the workforce, others consider that the real attraction was the welfare services offered by the unions. A third interpretation links the increase in female unionization to women's increased participation in urban popular movements (neighbourhood movements, Christian Base Communities, and so on) during the 1970s. In this sense, the process of female unionization was registered as part of the overall movement to appropriate and reformulate public space. (Blay, 1982) What is certain is that, even with the growth of unionization, women do not substantially participate in unions (Souza Lobo, 1984) and women's demands are not incorporated into the final stages of union negotiations.

Analysts and actors coincide in the view that there is an emergence of the woman's question in Brazilian unionism. What has led to its appearance in the unions' discourse? It is due in part to the restoration of union practices that came about at the end of the 1970s (work centred on factory matters and changes in the forms of articulating neighbourhood demands) and in part to the activities of women's movements which, by giving greater 'visibility' to women, legitimized the treatment of these issues at union level. (Souza Lobo,

1984; Castilhos Brito, 1984)

The two forms of action taken by women unionists were: the formation of women's commissions in the unions, which took on board relations between women workers and the union, and the struggle to integrate women into the union structure. (Souza Lobo, 1984a) These strategies, however, were not wholly successful because of different practices between the sexes, as was proved by the lack of continuity in organizational experiences. This situation led to some sectors suggesting that if the two sexes had different issues, practices and forms of participation, then the strategies adopted by the unions should reflect this. More specifically, it has been suggested that the fact that women have collective forms of resistance within the factory could be of greater importance than their participation in the union. (Castilhos Brito, 1984)

Opinion was divided within the women's movement and between unionists with regard to the question of women's sections in unions. Some women and men favoured the creation of women's commissions to help organize women's struggles and to raise the level of awareness about women's problems within the union. Other women felt that these commissions could marginalize women's struggles within the unions. (TIE report, s.f., no 17)

Women's union participation in Brazil culminated in the now renowned First Congress of Women Metal Workers, which took place in January 1978, organized by the leaders of the metal workers union of San Bernardo. This experience was later extended (from 1980 onwards) to other branches of production and to other cities. In the first place, as in many other cases, the Congress was organized with the intention of attracting women to the general union struggle and not with a view to mobilizing them around their own situation as women workers. (Humphrey, 1983)

The majority of women who participated in the Congress later lost their jobs. There was a wide range of denunciations and claims, many of which related to women's specific working conditions: differences in salaries (women earned on average 60 per cent of men's wages); disastrous hygiene and safety conditions for women; supervisors' strict control of the use of the toilets; obligatory overtime and threats of dismissal if workers refused; constant increases in the rhythm of production; lack of stability in employment (marriage and pregnancy were the main reasons for dismissal); racial discrimination; and sexual harassment by managers and supervisors.

In summary, although it was difficult to maintain women's permanent participation in union activities due to the social circumstances that define women's role, their high level of participation in the 1978–79 strikes constitutes an outstanding example of learning, of the possibilities of participation, and of overcoming some of the barriers imposed by female socialization in exercising political activities. (Castilhos Brito, 1984)

The Argentine case

The situation of women in Argentina is not fundamentally different from that in the region as a whole. Women workers are found at the delegate level but generally they do not obtain high posts in the hierarchy within their respective organizations. (Gil, 1970) This was clearly the situation in Argentina at the beginning of the 1970s. Within this framework, women's secretariats began to be created in some of the service occupational groups (insurance and banking). In addition, during the last Peronist government (1973–76) there was an attempt to organize the first women's congress of the General Worker's Confederation. But because of the general situation of crisis in the country and within the Peronist movement at the time, this did not take place.

Trade union organizations were dismantled during the dictatorship, but what was the situation with the return of a constitutional regime?

Firstly, some facts are drawn to the attention of the observer: the creation of women's sections or secretariats in a growing number of trade unions;[4] the appeal to women in the 1984 union election campaigns; the formation at the end of that year of the Women Unionists Board (formed by 14 trade unions, mainly of the service sector) and more recently (July 1985) the creation of the National Movement of Union Women, both of which defined their objective as contributing to the organization of women workers but departing from different internal tendencies within the union and from different approaches to women's issues. Can we consider this to be the emergence of the 'women's question' within Argentine unionism?

If this is the case, then the phenomenon is coming about in a very different context to that of Brazil. The participation of Argentine women workers in the manufacturing sector has decreased over the past 20 years, at first due to technological modernization at the beginning of the 1960s but later because of the economic policies of the military dictatorship. (Sautu, 1985)

Argentine unionism finds itself in the middle of profound changes connected with the process of political democratization (Palomino, 1985; Abos, 1985) and reflected in: greater political pluralism in proceedings; growing connections with other social movements; changes in the relative power of certain trade unions as a result of the economic crisis, among other factors. Under these conditions, there is possibly more receptivity than in the past to such challenges as the recognition of women's issues.

Only time will tell what will happen to these tentative attempts to achieve greater participation of women in the trade union sphere. For the moment, one can formulate the hypothesis that contacts with feminist groups and political women, as well as some union leaders' experience of exile during the dictatorship, have exerted a certain degree of influence on some of the women who are instigating these orientations in the sense of encouraging proposals of equality but also through a growing reassessment of women's role in society.

The Chilean case
Women's participation in trade union organizations in Chile is faced with additional problems to those already mentioned in this section. The repressive situation, which has existed for over a decade, and the acute economic crisis are reflected in very high unemployment figures. As Galvez and Todara show, the situation is very similar to the rest of the region as regards the factors that bring women into the job market and which are closely linked to the possibilities of

trade union organization: women are concentrated in occupations in which it is more difficult to organize unions and where their derived benefits are fewer.

Permanent harassment and lack of recognition of rights by the company and in the daily routine of the working world lead to a rejection of the work environment by women workers, making the possibilities of organization even more difficult and resulting in a sort of idealization of domestic work, which comes to be seen as a refuge. But signs are beginning to appear of an ideology questioning both these roles.

Furthermore, if we take into account the fact that women's union organization is limited by domestic functions, both in terms of material (time, working hours) and ideological obstacles (rejection of 'politics', fear of participating in public, and so on) then the overall outlook is disappointing. In this context, it is not surprising that women participate more enthusiastically in those union activities linked to services (the annual outing, the Christmas presents given by the union, and suchlike) than in the process of struggle or negotiation, which appear more distant and, in effect, are risky.

In the repressive conditions of the Chilean regime the parties and unions have adopted a distant attitude to the problems of women workers and given greater priority to other subjects. First, as in other countries, class contradictions tend to obscure awareness of gender. This is evident in the somewhat generalized belief that gender problems are individual problems that do not require collective action. The trade union organizations themselves scarcely consider the specific problems of women workers and do not take them on board as collective problems of the workforce. Furthermore, women unionists themselves recognize that they have not yet found alternatives to the working methods used traditionally in the trade union sphere and therefore have no way of taking into account women's specific work relationships and removing the above-cited obstacles to their participation indicated above.

In the union world, attempts to create a forum to mobilize women (such as the creation of a Women's Department in the National Union Co-ordinator in 1979, which organized a number of national women's meetings) typify the tensions aroused in these cases. The objective on the part of the union movement appeared to be to motivate women's participation in the struggle for democracy in the terms put forward. The existence of an important feminist movement in the country, which has led numerous demonstrations in opposition to the regime, combining the issue of democracy with demands for social changes in women's role, necessarily affects women in the unions as well. The dilemma of whether to incorporate women into male union organizations or search for autonomous organizational alternatives is very salient today in Chile.

The peasants of Bolivia

The identity of peasant women is more complex than that of women workers whose role is defined by the labour market. Who is a peasant woman, in what capacity does she become a member of women's organizations? How is the potential scope of membership defined? Applying parallel criteria to those used in union organization — and the peasant movement, particularly in Bolivia but also in other countries, is indeed organized and forms a part of the workers' movement — the labour situation ought to define the peasant, that is, agricultural work with different characteristics. But what does being a peasant woman imply? The definition of this role does not appear to be the labour situation but more precisely the family situation: to be a member of a peasant family. Labour does not define status. In the first place, the scope of women's productive work in this social organization can be very varied, depending on the presence of men or their absence due to migration, and the tasks of marketing or transport outside the domestic peasant unit as part of the actual organization of production. Secondly, it always includes tasks aimed at daily and generational reproduction. These tasks might be called 'domestic' in other social organizations but in the peasant sphere their specifically reproductive character is confused with productive tasks. Women who are physically separated from their peasant families (domestic workers in the city, for example) can also be called 'peasants', as their work is part of a diversification strategy in the division of labour scheme within the peasant family. In summary, what defines or characterizes peasant women is the fact that they function within or belong to a peasant family and not the fact that they carry out specific tasks outside the domestic sphere.

This multiplicity of tasks and lack of definition of roles influence forms of organization and participation. The organization of peasant women studied by Rosario León, the Bartolina Sisa Federation of Peasant Women, follows the union format in its organization. But the reality of peasant women renders such organizations inadequate. The combination of contradictions resulting from the position of peasant women (without mentioning women leaders) is reflected in the interviews of their leaders:

> When women try to organize themselves, they ask their husbands first; women don't make decisions on their own. But the time has come for we women to think for ourselves and form our own organizations. I think that women must also learn how to govern. Why should it only be men who rule? Just as Bartolina Sisa struggled alongside Tupac Katari, so too must peasant women struggle beside their husbands. A lot is said about peasant liberation but they only seem to take men into account. What about women? Don't women also need to be liberated? (Mejía de Morales, 1984, p. 10)

> We were really happy when we heard that a woman had been named President.[5] We said: 'There will be a solution because she's a woman, she'll regard us as her sisters.' Thinking this, a group of women from my community went to give her a present, a *tarilla*[6] which had the name of Bartolina Sisa and of our community woven into it. But she refused to see us, even though we pleaded. She made us wait there all day and finally when she saw us in the afternoon, it was only in the waiting room. We also wanted to shower her with confetti but she didn't want that either. She said she had to go somewhere and anyway we would dirty the floor, that's what she said

to us. So we presented her with the *tarilla* and a document asking for support. Then we left.

When we returned to our community we arrived almost at the same time as news of the economic measures which she had authorized. Our male colleagues made fun of us: 'So there you have it, nice isn't it? You go and congratulate her and now she's punishing us with these measures'. That's what they said to us. We felt morally defeated but we also learned from this. Just because we are all women doesn't mean we are all the same. (Mejía de Morales, 1984, p. 16)

We don't know whether she's a peasant woman or not, if she has a cause or not, if she has suffered or not, but she can't be a peasant. We have known suffering, ours is an uphill struggle. We will disown her because she is betraying women. This union is a disunion.

If she were really a peasant woman, she would know that in joint meetings with men, we women find it difficult to speak, men always outdo us because we're afraid to speak. But in women only meetings, we have a good discussion, we're not afraid to throw out ideas, we understand each other quickly without needing so many words and we talk about women's things which we cannot do in front of men. But in a mixed group we clam up. Now we know what we would be losing if we joined with men. That's why we will fight so as not to lose what we have already won. (Mejía de Morales, 1984, p. 18)

We are beginning to grow up, as a young girl dependent on her father becomes aware and breaks away, so have we. Women could not have formed the Federation at that time because we didn't know the steps to take. But we have organized the Confederation by our own means . . .

We organized courses on handicrafts and cooperatives, to keep in touch, so the organization didn't lose strength. These served to keep us informed about how the organization was going, what was happening in each section. We met in the parishes, where we cooked, slept, did everything. (Mejía de Morales, 1984, p. 43)

The initial organizational practices followed the logic of the Single Confederation of Bolivian Rural Workers Unions (CSUTCB), the institution that promoted the women's organization. The Federation of Peasant Women was created from the top down, by setting-up national structures first, and later, as a result of leaders' visits, establishing unions in different localities. Nevertheless, this form of union organization and participation does not go against but rather complements forms of organization in daily life: networks of provisions, kinship and inter-local solidarity. Inasmuch as these forms of association of peasant women are part of daily life and their domestic and local sphere, they go unnoticed, they are socially invisible. This is why in times of social and political repression they are able to play a 'clandestine' role, which is what happened following the *coup d'état* in July 1980. Unions gave way to alternative forms of organization that were used to plan the resistance.

The activities of the Federation of Peasant Women began in 1982 with the return of a democratic regime in Bolivia. The period that followed was characterized by differences and conflicts among its leadership and by attempts to manipulate politically an organization that had demonstrated its mobilizing power.

Predictably, the conflictive nature of Bolivian society began to manifest itself openly within the Federation and in relations between the Federation and left-wing political parties on the one hand, and the Confederation on the other. The Confederation attempted to neutralize the Federation's autonomy, creating a portfolio of 'Female Membership' whose activities included taking charge of peasant stores, which in effect was a return to women's traditional role. At the same time, the Federation's development led to greater co-ordination with other women's organizations, to learning about other forms of action and to a transformation of women's demands.

A digression: 'We want to retrieve our past'

> We want to retrieve our past, our history, to combine it with the history we are making now, because in order to advance you need to look at what went before. (Mejía de Morales, 1984, p. 83)

The evidence of the formation of women's movements in rural areas in the past decade leads immediately to the question of whether this is new or whether there is a record of such movements in the past. How did the identification with Bartolina Sisa arise? Or in more abstract terms: Which cultural pattern led to the emergence of these practices?

The memory of Bartolina Sisa is of a woman fighter who accompanied Tupac Katari. This role of peasant women is also clear in the testimonies and recollections of peasant struggles prior to 1952. (Rivera, 1987) Women carried out a great variety of activities in the process of peasant struggles, both in reclaiming territories and in resisting the expansion of estates or resisting forced and violent recruitment of the workforce for the army or production. For the mothers, wives and daughters of peasant leaders to accompany them in their struggles was considered a priority.

The position of the leaders' female family members was different from that of other peasant women. Whereas the former had to give their support to the men's militancy and replace them in productive work, the dominant tone of the latter was passive resignation in the face of forces over which they had no control. This is reflected in the testimonies:

> No, no they didn't participate . . . women only stayed at home.

> I only know how to listen, I don't know how to participate in anything, I don't know how to get involved in men's things.

They didn't understand, women have little intelligence. That's what they're like.
(Oral History Workshop, Chapter 6 of this book)

This resigned acceptance of decisions by women raises two questions. Firstly, could it be that they were hiding resistance practices which were neither mentioned nor accorded social recognition? Secondly, how did women begin to participate actively and consciously?

The methodology for finding an answer to these questions is clear: the search must begin by investigating the daily life of peasant women, as this is what shapes their perception of the world and society. In apparently trivial events that went unnoticed, in numerous insignificant daily and domestic chores, women developed a practice — often not accompanied by a concurrent reflection on the matter — of resistance and change. First, let us consider some images of the position of women and the complementarity between men and women:

Between themselves, man and woman have to help each other. But the woman works more: she has to cook the food, wash the clothes, carry the babies, graze the sheep, weave ponchos, sacks, *lliqllas* for babies, women must do all this. Perhaps you don't work very hard, but here in the countryside women have to take the cows out, take all sorts of things into town, sow potatoes and grains . . . phew! A woman has to do a bit of everything. She has to help her man a lot if she loves him. Do you think he can manage on his own? If we cut the wing off a bird, will it be able to fly? With only one wing it can't. Man–woman are always willing to do anything, but the woman does more.

My husband went to the meeting where they spoke of many things, what could they have been talking about? But my husband didn't tell me everything they had said, just a few things and when I asked him what had happened, he said: 'This and that'.
But I knew they had said a lot more. So I followed him to hear what they were talking about and find out everything. Some men go on their own and then they tell us very little. I want to know a lot more. but if they don't want me to speak, I say: 'If a woman knows then she can express her opinion and discuss with the rest. We women could learn and speak together, just among ourselves and it would be good, there would be enough of us then. I and other women could participate better with women that have a mind like yours. If there were ten with a good brain we could do a lot: many women could meet together with everything that we are told and what we learn.'

Everyday practices are linked to the defence of life; some of them develop out of resignation and passivity while others generate important collective action. Women's activities are rooted in a very strong cultural image of the complementary (hierarchical) couple. This defines their activities, which are almost always accompanied by rituals:

* taking over when men weaken;
* complementing jobs in agricultural production, reproduced in resistance practices;
* lessening the effects of defeat, as 'women will humble themselves and beg the master's forgiveness with the intention of at least saving their partner's life and regrouping the community'. (Chapter 6, Oral History Workshop)

It is traditional for Andean women to express resistance to the impositions of an oppressive society through their clothing.

> The tenacity of this act of defiance, carried out in silent but meaningful gestures, illustrates that women were very conscious of the symbolism of their clothing and weaving. We consider that this sensitivity is due not only to the fact that women are the producers of the family's clothing but also because in the woven textiles, as in a silent text, they generate a language full of complex meanings which enables them to express the distinct identity of the community. (Chapter 6)

Finally, there is the role of cultural resistance through rituals, which appears to be linked to mediation with malicious forces that penetrate the community's boundaries.

By examining the underlying cultural elements involved in these practices of resistance and affirmation of an ethnic identity, new significance can be attributed to women's silent message:

> In the light of these reflections we would suggest that the 'silence' of Andean women in the context of inter-cultural relations, is a deliberate form of anonymity, which contrasts with their verbal eloquence within the *ayllu* or family. This anonymity complements the male activity relating to the *q'ara* world by means of the word (files, documents, petitions) which places the man in a vulnerable and intermediary space. Female silence could therefore be said to constitute a cultural self-defence mechanism: to protect the man from the dangers of his links with the *q'ara* world and to reproduce the cultural and moral values of their own origins. (Chapter 6)

In the face of recollections of cultural resistance, the present situation of the peasant women's organization appears enigmatic. The multiplicity of meanings and symbols involved in the process of forming the Federation is accompanied by a multidimensional range of identities each trying to assert itself: increasingly less perfunctory and more combative demands for women's equality, coexisting with the importance of being *de pollera* (wearing indigenous dress) together with all the connotations of cultural resistance surrounding this symbol of traditional dress; the appeal to the figure of Bartolina Sisa — deeply rooted in the complementary hierarchy of the couple

— to request an autonomous women's movement. In summary, a proposal that essentially questions accepted forms of social organization but which stems from the collective memory of traditional cultural resistance.

Conclusions

This section is comparatively less rich in information and working hypotheses than those referring to women's participation in other spheres of social life, except in the case of peasant women and the retrieval of their historical memory. There are a number of reasons for this. The most obvious is that women, due to the factors referred to in this section, have not been actively incorporated in our society's trade unions. To what extent can this be said to be a true absence, and to what extent is it a matter of degrees of 'social visibility' or of gaps in knowledge? Are not women's experiences in unions also a part of these struggles, which by their very nature tend to be left out of historical records and therefore need to be retrieved from oblivion? Some data found in historical studies on women's union activities do indicate that struggles for participation are not new in this sphere, although they were never massive. (Navarro, 1986)

Women's limited participation in the union sphere, difficult at the best of times, is even more reduced under socio-political circumstances such as those imposed by dictatorial governments that repress all forms of participation. Unionism is an especially vulnerable target in these situations because it is a channel of participation for subordinate sectors, highly institutionalized, easily recognizable and visible to government agencies. If a target is to be chosen for repression, the union movement is the easiest: much easier than spontaneous non-institutional social movements, because of its visibility; much easier than other organizations (those of the Church for example) because of its overt identification with the interests of the subordinate social sectors.

This curb on participation obviously affects men as well as women, but it does not affect them in the same way. The historical juncture we are analysing occurred at a time when on other fronts — both at the Latin American level and more especially at the international level — the question of women's status was gaining relevance and bearing, if not legitimacy, as a social issue to be confronted by the state and by social organizations. The fact that, at the time, unionism was restricted in its scope of action meant a considerable delay in the formulation of the issue. But as we have seen in the Argentine and Brazilian cases, we can begin to detect new embryonic forms of participation and especially new ways of putting forward women's issues in the union world. Something similar is happening in Uruguay. For example, the Commission of Uruguayan women, created in 1983 by housewives linked to the Construction Union, has as members women from neighbourhood groups, workers and students. One of its objectives is to ensure that women's demands are taken up by unions and that women have greater participation in union life. (Rodríguez Villamil, 1984)

Evidently, the coincidence between democratic opening and the appearance or deepening of the theme of women within the trade union sphere is not fortuitous. Nevertheless, global recognition of the existence of a specific issue related to women and the difficulties they encounter in participating are longer-term issues linked to union structure. Equality in terms of power within labour organizations is a demand that is still not mentioned, that is silenced.

Daily life in politics or women and a democratic utopia

In a certain sense, the social action and movements we have analysed here are prototypes that arise 'naturally' out of daily life. Women's lives and identities are made up of daily events: the habitual, the trivial and insignificant, the invisible. The world of big events has little to do with them, at least for most of them. And yet in their daily reality, women live the manifestations and consequences of great historical dramas. At the same time, daily life can be transformed and come to influence public, social life. Because of their social position, women can become the key social protagonists in forming social movements that question the traditional way of engaging in politics, the relation between politics and social life, and the very nature of social relationships. For this to happen and how it will happen depends on the historical conditions and the development of the social forces themselves. And it is here that we can finally move on from the level of description and interpretation of reality, to the level of social utopias and potential for change in women's daily practices.

The attempt of authoritarian regimes, which devastated the region (or which are still doing so) to redefine the limits of legitimacy of political action contributed paradoxically to the politicization of spheres traditionally considered non-political. This phenomenon has been particularly clear in the case of women, who in various cases organized themselves in new ways, having recognized the political profile of their family roles. (Feijoo, 1983; Jelin, 1984) Without a doubt the most significant has been women's mobilization to denounce violations of human rights. Although recognizing that this phenomenon is more widespread than the Argentine case,[7] in some ways the Mothers of the Plaza de Mayo have become the paradigm of women's struggles in defence of human rights.

The Mothers raise new ethical banners; the appeal for a fundamental system of values: 'life, truth and justice, expound an ethical need for humanitarian principles' then becomes a project: 'human rights are now no longer just those that existed before and must be respected, but those which follow and must be established. They are presented as a horizon, as a utopia.' (Sondereguer, 1985)

The type of action in which these women engage does not restrict itself to the traditional rules of politics but attempts to give a new meaning to politics: 'We don't defend ideologies, we defend life.'

The case of the Mothers of the Plaza de Mayo must be similar to other women's movements where participation was provoked by political events that 'hit them' and which — without their doing anything — began changing women's consciousness and role. By emphasizing matters such as justice, liberty or solidarity, the Mothers in a certain sense defied the privatization and isolation of women. They also shattered the myth that women are incapable of uniting and of showing solidarity among themselves and, more fundamentally, they buried the image of resignation and weakness.

Although the Mothers movement is 'new' in so far as it responds to a painful and exceptional circumstance, it is possible to recognize some traits in common with other women's movements in defence of the standard of living, women's rights, and so on. In synthesis, identity (mother, housewife, woman) is a key element in understanding these movements; they all erect an ethical dimension (right to life, to a dignified life, no discrimination, for example) and finally, they work more towards gaining control of an autonomous or independent field in the face of the system, than winning political power. These common features mean that they are confronted with similar problems, basically 'their link with politics', and the fact that, for their demands to be considered they must wait until 'later': a consolidated democracy, improvements in the economic indicators, a more modern society.

It is a movement that does not distinguish between the pragmatic effectiveness of action and normative reforms but rather expounds an ethical commitment which is un-negotiable and is stated as a political utopia stemming from feelings and convictions. Theoretically, their proposal can be widened to cover a transformation of the socio-political space, starting from an adjustment to the world of the future, as in the Antigone paradigm:

> The standpoint of Antigone is of a woman who dares to challenge public power by giving voice to familial and social imperatives and duties. . . . To recapture that voice and to reclaim that standpoint, and not just for women alone, it is necessary to locate the daughters of Antigone where, shakily and problematically they continue to locate themselves: in the arena of the social world where human life is nurtured and protected from day to day. This is a world women have not altogether abandoned, though it is one both male-dominant society and some feminist protests have devalued as the sphere of 'shit-work', 'diaper-talk', and 'terminal' social decay. This is a world that women, aware that they have traditions and values, can bring forward to put pressure on contemporary public policies and identities . . . To define this world simply as the 'private sphere' in contrast to the 'public sphere', is to mislead. For contemporary Americans, 'private' conjures up images of narrow exclusivity. The world of Antigone, however, is a social location that speaks of and to, identities that are unique to a particular family, on the one hand but, on another more basic level, it taps a deeply buried human identity; for we are first and foremost not political or economic man but family men and women. (Elshtain, 1982, pp. 55–6)

But we should not deceive ourselves. The existence of ethical and democratic forces is not a 'natural' part of being a woman. They are historical constructions and aspirations which, departing from the identification of women with procreation and the gestation of life, can be incorporated into a desirable future society, But what is not feasible, is to imagine any sort of necessary and total automatic liberation.

The global significance of social movements: citizenship and identity

From a theoretical perspective we can distinguish two ways of interpreting social movements based on their inclusion in the macro-social plan. One way of understanding them, linked to the social recognition of subordinate sectors in critical moments of historical processes, involves seeing social movements as mechanisms of struggle to widen socio-political citizenship. It is a struggle for the recognition and legitimacy of the social presence of specific groups of the population. It is a struggle for equal rights, justice, and the homogenization of society in terms of the recognition of a minimum threshold of rights associated with belonging to and inclusion in the social system. In this sense, the history of the struggle for legal equality (first suffrage, now equal parental authority) is paradigmatic.

A second way of seeing social movements is linked to the collective social search for identity and for the appropriation of a cultural field, as an affirmation of the right to specificity and difference. As discussed by Melucci in relation to feminism:

> The objective of the movement is not only equality of rights but rather the right to be different. The struggle is against discrimination, and in favour of a more equitable distribution in the economic market and, in the political realm the struggle is still for citizenship. The right to be recognized as different is one of the deepest needs in post-industrial and post-material society. (Melucci, 1984, pp. 830–31)

Both elements are present in the Latin American social situations we have studied. It is a struggle to widen citizenship while simultaneously claiming social recognition of specificities — a political struggle in terms of access to the mechanisms of power but also cultural in the search for different identities. Perhaps the Bartolina Sisa movement of peasant women is the best archetype: women with no previous political experience are instigated from above (by men), but at the same time, recognize and claim their ethnic and gender specificity, and their membership of the peasant class. Reality and slogans can only be contradictory, as they are inserted in different logics of action, stemming from superimposed social positions. The historical meeting, or the temporary synchronism of processes, which we tend to view as being logically and historically successive, is potentially (when not actually) innovative, both in the form and content of collective action.

The search for citizenship and the creation of an identity are both collective and active processes. The fact that we can currently study these aspects among women in Latin America is in itself an indication of who women (or at least some women) are. They are not passive beings taking refuge in privacy. They are there outside, building. But there is no guarantee of success. Moreover, the critieria of what constitutes 'success' are also being shaped along the very course of history.

Notes

1. Literature on feminism in Latin America is relatively rich in historical analyses (Kirkwood, 1984; Feijoo, 1981; Hahner, 1981; Rodríguez Villamil and Sapriza, 1983; Villavicencio, 1983; Lavrin (ed.) 1985). As regards the present situation, the most complete source of reference is to be found in publications of the Women's Alternative Communication Unit of the ILET (Latin American Institute for Transnational Studies) especially their 'Mujer/ILET' Bulletin.

2. For example, Baxandall (1976) suggests that women's awareness of their double role — as workers and consumers — would generate greater motivation to struggle for other demands unrelated to wages (humanization of work, childcare provision, and so on) which are neglected by workers' movements led by men.

3. A recent report of the situation of women in Argentine unionism (Gogna, 1986) indicates that they have women's departments or secretariats in the following trade unions: Insurance Union; Banking Association; Argentine Teachers' Union; Association of Public Employees; Argentine Graphic Union; Union of Tobacco Workers; Argentine Federation of Public Health Workers; University of Buenos Aires Personnel Association; and National Civil Servants Union.

4. I am grateful to Mónica Gogna for her collaboration in the preparation of this and the following section.

5. This refers to Lidia Gueiler elected as President of Bolivia.

6. See Glossary for a translation of *tarilla* and other Quechua and Aymara words.

7. So, for example, several of the human rights' organizations in Uruguay — Mothers and Relatives of those Tried by Military Justice; Relatives of the Disappeared; Relatives of Exiles — are almost exclusively made up of women. (Rodríguez Villamil, 1984) In Chile after 1974, organizations were formed whose aim was to denounce the violation of basic human rights and which were composed mainly of women, many of them without previous experience of organizations. (Delsing et al, 1983) In Peru and Guatemala women are also organizing around the defence of human rights.

Bibliography

Introduction

Evers, Tilman. 'Identidade: a face oculta o movimentos sociais', *Novos Estudos* 2 (4): 11–23, 1984.

Germani, Gino. *Política y sociedad en una epoca de transición*. Paidós, Buenos Aires, 1964.

Jelin, Elizabeth. *Familia y unidad doméstica: mundo público y vida privada*. Estudios CEDES, Buenos Aires, 1984.

Lechner, Norbert. '¿Qué significa hacer política?', in N. Lechner *Qué significa hacer política*. DESCO, Lima, 1982.

Melucci, Alberto. *L'invenzzione del presente: Movimenti, identitá, bisogni individuali*. Il Mulino, Bologna, 1982.

Stavenhagen, Rodolfo. *Las clases sociales en las sociedades agrarias*. Siglo XXI, Mexico, 1969.

Chapter 1

Altamirano, Teófilo. *Presencia andina en Lima Metropolitana*. PUC, Lima, 1984.

Alternativa. 'Algunos datos sobre San Martín de Porres', ms., 1983.

Barnet, Miguel. *Biografía de un cimarrón*. Ed. Letras Cubanas, La Habana, 1980.

Barrig, Maruja. 'Servicios urbanos y mujeres de bajos ingresos. Apuntes para una definición', Grupo de Trabajo SUMBI, Lima, mimeo, 1983.

Barrig, Maruja and Riofrío, Gustavo. 'Los programas de promoción dirigidos a la mujer en los barrios de Carmen de la Legua y El Agustino', Centro de Capacitación y Asesoría LEWCA, Lima, mimeo, 1982.

Barrig, Maruja, Chueca y Yáñez. *Anzuelo sin carnada*. Ed. ADEC, Mosca Azul, Lima, 1985.

Blondet, Cecilia. 'En las barriadas nos hicimos mujeres', *Cultura Popular* 11–12, CELADEC, Lima, 1984.

—— 'Neuvas formas de hacer política: las amas de casa populares', *Allpanchis* (forthcoming), Cusco, Perú, 1985.

Collier, David. *Squatters and Oligarchs: Authoritarian Rule and Policy Change in Peru*. Johns Hopkins University Press, Baltimore, 1976.

Cotler, Julio. 'The mechanics of internal domination and social change in Peru', *Studies in Comparative International Development* 3 (12), 1968.

—— 'Clases, estado y nación en el Perú', *Perú Problema* 17, IEP, Lima, 1978.

—— Proyecto 'La política y los jóvnes de las clases populares en Lima', IEP, Lima, mimeo, 1985.

de la Cadena, Marisol. 'La comunera como proeuctora', *Allpanchis* XXI (25), año XV, Cusco, Perú, 1985.

Derpich, Vilma. *Testimonio: hacio la sistematización de la historia oral.* Ed. Universidad de Lima, Lima, 1983.

Feijoo, María del Carmen. 'Las luchas de un barrio y la memoria colectiva', *CEDES* 4 (5), Buenos Aires, 1981.

—— 'Buscando un techo: familia y vivienda popular', Estudios CEDES, Buenos Aires, 1983.

—— 'Las mujeres en los barrios: de los asuntos locales a alos problemas de género', *Materiales para la Comunicación Popular* 5, IPAL, Lima, 1984.

Figueroa, Adolfo. *La economía campesina de la sierra del Perú.* PUC, Lima, 1981.

Golte, Jürgen and Adams, Norma. 'Los caballos de Troya de los conquistadores', IEP, Lima, mimeo, 1984.

Jelin, Elizabeth. 'Las relaciones sociales del consumo: el caso de las unidades domésticas de sectores populares', Documento de Trabajo 14, The Population Council, Mexico, 1983.

—— 'Participación de la mujer en América Latina: una guía para la investigación', Buenos Aires, mimeo, 1984.

—— 'Familia y unidad doméstica: mundo público y vida privada', Estudios CEDES, Buenos Aires, 1984.

Chapter 2

Alvarez, Sonia. 'The politics of gender and the Brazilian Abertura process: alternative perspectives on women and the state in Latin America', document presented to the XII International LASA Convention, Albuquerque, 1985.

Blachman, Morris. 'Selective omission and theoretical distortion in studying the political activity of women in Brazil', in June Nash and Helen Safa (eds) *Sex and Class in Latin America.* Praeger Publishers, New York, 1976.

Blay, Eva Alterman. 'Mulheres e movimentos sociais urbanos no Brasil: Anistia, custo de vida e creches', in *Encontros com a Civilização Brasileira* 26: 63–70, 1980.

—— 'Do espaço público ao privado: a conquista da cidadania pela mulher no Brasil', document presented to the VI Annual Conference of ANOPCS, Friburgo, mimeo, 1982.

Bosi, Ecléa. *Memória e sociedade — Lembranças de Velhos.* T. A. Queiroz, São Paulo, 1979.

Caldeira, Teresa Pes de Rio. *A política dos outros.* Brasiliense, São Paulo, 1984a.

—— 'A luta pelo voto em um bairro da periferia', *Cuadernos CEBRAP* 1, 1984b.

Cardoso, Ruth. 'Las neuvas formas de participación política: las mujeres en el Brasil', CEPAL, Santiago, mimeo, 1983a.

—— 'Nem tudo que reluz dá ouro', research report, CEBRAP, São Paulo, mimeo, 1983b.

—— 'Movimientos sociais urbanos: balanço critico', in Bernardo Sorj and María Herminia T. Almeida (eds) *Sociedade e política no Brasil pós — 64.* Brasiliense, São Paulo, 1983c.

—— 'Formas de participação popular no Brasil pós — 64', research report, CEBRAP, São Paulo, mimeo, 1984.

Castells, Manuel. *The City and the Grassroots.* Edward Arnold, London, 1983.

Chiriac, Jane and Padilla, Solange. 'Características e limites das organizações de base femenina', in Fundação Carlos Chagas (ed.) *Trabalhadoras do Brasil.*

Brasiliense, São Paulo. 1982.

Durham, Eunice. 'Movimentos sociais — a construção da cidadania', *Novos Estudos* 10: 24–30, 1984.

Evers, Tilman. 'Os movimentos sociais urbanos: o caso do movimento do custo de vida', in José Alvaro Moisés et al. *Alternativas populares de democracia: Brasil anos 80*. Petrópolis, São Paulo/Vozes, CEDEC, 1982.

——— 'Identidade: a face oculta dos movimentos sociais', *Novos Estudos* 2 (4) 11–23, 1984.

Evers, Tilman; Muller-Platenberg, Clarita and Spessart, Stefanne, 'Movimentos de bairro e estado: lutas na esfera da reprodução na América Latina', in José Alvaro Moisés *et al. Cidade, povo e poder*. Rio, CEDEC/Paz e Terra, São Paulo, 1982.

Gohn, María da Glória. 'Lutas populares urbanas — um estudo sobre os movimentos sociais destacando — se a luta por creches em São Paulo', PhD thesis, FFLCH, São Paulo University, 1983.

Grossi, María. 'El cuestionamiento de la política partidaria: los movimientos de base en Brasil', S/l., mimeo, s.f.

Jacobi, Pedro. 'Movimientos sociales urbanos no Brasil', *Bib* 9: 22–30, 1980.

——— 'Movimentos populares urbanos e resposta do estado: autonomia e controle vs. cooptação e clientelismo', in Renato Boschi, *Movimentos colectivos no Brasil urbano*. Zahar, Río de Janeiro, 1983.

Jacobi, Pedro and Nunes, Edison. 'Movimentos por melhores condições de Saúde: Zona Leste, a Secretaria de Saúde e o Povo'. ANPOCS, Friburgo, 1981.

Karner, Hartmut. 'Los movimientos sociales: revolución de lo cotidiano', in *Nueva Sociedad* 64: 24–32, 1983.

Lavinas, Lena and Le Doaré, Hélène. 'Mobilisations et organisations feminines dans les secteurs populaires', *Cahiers de Amériques Latines* 26: 39–58, 1982.

Lechner, Norbert. ¿*Qué significa hacer política?* DESCO, Lima, 1982.

Massolo, Alejandra and Díaz Ronner, Lucila. 'La participación de las mujeres en los movimientos sociales urbanos en la ciudad de México: un proyecto de investigación', CEPAL, Santiago, mimeo, 1983.

Moraes, María Lidia. 'Familia e feminismo: reflexões sobre papeis femeninos na imprensa para mulheres', PhD thesis, FFLCH, University of São Paulo, 1982.

Paoli, Maria Celia. 'Mulheres: lugar, imagem, movimento', in *Perspectivas antropológicas da mulher* 4: 63–100, 1985.

Schmink, Marianne. 'A Woman in Brazilian "Apertura" Politics', in *Signs* 7 (1): 115–34, 1981.

Singer, Paul. 'O feminino e o feminismo', in Paul Singer and Vinicius Caldeira Brandt (eds) *São Paulo: o povo em movimento*. Petropólis, CEBRAP/Vozes, São Paulo, 1980.

Touraine, Alain. *La voix el le regard*. Seuil, Paris, 1978.

Chapter 3

Arendt, Hannah. *La condición humana*. Seix Barril, Barcelona, 1974.

Bousquet, Jeanne Pierre. *Las locas de Plaza de Mayo*. El Cid Editor, Buenos Aires, 1983.

Braudel, Fernando. *Historia y ciencias sociales: la larga duración*, 1968.

Caldeira, Teresa. 'Women, Daily Life and Politics', Chapter 2 of this book.

Cano, Inés. 'El movimiento feminista argentino en la década del 70', in *Todo es Historia*. Buenos Aires, August 1982.

Casas, Nelly. 'Qué pasó con las mujeres políticas a partir del 51', in *Formación política para la democracia*, Redacción, Buenos Aires, 1982.

—— 'Se hace camino al andar', *Tiempo, La Mujer*, 10 March 1984.

CONADEP. *Nunca Más*. EUDEBA, Buenos Aires, 1984.

Elshtain, Jean. 'Antigone's daughters', *Democracy* 2 (2), April 1982.

Entel, Alicia. 'Los nuevos refugiados', in *Clarín*, Buenos Aires, 28 October 1983.

Feijoo, María del Carmen. *Las feministas, la vida de nuestro pueblo*. CEAL, Buenos Aires, 1982a.

—— 'La mujer en la historia argentina', in *Todo es Historia*, Buenos Aires, 1982b.

—— 'Mujer y política en América Latina: viejos y neuvos estilos', mimeo, 1983.

—— 'Mujeres en barrios: de los problemas locales a los problemas de género', in *Materiales para la Comunicación Popular* 5, October 1984.

Feijoo, María del Carmen and Jelin, Elizabeth. 'Las mujeres piden más', in *Clarín*, Buenos Aires, 13 December 1983.

Fontán, Dionisia. *Nueva presencia*. Buenos Aires, 17 September 1982.

Frenkel, Roberto. *Las recientes políticas de estabilización en la Argentina: de la vieja a la nueva ortodoxia*. Institute of International Relations, Pontificia Universidad Católica, Argentina, 1980.

Gogna, Mónica. 'Día international de la mujer: presencias y ausencias', in *Debates* 1, September–October 1984.

González Bombal, Inés. 'El movimiento de derechos humanos en la Argentina', mimeo, 1984a.

—— 'El movimiento vecinal en el Gran Buenos Aires', FLACSO thesis, 1984b.

Jelin, Elizabeth. 'Las mujeres y la participación popular: ideas para la investigación y el debate', in *Diálogos sobre la Participación* 2, UNRISD, Geneva, 1982.

Jelin, Elizabeth and Feijoo, María del Carmen. 'Trabajo y familia en el ciclo de vida femenino: el caso de los sectores populares de Buenos Aires', in *Estudios CEDES*, Buenos Aires, 1980.

Kaplan, Temma. 'Female consciousness and collective action: the case of Barcelona, 1910–1918', in *Signs* 7 (3), 1982.

Kirkwood, Julieta. 'Feministas y políticas. Práctica o teoría?', document presented to the Research Seminar on Women and Feminist Research: Balance and Perspectives of the Women's Decade in Latin America, Montevideo, 8–11 December 1984.

Landi, Oscar. *La tercera presidencia de Perón: gobierno de emergencia y crisis politica*. CEDES, Documento de Trabajo 10, Buenos Aires, 1978.

Lechner, Norbert. 'Especificando la política', in *Crítica y Utopía* 8, 1982.

Leffort, Claude. 'Direitos do homen e política', in *Libre* 7, Payot, 1980.

Llovet, Juan José. *Servicios de salud y sectores populares. Los años del Proceso*. Estudios CEDES, Buenos Aires, 1984.

Melucci, Alberto. 'The new social movements: a theoretical approach', in *Social Science Information* 19 (2): 199–226, 1980.

—— 'The hypotheses for the analysis of new movements', in D. Pinto (ed.) *Contemporary Italian Sociology*. Cambridge University Press, Cambridge, 1981.

Navarro, Maryssa. *Evita*. Corregidor, Buenos Aires, 1981.

Offe, Claus. 'Competitive party democracy and the Keynesian welfare state', mimeo, 1981.

Palermo, Vicente and García Delgado, Daniel. 'El movimiento de derechos humanos en la transición a la democracia', mimeo, 1983.

Paramio, Ludolfo. 'El desencanto espanol como crisis de una forma de hacer politica', in Norbert Lechner *¿Qué Significa Hacer Política?*, 1982.

Quevedo, Luis Alberto. 'Discurso politico y orden social', unpublished thesis (Licenciatura), University of El Salvador, 1984.
Rossanda, Rossana. *Las otras*. Gediva, Barcelona, 1982.
Rowbotham, Sheila. *Women, Resistance and Revolution*. Penguin Books, London, 1972.
—— *Hidden from History*. Vintage Press, London 1976.
Swerdlow, Amy. 'Ladies day at Capitol: women strike for peace vs HUAC', in *Feminist Studies* 8 (3), 1982.
Varela-Cid, Eduardo and Vicens, Luis. *La imbecilización de la mujer*. El Cid Editor, Buenos Aires, 1984.
Vega, Juan Enrique. 'América Latina: la conquista del reino de este mundo', in *América Latina 80: democracia y movimiento popular*. DESCO, 1981.
Weber, Max. 'Politics as a vocation', in *From Max Weber: Essays in Sociology*. Routledge & Kegan Paul, London 1970, p. 121.
Weisstein, Naomi. 'La psicología construyendo a la mujer', 1981.

Newspapers, Magazines and Journals

Alfonsina
Aquí Nosostras
Boletín de Dima
Clarín
Diario Popular
El Bimestre
El Periodista
El Porteño
Humor
La Nación
La Voz
Madres de Plaza de Mayo
Mate Amargo
Mujer
Paz y Justicia

Chapter 4

Barrera, Manuel. 'La demanda democrática de los trabajadores chilenos', Centro de Estudios del Desarrollo, June 1984.
Campero, Guillermo and Valenzuela, José A. *El movimiento sindical en el régimen militar chileno 1973-1981*. Estudios ILET, May 1984.
Departamentos Femeninos de Confederaciones Unidad Obrero Campesina — Nehuén — El Surco. 'Situación actual y laboral de la mujer campesina', May 1985.
Díaz, Eugenio. *Manual sobre negociación colectiva*. Programa de Estudios Sindicales, VECTOR, Centro de Estudios Económicos y Sociales, September 1984.
Espinoza, María Paulina. 'Informe estadistico', from the research project 'Modos de inserción de la mujer trabajadora en el sector informal: bases para la acción', by Ximena Díaz and Eugenia Hola, April 1984.
Gómez, María Soledad and Mallea, Ana María. 'Gremios y asociaciones en el período 1973-83', *Materiales para discusión* 55, Centro de Estudios del Desarrollo, November 1984.

Instituto Nacional de Estadisticas INE. 'Encuesta Nacional del Empleo 1980, October–December'.

Kergoat, Danièle. '¿Obreros igual obreras?', in *Crítica de la Economía Política Edición Latinoamericana* 14–15, La Mujer Trabajo y Política, Ediciónes El Caballito, Mexico, 1980.

Le Garrec, Evelyne. *Las Mensajeras*. Tribuna Feminista, Editorial Debate, 1977.

Martínez, Javier and León, Arturo. 'La involución del proceso de desarrollo y la estructura social', *Materiales para discusión* 53, Centro de Estudios del Desarrollo, November 1984.

Maruani, Margaret. *Les syndicats à l'épreuve du féminisme*. Editions Syros, 1979.

Ruiz Tagle, Jaime and Campero, Guillermo. *Legislación laboral y modelo económico*. Manual de Educación Popular, Programa de Economia del Trabajo, Vicaría de Pastoral Obrera.

Zylbergerg-Hocquard, Marie Hélène. *Femmes et féminisme dans le mouvement ouvrier français*. Les éditions ouvrières, Paris, 1981.

Chapter 5

Albó, Xavier. 'Achacachi, medio siglo de lucha campesina', CIPCA, La Paz, 1979.

——— Rebelión e ideología: luchas del campesinado aymara del altiplano boliviano 1919–1920', in *Historia Boliviana* 1/2 1981a.

——— 'Chuquiyawa, la cara aymara de La Paz', CIPCA 1 (20), La Paz, 1981b.

——— 'Bases étnicas y sociales para la participación aymara', in Calderón and Dandler (eds) *Bolivia: la fuerza histórica del campesinado*. UNRISD–CERES, Geneva, 1986.

Albó, Javier and Barnadas, Joseph. *La cara campesina de neustra historia*. UNITAS, La Paz, 1983.

Arauco, María I. *Mujeres en la revolución nacional: las barzolas*. Distribuidora CINCO, La Paz, 1984.

Barrios de Chungara, Domitila. *Let me speak: testimony of Domitila, a woman of the Bolivian mines*. Monthly Review Press, New York, 1978.

Blanes, José and Calderón, Fernando. 'Bolivia: diferenciación y cambio social: 1954–82', CERES, La Paz, 1983.

Calderón, Fernando. 'Los pueblos quechuas y aymaras en la formación y desarrollo de la sociedad boliviana', in John Rex (ed.) *Raza y clase en la sociedad colonial*. UNESCO, Paris, 1977.

——— *La política en las calles*. CERES, La Paz, 1983.

——— *Urbanización y etnicidad: el caso de La Paz*. CERES, Cochabamba, 1984.

Calderón, Fernando; Carafa, Carlos and Pérez de Castaños, María. *Mujer, clase y discriminación social*. UNICEF, Bolivia, 1984.

Calderón, Fernando and Dandler, Jorge (eds), *Bolivia: la fuerza histórica del campesinado*. UNRISD–CERES, Geneva, 1986.

CSUTCB. 'Plataforma de lucha de la Confederación Sindical Unica de Trabajadores Campesinos de Bolivia', 11th National Congress, 1983.

Dandler, Jorge. *El sindicalismo campesino en Bolivia*. CERES, La Paz, 1984.

Dandler, Jorge; León, Rosario *et al*. 'Economía campesina en los valles y serranías de Cochabamba: procesos de diversificación y trabajo', CERES (preliminary reports), Cochabamba, 1982.

Feijoo, María del Carmen. 'Las luchas de un barrio y la memoria colectiva', *CEDES* 4 (5), Buenos Aires, 1981.

García, Antonio. 'Los sindicatos en el esquema de la revolución nacional', in

Trimestre Económico, November–December, 19?, Mexico, pp. 597–629.

Iriarte, Gregorio. 'Sindicalismo campesino: ayer hoy y mañana', CIPCA, La Paz, 1980.

Jelin, Elizabeth. 'Women and the urban labour market', ILO working paper 77, 1979.

—— 'Women and popular participation: ideas for research and debate', in *Dialogue about Participation* 2, UNRISD, Geneva, 1982.

—— 'Las relaciones sociales del consumo: el caso de las unidades domésticas de sectores populares', *CEDES*, Buenos Aires, mimeo, 1983.

—— *Familia y unidad doméstica: mundo público y vida privada*. Estudios CEDES, Buenos Aires, 1984.

Larson, Brooke. *Explotación agraria y resistencia campesina en Cochabamba*. CERES, Cochabamba, 1984.

Larson, Brooke and León, Rosario. 'Contexto etnohistórico y relaciones de intercambio en Tapacarí: una perspectiva a largo plazo', SSRC/CERES, Sucre, Bolivia, 1983.

León de Leal, Magdalena *et al.* 'Mujer y capitalismo agrario', ACEP, Bogota, 1980.

León, Rosario. 'Minera, campesina y comerciante: tres dimensiones de participación en Cochabamba', CERES–UNRISD, Cochabamba, 1982.

—— 'El sistema de ferias en Tapacarí: negociar para vivir', CERLAC/FLACSO, La Paz, 1983.

—— 'Organizaciones alternativas de la mujer en Cochabamba (1980–82)', paper presented at the LASA Congress, México, 1983.

Mejía de Morales, Lucila *et al.* *Las hijas de Bartolina Sisa*, compiled by Javier Medina. La Paz, 1985.

Muñoz, Blanca. 'La participación de la mujer campesina en Bolivia: un estudio del Altiplano', abridged version, in Calderón and Dandler (eds) *Bolivia: la fuerza histórica del campesinado*.

Nash, June and Rocca, Manuel. *Dos mujeres indígenas: Brasilia y facundina*. Instituto Indigenista Interamericano, México, 1976.

Rivera Cusicanqui, Silvia. 'Medio siglo de luchas campesinas en Bolivia', *Ultima Hora* (special edition), La Paz, 1979.

—— 'Luchas campesinas en Bolivia: el movimiento katarista', in *Bolivia Hoy*, Siglo XXI, Mexico, 1983.

—— *Oppressed but not Defeated: Peasant Struggles among the Aymara and Qhechwa in Bolivia, 1900–1980*. UNRISD, Geneva, 1987.

Sostres y Ardaya. *Prácticas de la resistencia y reivindicacion de la mujer campesina: el caso de las Bartolinas*. FLACSO, La Paz, 1984.

UNICEF. 'Participación económica y social de la mujer peruana', Lima, 1981.

Wolf, Eric. *Peasant Wars of the Twentieth Century*. Faber & Faber, London, 1971.

Wainerman, Catalino; Jelin, Elizabeth and Feijoo, María del Carmen. *Del deber ser y el hacer de las mujeres: dos estudios del caso en Argentina*. PISPAL, El Colegio de México, México, 1983.

Chapter 6

Aguiló, Federico. 'Una posible pista sobre la presencia de *mitmakuna* en la zona de pampa Yampara', in *Historia Boliviana* III (2), Cochabamba, 1983.

Bastien, Joseph. *Metaphor and Ritual in an Andean Ayllu*. West Publishing Co., Minnesota, 1978.

Bouysse-Cassagne, Thérèse. 'Tributo y etnias en Charcas en la época del Virrey

Toledo', in *Historia y Cultura* 2, La Paz, 1976.

Cereceda, Verónica. 'Sémiologie du tissu andin', in *Annales ESC* 33 (5–6), Paris, 1978.

Jelin, Elizabeth. *Familia y unidad doméstica: mundo público y vida privada*. Estudios CEDES, Buenos Aires, 1984.

Larson, Brooke. 'Producción doméstica y trabajo femenino indígena en la formación de una economía mercantil colonial', in *Historia Boliviana* III (2), Cochabamba, 1983.

Ortner, Sherry. 'Is female to male as nature is to culture?', in Zimbalist and Lamphere (eds) *Woman, Culture and Society*. Stanford University Press, California, 1974.

Platt, Tristan. *Espejos y maíz*. Cuadernos CIPCA, La Paz, 1976.

—— *Estado boliviano y ayllu andino*. IEP, Lima, 1982.

Rivera Cusicanqui, Silvia. 'Lo infrapolitico en Quimera', 1985.

THOA (Andean Oral History Workshop). *El indio Santos Marka T'ula, cacique principal de los ayllus de Qallapa y apoderado general de las comunidades originarias de la republica*. THOA, La Paz, 1984.

Ticona, Esteban. 'Archivos cacicales y fondos documentales orales, una alternativa archivística: el caso de la familia Marka T'ula', paper presented to the IV Consultative Meeting on Bolivian archives, Cochabamba, November 1985.

Chapter 7

Abos, Alvaro. 'Los diez desafíos del movimiento obrero argentino', in *UNIDOS* 3 (6): 126–42, Buenos Aires, 1985.

Abramo, Lais. 'Los mecanismos que mantienen la discriminacion de las mujeres de los sectores populares en America Latina', paper presented at a comparative research conference, mimeo, 1985.

Baxandall, Rosalyn. 'Women in American trade unions: an historical analysis', in Juliet Mitchell and Ann Oakley (eds) *The Rights and Wrongs of Women*. Pelican Books, London, 1976.

Blay, Eva Alterman. 'Do Espaço privado ao publico: a conquista da cidadania pela mulher no Brasil', paper presented to the VI Annual Meeting of the ANOPCS, mimeo, 1982.

Castilhos Brito, María Noemí. 'Participación sindical femenina no processo de redemocratizaçao no Brasil', mimeo 1984.

CEPAL (Economic Commission for Latin America). *La mujer en el sector popular urbano — America Latina y el Caribe*. CEPAL, Santiago de Chile, 1984.

Chang, Ligia and Ducci, María Angélica. *Realidad del empleo y la formación profesional de la mujer en América Latina*. CINTERFOR, Montevideo, 1977.

Delsing, Riet *et al. Tipología de organizaciones y grupos de mujeres pobladoras*. Estudios SUR, working paper 17, 1983.

Donzelot, Jacques. *The Policing of Families*. Panthem Books, New York, 1979.

Elshtain, Jean. *Public Man, Private Woman*. Princeton University Press, Princeton, 1981.

—— 'Antigone's daughters', *Democracy* 2 (2), April 1982.

Feijoo, María del Carmen. 'Mujer y política en América Latina: viejos y nuevos estilos', mimeo, 1983.

—— 'Mujeres: el derecho al cuerpo', *Debates* 1 (1), September–October 1984.

Feijoo, María del Carmen and Gogna, Mónica. 'Las mujeres en la transición a la democracia', in E. Jelin (ed.) *Los nuevos movimientos sociales*. CEAL, Buenos Aires, 1985.

Gil, Elena. *La mujer en el mundo del trabajo*. Libera, Buenos Aires, 1980.

Gitahy, Leda *et al*. 'Operarias: sindicalisaçao e reivindicaçoes (1970–80)', *Revista de Cultura e Politica* 8, CEDEC, July 1982.

Gogna, Mónica. 'Mujeres y sindicatos', mimeo, Buenos Aires, 1986.

Hahner, June E. *A mulher brasileira e suas lutas sociais e politicas: 1850–1937*. Brasiliense, São Paulo, 1981.

Hartman Strom, Sharon. 'Challenging "women's place": feminism, the left and industrial unionism in the 1930s', *Feminist Studies* 9 (2), 1983.

Humphrey, John. 'Sindicato: un mundo masculino', *Novos Estudos*, CEBRAP 2 (1), 1983.

Jelin, Elizabeth. *Familia y unidad doméstica: mundo público y vida privada*. Estudios CEDES, Buenos Aires, 1984.

Kirkwood, Julieta. 'Feministas y politicas. ¿Práctica o teoria?', paper presented to the Seminar on Research on Women and Feminist Research; Balance and Perspectives of the Women's Decade in Latin America, Montevideo, 8–11 Dec. 1984.

Lavrin, Asunsión (ed.). *Las mujeres latinoamericanas; perspectivas históricas*. Fondo de Cultura Economica, México, 1985.

Mejía de Morales, Lucila *et al*. *Las hijas de Bartolina Sisa*. Hisbol, La Paz, 1984.

Melucci, Alberto. 'An end to social movements?'. Introductory paper to the sessions on 'New movements and change in organizational forms', *Social Science Information* 23 (4/5): 819–35, 1984.

Navarro, Marysa. 'Mujeres, trabajo y sindicatos en la Argentina', mimeo, 1986.

Palomino, Héctor. 'El movimiento de democratización sindical', in E. Jelin (ed.) *Los nuevos movimientos sociales*. CEAL, Buenos Aires, 1985.

Rivera Cusicanqui, Silvia. *Oppressed but not defeated: Peasant Struggles among the Aymara and Quechwa in Bolivia, 1900–1980*. UNRISD, Geneva, 1987.

Rodríguez Villamil, Silvia. 'Los movimientos sociales de mujeres en la transición a la democracia', mimeo, 1984.

Rodríguez Villamil, Silvia and Sapriza, Graciela. *Mujer, estado y política en el Uruguay del siglo XX*. Ediciones de la Banda Oriental, Montevideo, 1984.

Rossanda, Rossana. 'Nuevos enfoques para un dilema', *La Razón*, p. 34, 22 August 1985.

Sautu, Ruth. Paper presented to the seminar on 'Women and Work', organized by the Dirección Nacional de la Mujer y la Familia, Buenos Aires, 1985.

Sondereguer, María. 'El movimiento de derechos humanos en Argentina', mimeo, 1985.

Souza Lobo, Elizabeth. 'La clase obrera en femenino: prácticas obreras y prácticas de las obreras en San Pablo', mimeo, 1984.

TIE (Transnationals Information Exchange). 'The new militancy', *Report 17*, pp. 36–7, Amsterdam, 1984.

Villavicencio, Maritza. 'Raíces del movimiento femenino en el Perú', paper presented to the Seminar on Women and Politics in Latin America, Grupo de Trabajo sobre Condicion Femenina, CLACSO, Buenos Aires, mimeo, 1983.

Index